Math in Focus®

Singapore Math®
by Marshall Cavendish

Consultant and Author
Dr. Fong Ho Kheong

Authors
Chelvi Ramakrishnan and Bernice Lau Pui Wah

U.S. Consultants
Dr. Richard Bisk
Andy Clark
Patsy F. Kanter

Marshall Cavendish
Education

U.S. Distributor

Houghton
Mifflin
Harcourt

© 2015 Marshall Cavendish Education Private Limited

Published by Marshall Cavendish Education
An imprint of Marshall Cavendish Education Private Limited
Times Centre, 1 New Industrial Road, Singapore 536196
Customer Service Hotline: (65) 6213 9444
U.S. Office Tel: (1-914) 332 8888 Fax: (1-914) 332 8882
E-mail: tmesales@mceducation.com
Website: www.mceducation.com

Distributed by
Houghton Mifflin Harcourt
222 Berkeley Street
Boston, MA 02116
Tel: 617-351-5000
Website: www.hmheducation.com/mathinfocus

First published 2015

Math in Focus® Student Book 1B
ISBN 978-0-544-19356-7

Printed in the United States of America

1 2 3 4 5 6 7 8   1401   20 19 18 17 16 15
4500463696   A B C D E

Contents

Look for **Practice and Problem Solving**

Student Book A and Student Book B	Workbook A and Workbook B
• **Let's Practice** in every lesson	• **Independent Practice** for every lesson
• Put on Your Thinking Cap! in every chapter	• Put on Your Thinking Cap! in every chapter

CHAPTER 11 Picture Graphs and Bar Graphs

Look for **Assessment Opportunities**

Student Book A and Student Book B	Workbook A and Workbook B
• **Quick Check** at the beginning of every chapter to assess chapter readiness • **Guided Learning** after every example or two to assess readiness to continue lesson	• **Chapter Review/Test** in every chapter to review or test chapter material • **Cumulative Reviews** eight times during the year • **Mid-Year** and **End-of-Year Reviews** to assess test readiness

CHAPTER 12 Numbers to 40

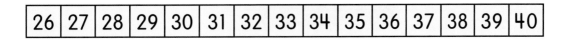

CHAPTER

13

Addition and Subtraction to 40

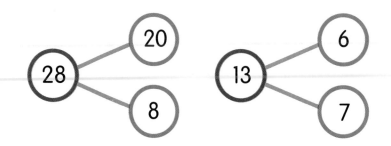

CHAPTER 15 Calendar and Time

CHAPTER 16 Numbers to 120

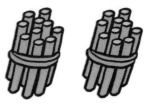

CHAPTER 17 Addition and Subtraction to 100

CHAPTER
18 Multiplication and Division

CHAPTER 19 Money

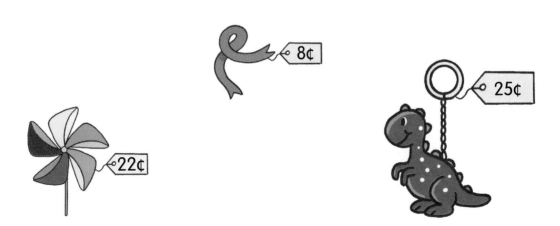

Welcome to
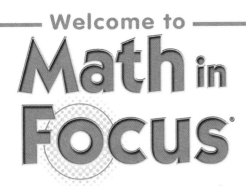
Math in Focus®

This exciting math program comes to you all the way from the country of Singapore. We are sure you will like all the different ways to learn math.

What makes *Math in Focus®* different?

- **Two books** You don't write in the ▢ in this textbook. This book has a matching **Workbook.** When you see  you will write in the **Workbook.**

- **Longer lessons** Some lessons may last more than a day, so you can really understand the math.

- **Math will make sense** Learn to use number bonds to understand better how numbers work.

In this book, look for

Learn	Guided Learning	Let's Practice	ON YOUR OWN
This means you learn something new.	Your teacher helps you try some problems.	Practice. Make sure you really understand.	Now try some problems in your own **Workbook.**

Also look forward to *Games, Hands-On Activities, Put on Your Thinking Cap!,* and more. Enjoy some real math challenges!

What's in the Workbook?

Math in Focus® will give you time to learn important math ideas and do math problems. The **Workbook** will give you different types of practice.

- *Practice* problems will help you remember the new math idea you are learning. Watch for this ▐ ON YOUR OWN ▐ in your book. That will tell you which pages to use for practice.

- *Put on Your Thinking Cap!*

    Challenging Practice problems invite you to think in new ways to solve harder problems.

    Problem Solving gives you opportunities to solve questions in different ways.

- *Math Journal* activities ask you to think about thinking, and then write about that!

Students in Singapore have been using this kind of math program for many years. Now you can too — are you ready?

10 Weight

BIG IDEA

The weight of things can be compared and measured with non-standard units.

Recall Prior Knowledge

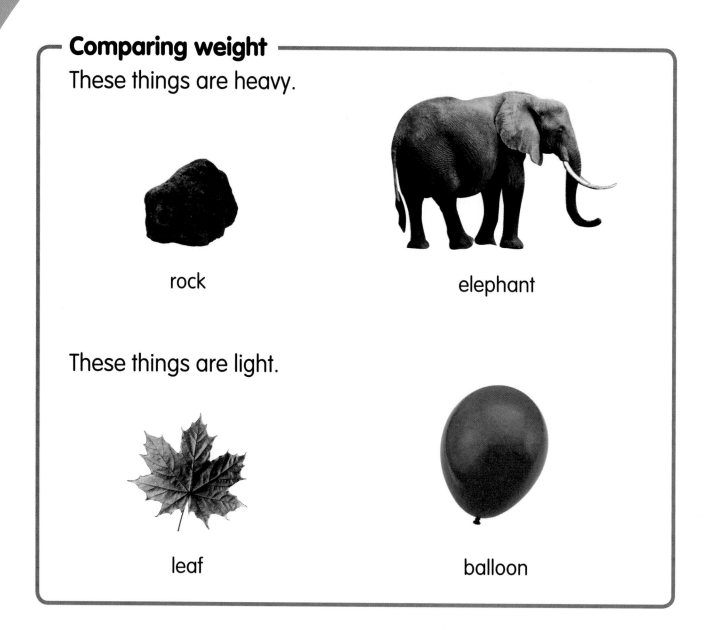

Comparing weight

These things are heavy.

rock

elephant

These things are light.

leaf

balloon

Comparing numbers

9 is less than 10.

8 is greater than 5.

Comparing length

Tim is taller than Sue.
Roy is taller than Tim.
So, Roy is taller than Sue.
Roy is the tallest.
Sue is the shortest.

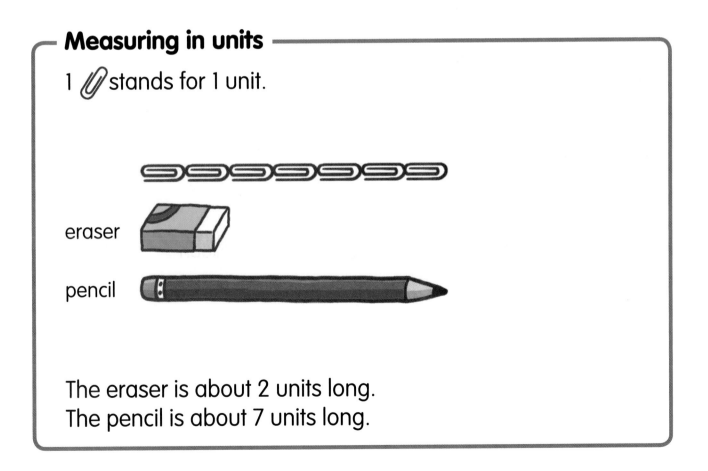

Sue   Tim   Roy

Measuring in units

1 🖇 stands for 1 unit.

eraser

pencil

The eraser is about 2 units long.
The pencil is about 7 units long.

Tell which things are heavy and which are light.

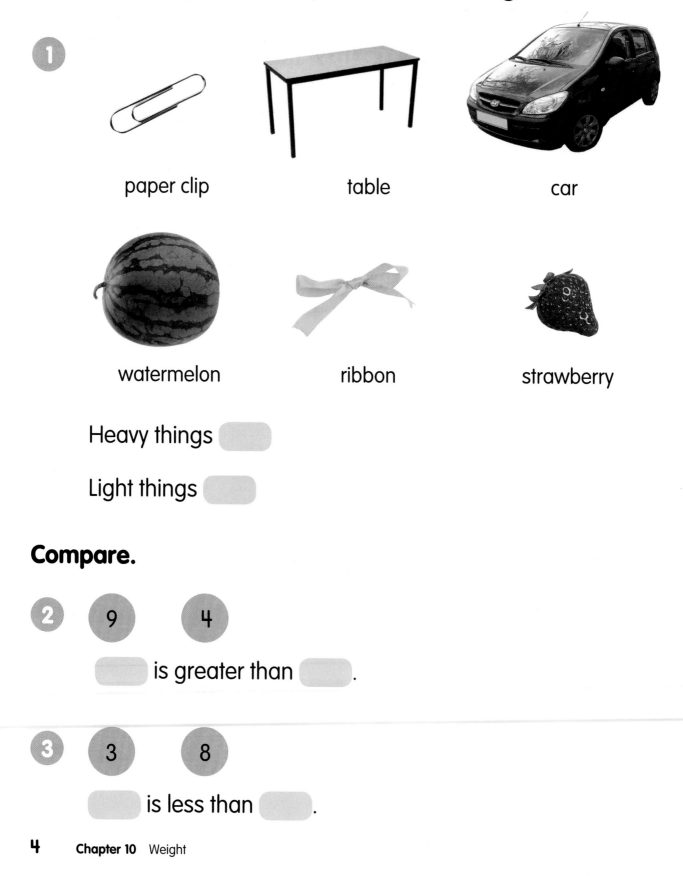

1

paper clip   table   car

watermelon   ribbon   strawberry

Heavy things

Light things

Compare.

2   9   4

___ is greater than ___ .

3   3   8

___ is less than ___ .

Choose shorter, shortest, or tallest.

4 The cat is ⬚ than the dog.

5 The dog is ⬚ than the horse.

6 So, the cat is the ⬚.

7 The horse is the ⬚.

Find the missing numbers.

1 ⬤ **stands for 1 unit.**

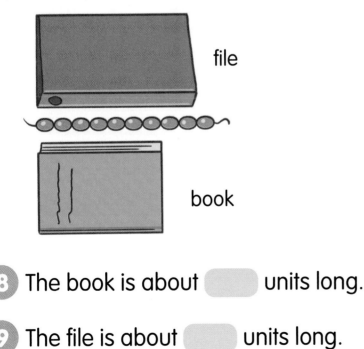

file

book

8 The book is about ⬚ units long.

9 The file is about ⬚ units long.

1 Comparing Things

Lesson Objectives

- Compare the weight of two things using the terms 'heavy', 'heavier', 'light', 'lighter', and 'as heavy as'.
- Compare the weight of more than two things using the terms, 'lightest' and 'heaviest'.

Vocabulary

heavy	heavier	heaviest
light	lighter	lightest
weight	as heavy as	

Learn

You can compare the weight of things.

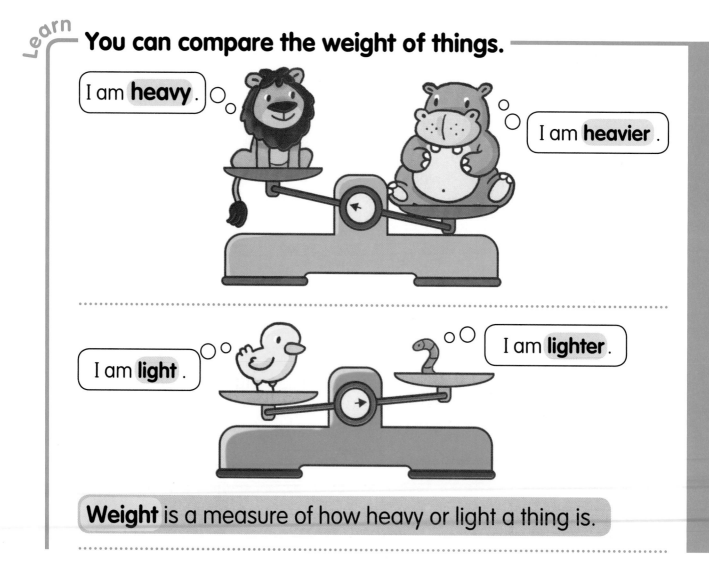

I am **heavy**.

I am **heavier**.

I am **light**.

I am **lighter**.

Weight is a measure of how heavy or light a thing is.

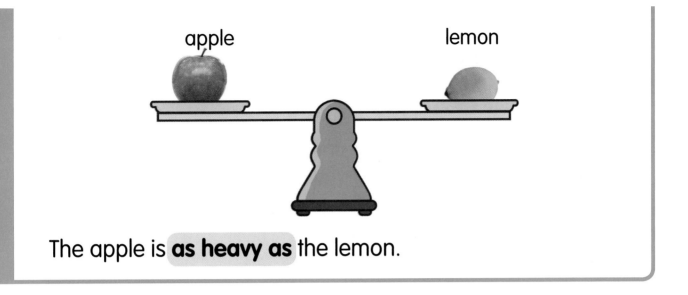

apple

lemon

The apple is **as heavy as** the lemon.

Guided Learning

Look at the pictures.

metal ball

 soft toy

A big thing may be lighter than a small thing.

Answer each question.

1 Which is heavier? The [ ] is heavier.

2 Which is lighter? The [ ] is lighter.

3 Is a big thing always heavier than a small thing? [ ]

 # Hands-On Activity

Guess which is heavier in each group.

Use a balance to check your answers.

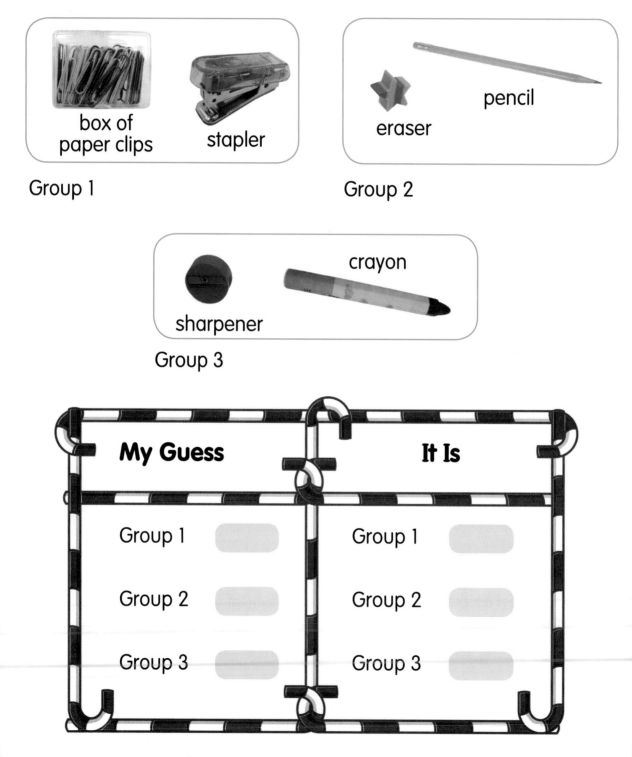

box of
paper clips

stapler

Group 1

eraser

pencil

Group 2

sharpener

crayon

Group 3

My Guess		It Is	
Group 1		Group 1	
Group 2		Group 2	
Group 3		Group 3	

Learn **You can compare the weight of two things by using another object.**

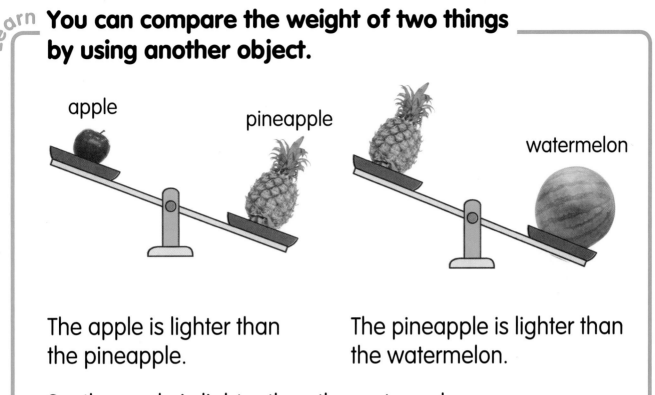

apple

pineapple

watermelon

The apple is lighter than the pineapple.

The pineapple is lighter than the watermelon.

So, the apple is lighter than the watermelon.

Guided Learning

Look at the pictures.
Complete.

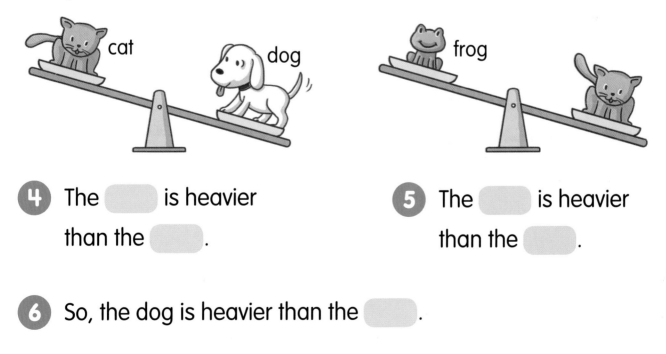

cat

dog

frog

4 The ⬜ is heavier than the ⬜.

5 The ⬜ is heavier than the ⬜.

6 So, the dog is heavier than the ⬜.

Learn **You can compare the weight of more than two things.**

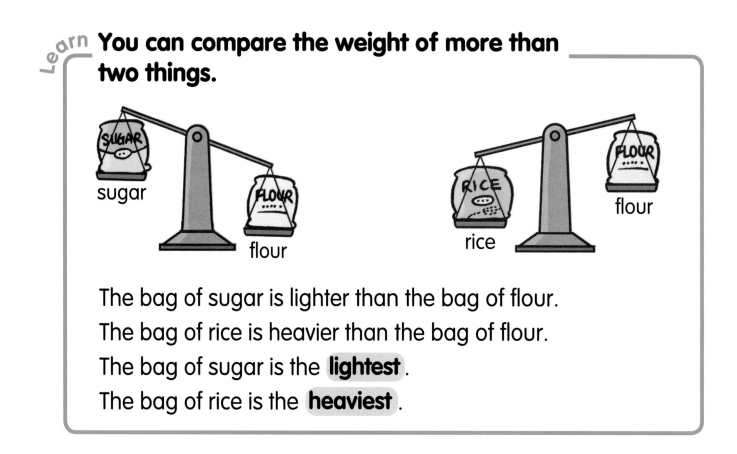

sugar

flour

rice

flour

The bag of sugar is lighter than the bag of flour.

The bag of rice is heavier than the bag of flour.

The bag of sugar is the **lightest** .

The bag of rice is the **heaviest** .

Guided Learning

Look at the pictures.
Complete.

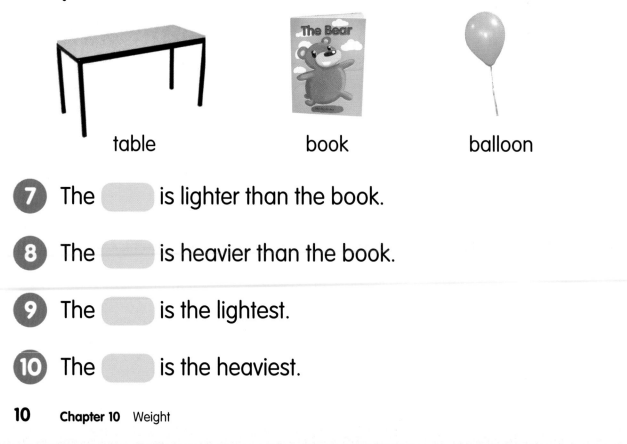

table

book

balloon

7 The _____ is lighter than the book.

8 The _____ is heavier than the book.

9 The _____ is the lightest.

10 The _____ is the heaviest.

Hands-On Activity

STEP 1

Put a pair of scissors on one side of a balance.
Use modeling clay to make a ball as heavy
as the pair of scissors.

Name it Ball A.

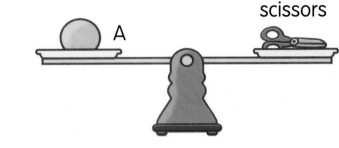

scissors

A

STEP 2

Put a calculator on one side of the balance.
Use the modeling clay to make another ball
as heavy as the calculator.

Name it Ball B.

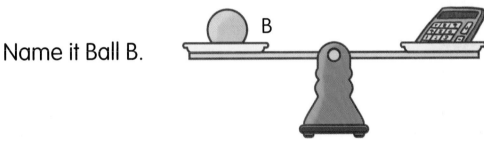

calculator

B

Answer these questions.

1 Hold the balls in your hands.
Which ball is heavier, A or B?

2 Which is heavier, the pair of scissors or the calculator?

Let's Practice

Look at the pictures. Choose lighter or heavier.

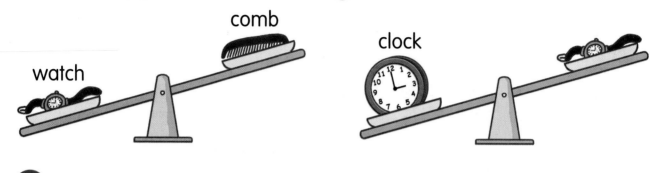

comb

watch

clock

1 The comb is ____ than the watch.

2 The clock is ____ than the watch.

3 So, the clock is ____ than the comb.

Use your answers to Exercises 1 to 3 to answer these questions.

4 Which is the lightest? ____

5 Which is the heaviest? ____

Complete.

6 Find three things heavier than your math book. ____

7 Find two things lighter than your math book. ____

8 Find one thing about as heavy as your math book. ____

ON YOUR OWN

Go to Workbook B:
Practice 1, pages 1–6

2 Finding the Weight of Things

Lesson Objectives

- Use a non-standard object to find the weight of things.

- Compare weight using a non-standard object as a unit of measurement.

Learn

You can measure weight with objects.

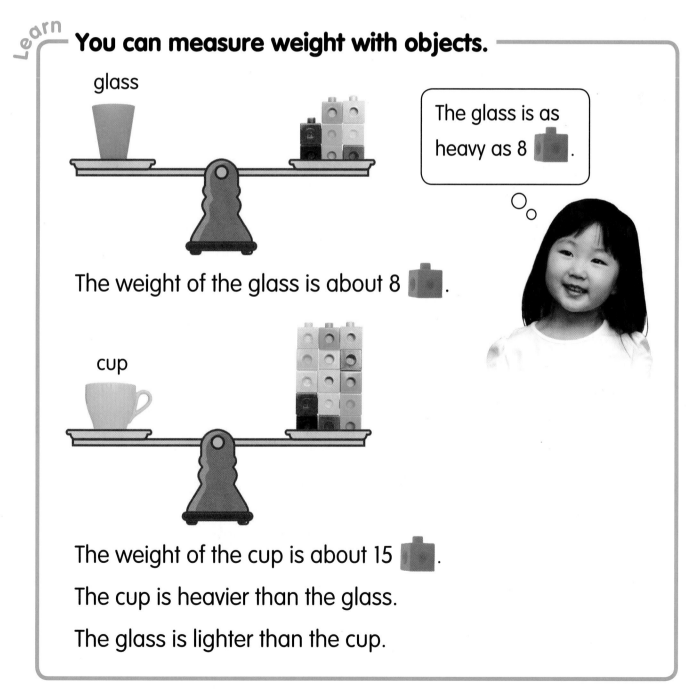

glass

The glass is as heavy as 8 ▪.

The weight of the glass is about 8 ▪.

cup

The weight of the cup is about 15 ▪.

The cup is heavier than the glass.

The glass is lighter than the cup.

**Look at the pictures.
Complete.**

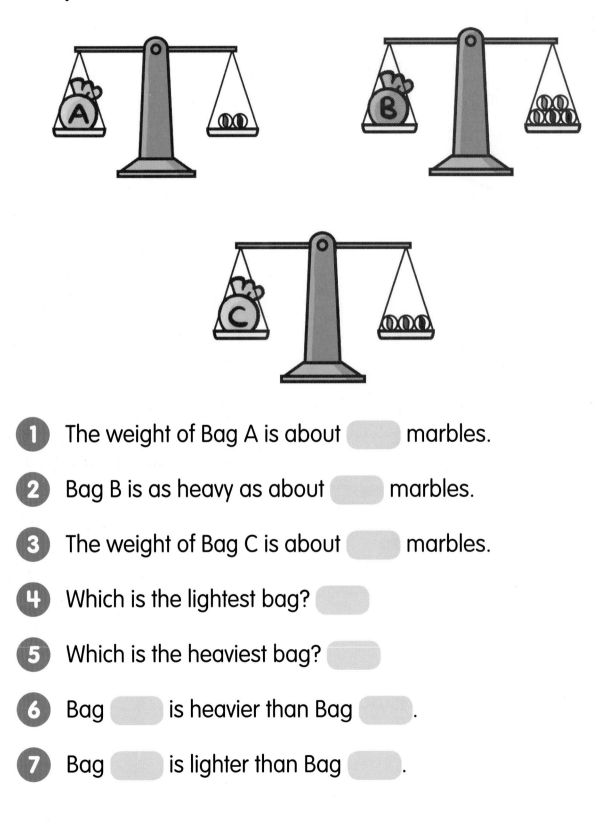

1. The weight of Bag A is about [   ] marbles.

2. Bag B is as heavy as about [   ] marbles.

3. The weight of Bag C is about [   ] marbles.

4. Which is the lightest bag? [   ]

5. Which is the heaviest bag? [   ]

6. Bag [   ] is heavier than Bag [   ].

7. Bag [   ] is lighter than Bag [   ].

Hands-On Activity

1 Use 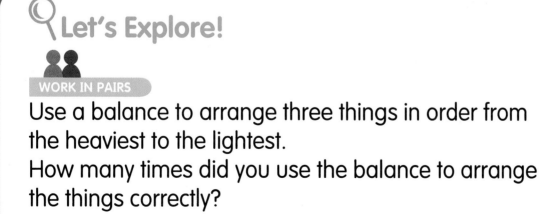 or and a balance to find the weight of each thing.

pencil case   a marker   a stapler

2 Use a box of things.
Pick one thing.

Find its weight using or .
Write its weight on a card.

> CLUE: My mystery thing weighs about 15 coins.

Show some friends the box of things and the card.
Ask them to guess what your mystery thing is.
They can use and a balance to check their guesses.

Let's Explore!

Use a balance to arrange three things in order from the heaviest to the lightest.
How many times did you use the balance to arrange the things correctly?

**Look at the picture.
Then fill in the blanks.**

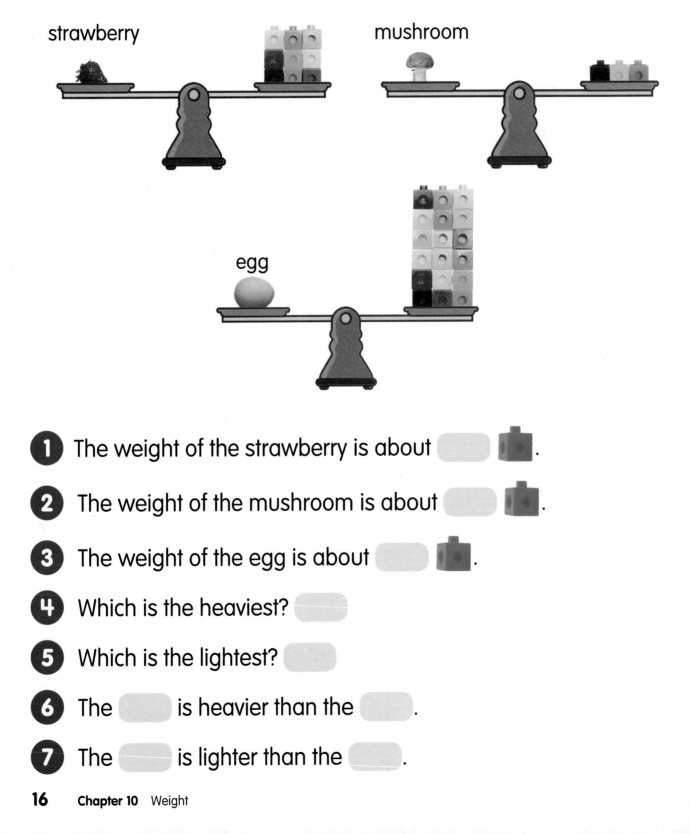

1. The weight of the strawberry is about ⬤⬤ ▪.

2. The weight of the mushroom is about ⬤⬤ ▪.

3. The weight of the egg is about ⬤⬤ ▪.

4. Which is the heaviest? ⬤⬤

5. Which is the lightest? ⬤⬤

6. The ⬤⬤ is heavier than the ⬤⬤.

7. The ⬤⬤ is lighter than the ⬤⬤.

Study the picture.
Complete.

scissors

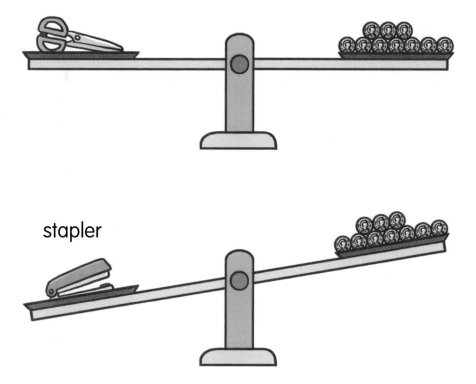

stapler

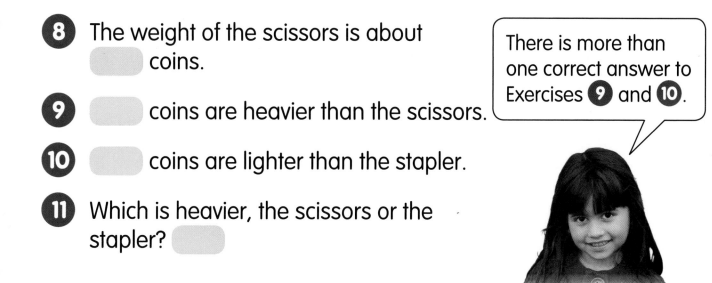

8 The weight of the scissors is about
[   ] coins.

9 [   ] coins are heavier than the scissors.

10 [   ] coins are lighter than the stapler.

11 Which is heavier, the scissors or the
stapler? [   ]

There is more than
one correct answer to
Exercises **9** and **10**.

ON YOUR OWN

**Go to Workbook B:
Practice 2, pages 7–10**

3 Finding Weight in Units

Lesson Objectives

- Use the term 'unit' when writing the weight of things.
- Explain why there is a difference in a measurement when using different non-standard units.
- Arrange things according to their weights.

Vocabulary
unit

Learn

You can measure weight in units.

1 Eraser stands for 1 unit.

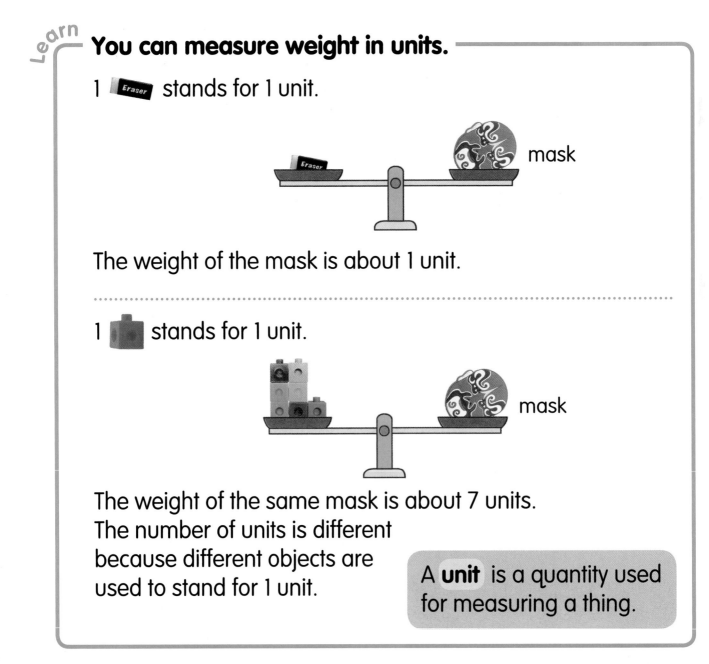

mask

The weight of the mask is about 1 unit.

1 ▢ stands for 1 unit.

mask

The weight of the same mask is about 7 units.
The number of units is different because different objects are used to stand for 1 unit.

A **unit** is a quantity used for measuring a thing.

✋ Hands-On Activity

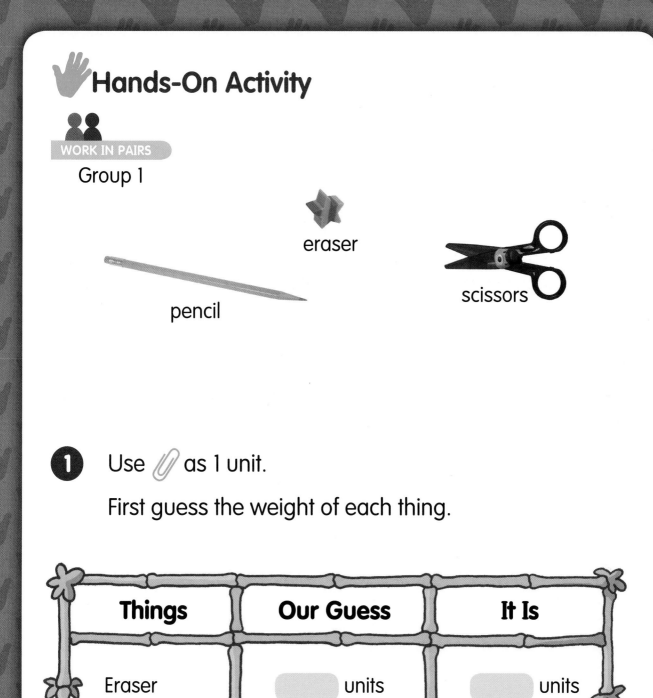

WORK IN PAIRS

Group 1

eraser

pencil

scissors

1 Use 📎 as 1 unit.

First guess the weight of each thing.

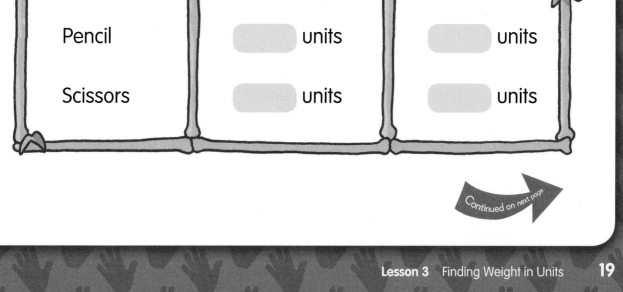

Things	Our Guess	It Is
Eraser	____ units	____ units
Pencil	____ units	____ units
Scissors	____ units	____ units

Continued on next page

Group 2

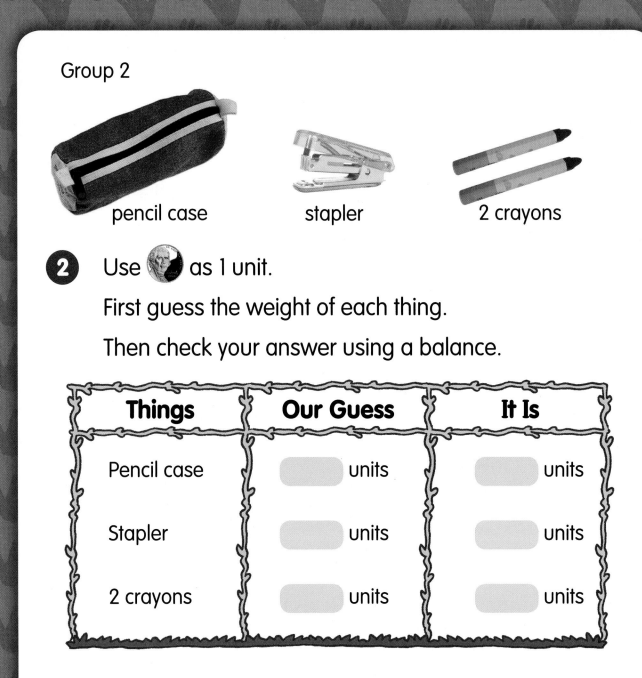

pencil case   stapler   2 crayons

2 Use 🪙 as 1 unit.

First guess the weight of each thing.

Then check your answer using a balance.

Things	Our Guess	It Is
Pencil case	_____ units	_____ units
Stapler	_____ units	_____ units
2 crayons	_____ units	_____ units

3 Now use 📎 as 1 unit to find the weight of the things in Group 2.

What happens?

4 Then, use 🪙 to find the weight of the things in Group 1.

What happens? Can you say why?

Guided Learning

Look at the picture.

1 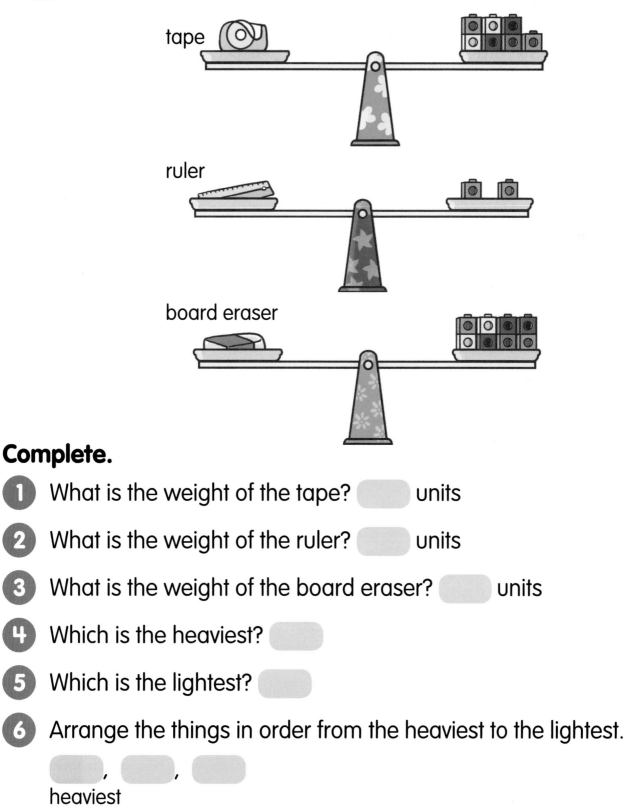 stands for 1 unit.

tape

ruler

board eraser

Complete.

1 What is the weight of the tape? ⬚ units

2 What is the weight of the ruler? ⬚ units

3 What is the weight of the board eraser? ⬚ units

4 Which is the heaviest? ⬚

5 Which is the lightest? ⬚

6 Arrange the things in order from the heaviest to the lightest.

⬚ , ⬚ , ⬚

heaviest

Let's Practice

Look at the pictures.
Complete.

Lesley has 1 watermelon slice, 1 apple, and a bunch of grapes.

1 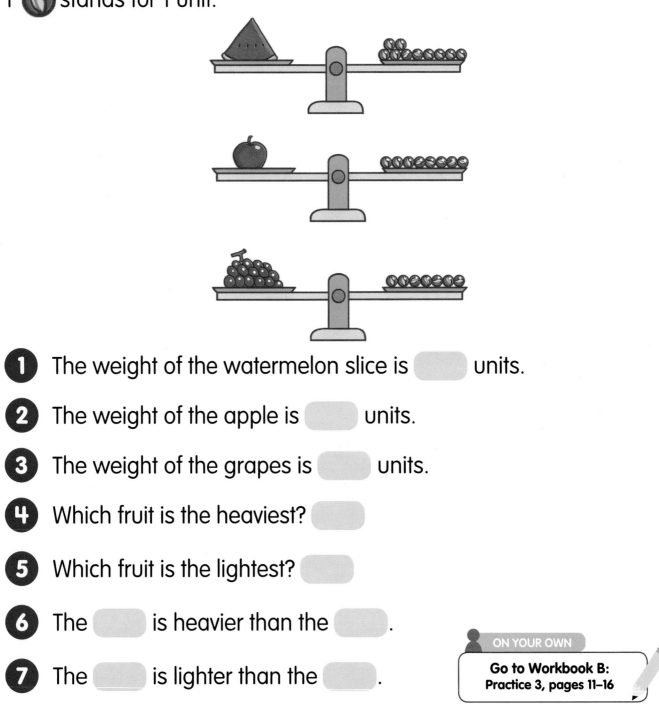 stands for 1 unit.

1. The weight of the watermelon slice is [   ] units.

2. The weight of the apple is [   ] units.

3. The weight of the grapes is [   ] units.

4. Which fruit is the heaviest? [   ]

5. Which fruit is the lightest? [   ]

6. The [   ] is heavier than the [   ].

7. The [   ] is lighter than the [   ].

ON YOUR OWN

Go to Workbook B:
Practice 3, pages 11–16

Put On Your Thinking Cap!

PROBLEM SOLVING

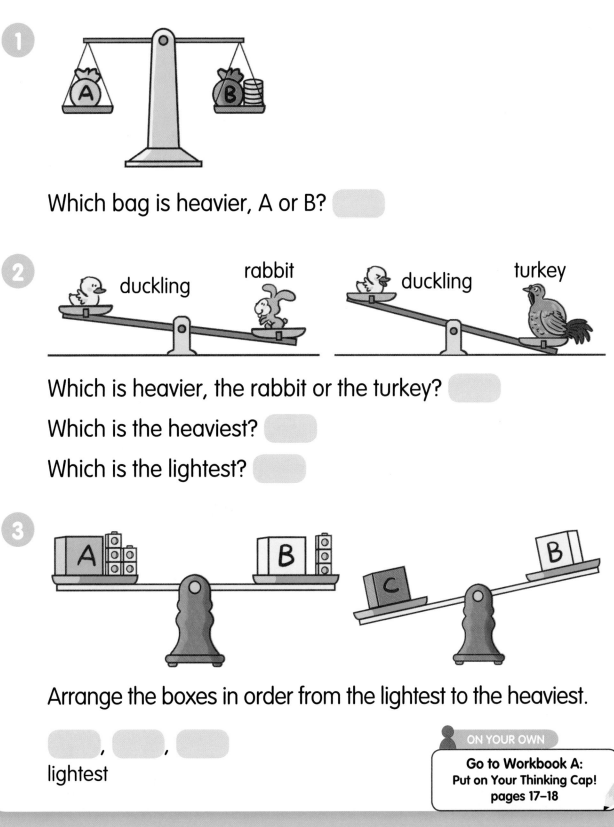

1

Which bag is heavier, A or B?

2

duckling   rabbit

duckling   turkey

Which is heavier, the rabbit or the turkey?

Which is the heaviest?

Which is the lightest?

3

A   B

C   B

Arrange the boxes in order from the lightest to the heaviest.

, ,

lightest

ON YOUR OWN

Go to Workbook A:
Put on Your Thinking Cap!
pages 17–18

Chapter Wrap Up

BIG IDEA The weight of things can be compared and measured with non-standard units.

You have learned...

to compare the weight of things.

 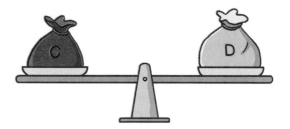

Bag A is lighter than Bag B.
Bag B is heavier than Bag A.
Bag C is as heavy as Bag D.

to compare the weight of two things by using another object.

 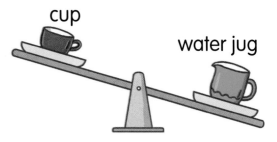

The fork is lighter than the cup.
The water jug is heavier than the cup.
So, the water jug is heavier than the fork.
The fork is the lightest.
The water jug is the heaviest.

to measure weight using non-standard units.

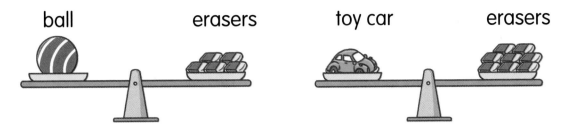

ball   erasers   toy car   erasers

The weight of the ball is about 5 erasers.
The weight of the toy car is about 8 erasers.

the number of units is different when different objects
are used to stand for 1 unit.

1 🔵 stands for 1 unit.   1 ⬜ stands for 1 unit.

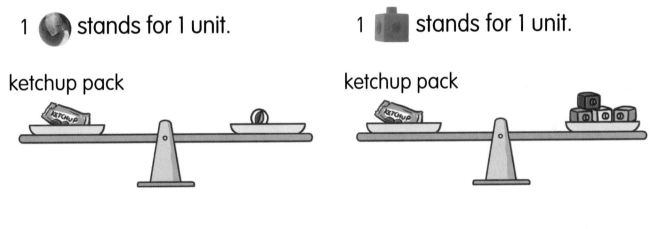

ketchup pack   ketchup pack

The weight of the pack of ketchup is about 1 unit
when you use 🔵.

The weight of the same pack of ketchup is about
4 units when you use ⬜.

to tell the weight of a thing in units.

to arrange things in order from the heaviest or the lightest.

1 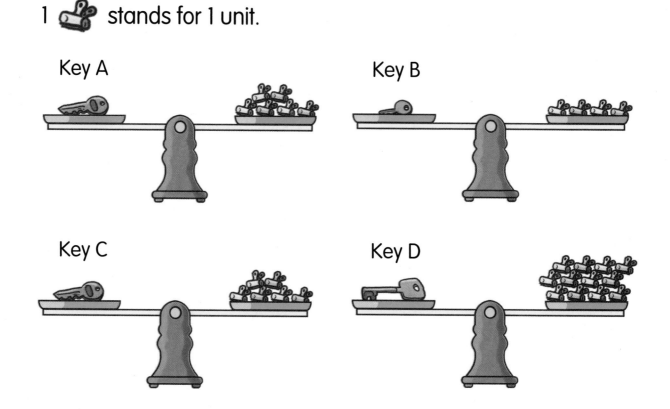 stands for 1 unit.

Key A   Key B

Key C   Key D

Key A weighs about 6 units.
Key B weighs about 4 units.
Key C weighs about 6 units.
Key D weighs about 12 units.

Key B is lighter than Key A.
Key A is heavier than Key B.
Key A is as heavy as Key C.
Key B is the lightest.
Key D is the heaviest.

ON YOUR OWN

Go to Workbook B:
Chapter Review/Test,
pages 19–24

Picture Graphs and Bar Graphs

Old MacDonald had a farm,
E - i - e - i - o
And on his farm he had some ducks,
E - i - e - i - o
With a quack, quack here,
and a quack, quack there,
Here quack, there quack,
Everywhere quack, quack.
Old MacDonald had a farm,
E - i - e - i - o!

Lesson 1 Simple Picture Graphs

Lesson 2 More Picture Graphs

Lesson 3 Tally Charts and Bar Graphs

BIG IDEA

Picture graphs, tally charts, and bar graphs can be used to show data.

Showing data with pictures

There are 5 .

There are 3 .

There are 3 .

There are 2 .

Solve.

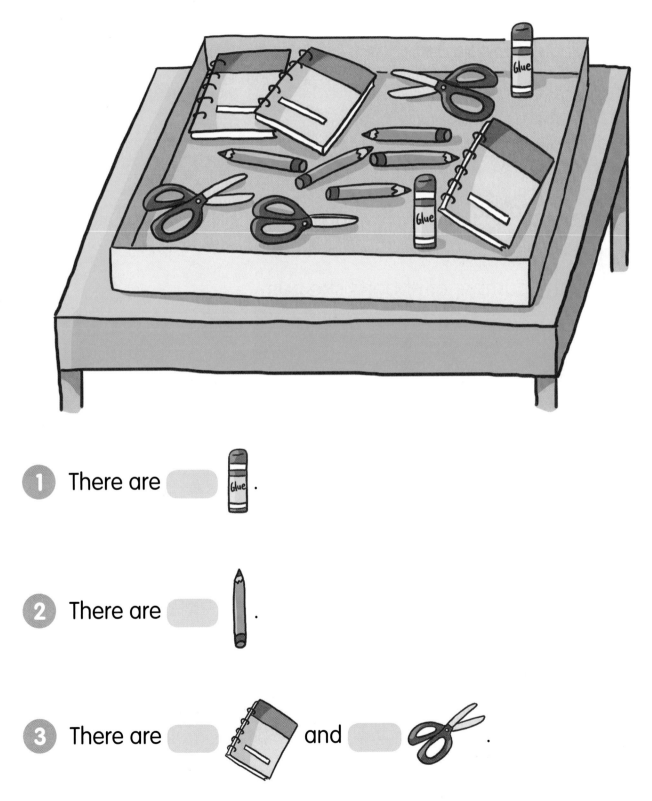

1 There are ⬭ .

2 There are ⬭ .

3 There are ⬭ and ⬭ .

Simple Picture Graphs

Lesson Objectives

- Collect and organize data.
- Show data as a picture graph.
- Understand the data shown in a picture graph.

Vocabulary

data	most
picture graph	fewest
more	fewer

Learn **You can collect data and show it as a picture graph.**

Sally loves ribbons!
Count the number of ribbons she has.

Data is information that has numbers.
Here the information is the number of ribbons and their colors.

Sally's Ribbons

Red	Blue	Yellow

You can show data as a **picture graph**.
Read the picture graph.

There are 5 red ribbons.

There are 7 blue ribbons.

There are 4 yellow ribbons.

Sally has the **most** blue ribbons.

She has the **fewest** yellow ribbons.

There are 2 **more** blue ribbons than red ribbons.

There are 3 **fewer** yellow ribbons than blue ribbons.

There are 16 ribbons in all.

> **Most** means the greatest number. **Fewest** means the least number.

A picture graph uses pictures or symbols to show data.

Guided Learning

Look at the picture graph.
Then solve.

There are three hens on Old Joe's farm.
The picture graph shows the number of eggs that each hen laid this week.

Eggs Laid This Week

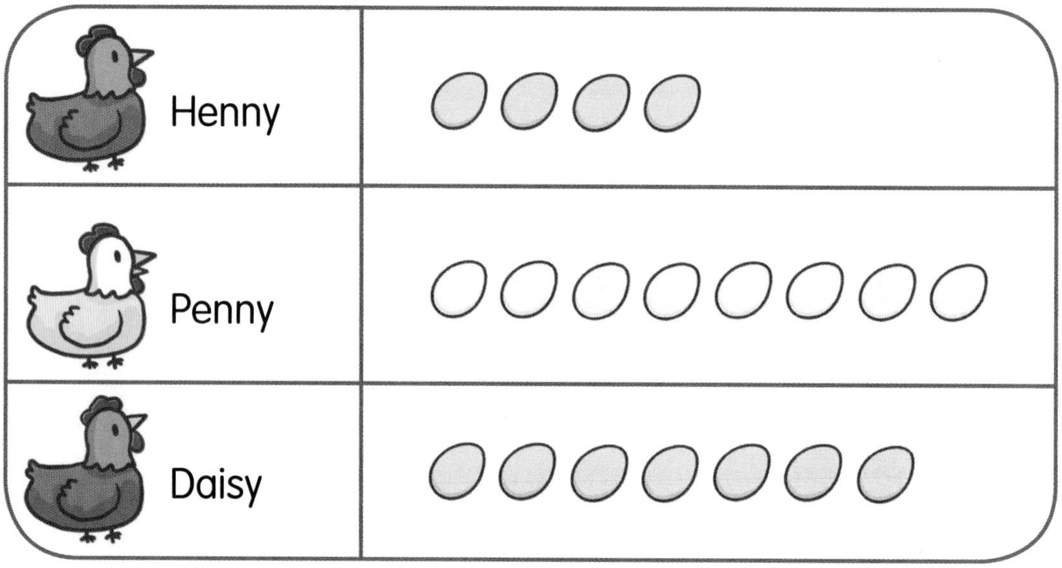

Henny	○ ○ ○ ○
Penny	○ ○ ○ ○ ○ ○ ○ ○
Daisy	○ ○ ○ ○ ○ ○ ○

1 Henny laid _____ eggs.

2 Penny laid _____ eggs.

3 Daisy laid _____ eggs.

4 _____ laid the most eggs.

5 _____ laid the fewest eggs.

6 Daisy laid _____ more eggs than Henny.

7 There are _____ eggs in all.

Look at the picture graph.
Then answer the questions.

Sea Animals Seen at the Seashore

Crab	
Squid	
Starfish	
Fish	

8 How many crabs are there?

9 How many squid are there?

10 How many starfish are there?

11 How many fish are there?

12 Which sea animal is seen most often?

13 Which sea animal is seen least often?

14 Are there more squid or fish?

How many more?

15 Are there fewer starfish or crabs?

How many fewer?

Look at the picture graph.
Complete.

Fruit Parade

Apple	🍎 🍎 🍎 🍎 🍎 🍎
Orange	🍊 🍊
Strawberry	🍓 🍓 🍓 🍓 🍓 🍓 🍓 🍓

1 There are ____ apples.

2 There are ____ oranges.

3 There are ____ more apples than oranges.

4 There are ____ fewer oranges than strawberries.

5 The number of ____ is the greatest.

6 The number of ____ is the least.

Look at the picture graph.
Complete.

Shapes

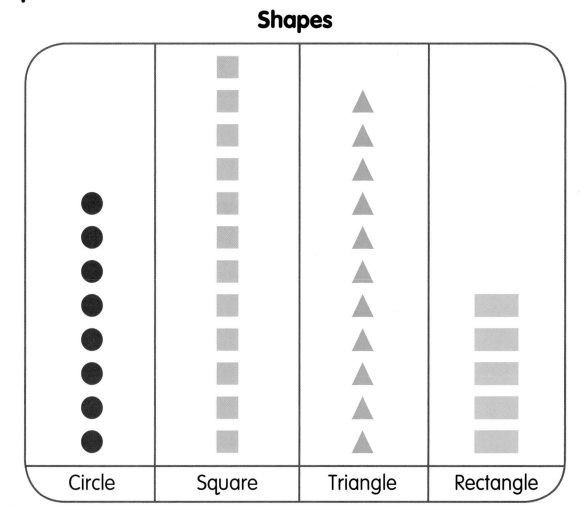

| Circle | Square | Triangle | Rectangle |

7 There are ___ squares.

8 There are 11 ___.

9 The number of ___ is the greatest.

10 The number of ___ is the least.

11 There are ___ more squares than circles.

12 There are ___ fewer rectangles than triangles.

ON YOUR OWN

Go to Workbook B:
Practice 1, pages 25–28

LESSON 2 More Picture Graphs

Lesson Objectives

- Collect and organize data.
- Draw picture graphs.
- Understand the data shown in picture graphs using symbols.

Learn

You can collect data to make a picture graph.

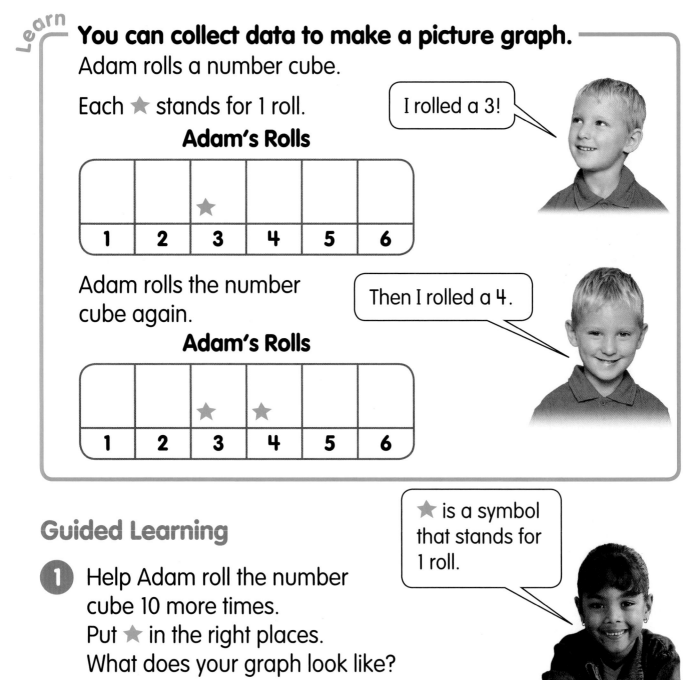

Adam rolls a number cube.

Each ★ stands for 1 roll.

I rolled a 3!

Adam's Rolls

		★			
1	2	3	4	5	6

Adam rolls the number cube again.

Then I rolled a 4.

Adam's Rolls

		★	★		
1	2	3	4	5	6

Guided Learning

★ is a symbol that stands for 1 roll.

1 Help Adam roll the number cube 10 more times.
   Put ★ in the right places.
   What does your graph look like?

Hands-On Activity

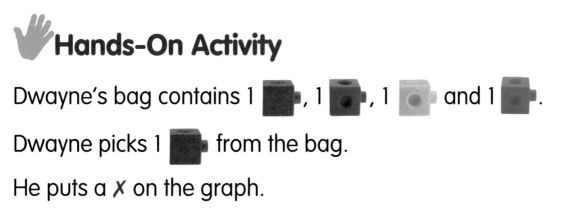

Dwayne's bag contains 1 [cube], 1 [cube], 1 [cube] and 1 [cube].

Dwayne picks 1 [cube] from the bag.

He puts a ✗ on the graph.

Dwayne's Picks

[cube]	✗
[cube]	
[cube]	
[cube]	

Dwayne puts the [cube] back into the bag.

Help him pick another one.

Put another ✗ on the graph.

Do this 10 times.

Which [cubes] did you pick most often?

Which [cubes] did you pick the fewest times?

Use ✗ to show each pick.

You can understand the data shown in a picture graph.

This picture graph shows the favorite toys of 18 children.

Our Favorite Toys

⭐				
⭐				
⭐		⭐		⭐
⭐	⭐	⭐		⭐
⭐	⭐	⭐		⭐
⭐	⭐	⭐	⭐	⭐
Teddy Bear	Doll	Ball	Toy Car	Cooking Set

Each ⭐ stands for 1 child.

4 children like cooking sets.
3 children like dolls.
The most popular toy is the teddy bear.
3 fewer children like toy cars than cooking sets.
The same number of children like balls and cooking sets.
There are 5 kinds of toys in all.

Guided Learning

Look at the picture graph.
Then answer the questions.

This picture graph shows the favorite colors chosen by a first grade class.

Our Favorite Color

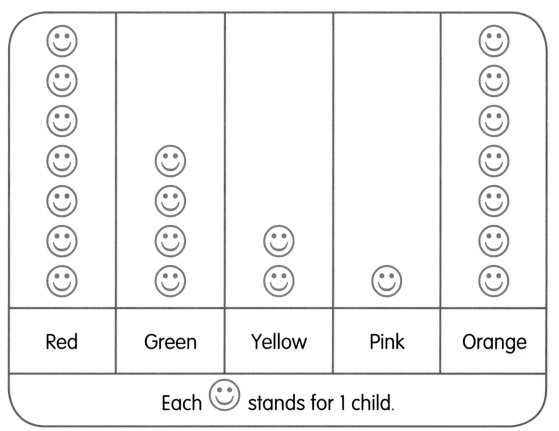

Each ☺ stands for 1 child.

2 How many children chose orange?

3 Which color did the children choose the least?

4 How many more children chose red than green?

5 How many fewer children chose yellow than orange?

6 How many children are there?

Let's Practice

Look at the picture graph.
Then answer the questions.

This picture graph shows some cars in a parking lot.

Cars in a Parking Lot

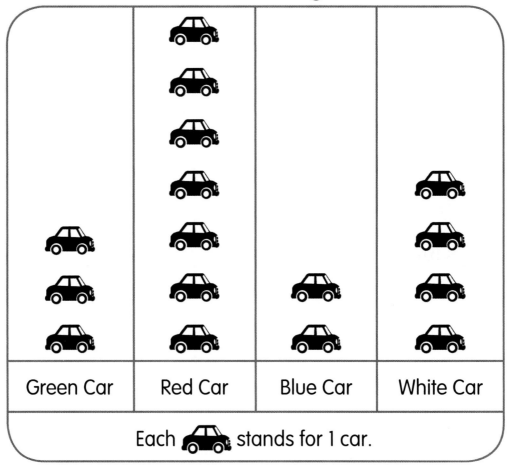

Each 🚗 stands for 1 car.

1. How many blue cars are there?

2. How many red cars and white cars are there in all?

3. How many more red cars than green cars are there?

4. How many cars are **not** green?

Look at the picture graph.
Then answer the questions.

This picture graph shows the favorite season of some children.

Favorite Seasons

Spring	● ● ●
Summer	● ● ● ●
Fall	● ●
Winter	● ● ● ● ● ●

Each ● stands for 1 child.

5 Winter is the favorite season of ____ children.

6 ____ is the favorite season of 4 children.

7 How many children chose spring or fall as their favorite season? ____

8 Which is the most popular season? ____

9 ____ is the favorite season of the fewest children.

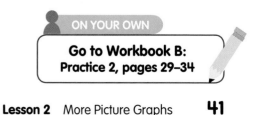

ON YOUR OWN

Go to Workbook B:
Practice 2, pages 29–34

3 Tally Charts and Bar Graphs

Lesson Objectives

- Make a tally chart.
- Show data in a bar graph.
- Understand data shown in a bar graph.

Learn **You can collect data and organize it using a tally chart and bar graph.**

Mrs. Hanson has her class paste pictures of their favorite sport on a sheet of paper like this.

Then she makes a tally chart with this data.
She checks ✔ the favorite sport of each child
and draws a **tally mark** / on the tally chart.

Soccer   tally

I check the favorite sport of one child and draw a tally mark.

I draw 4 tally marks like this ||||. To show 5 tally marks, I draw the fifth mark across the 4 tally marks. |||||

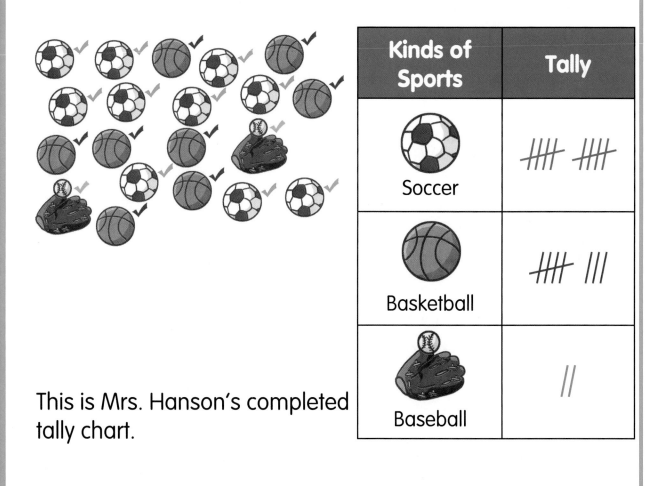

Kinds of Sports	Tally
Soccer	||||| |||||
Basketball	||||| |||
Baseball	||

This is Mrs. Hanson's completed tally chart.

Continued on next page

Then Mrs. Hanson counts the tally marks for each kind of sport.

Kinds of Sports	Tally	Number of Children
Soccer	ⵀⵀ ⵀⵀ	10
Basketball	ⵀⵀ |||	8
Baseball	||	2

The tally chart shows the number of children who choose each sport as their favorite.

Mrs. Hanson shows the data using a picture graph. She uses ■ to stand for 1 child.

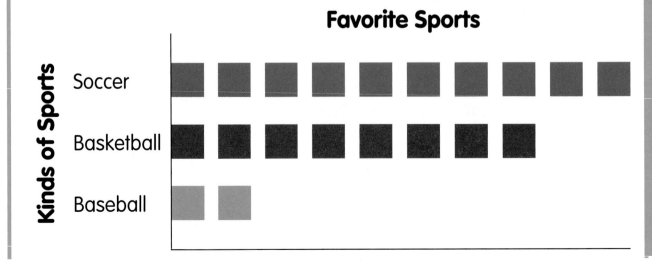

Favorite Sports

Then Mrs. Hanson shows the same data in a bar graph.

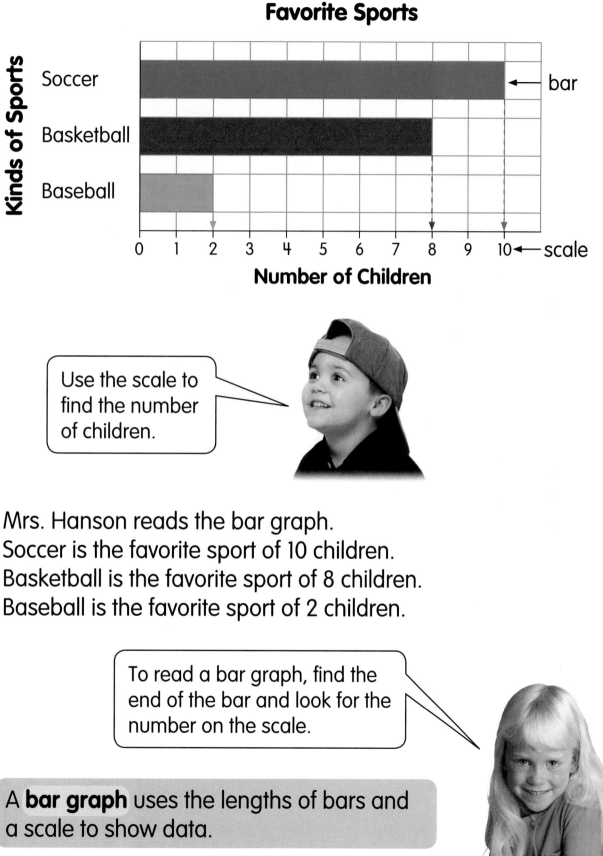

Favorite Sports

Use the scale to find the number of children.

Mrs. Hanson reads the bar graph.
Soccer is the favorite sport of 10 children.
Basketball is the favorite sport of 8 children.
Baseball is the favorite sport of 2 children.

To read a bar graph, find the end of the bar and look for the number on the scale.

A **bar graph** uses the lengths of bars and a scale to show data.

Guided Learning

Peter saw some animals at the zoo.

Use a copy of this tally chart.
Count and make a tally mark for each animal.

1

Kinds of Animals	Tally	Number of Animals
Lion		
Monkey		
Horse		

Complete.

2 There are ____ monkeys.

3 There are ____ animals in all.

This is the bar graph of the animals Peter saw.

Animals Peter Saw at the Zoo

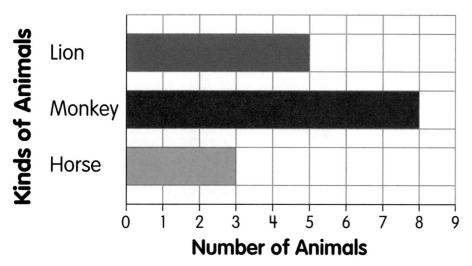

**Look at the bar graph.
Complete.**

4 There are ⬭ monkeys.

5 There are ⬭ lions.

6 There are ⬭ horses.

7 There are ⬭ more monkeys than horses.

8 There are ⬭ fewer lions than monkeys.

9 The number of ⬭ is the least.

10 The number of ⬭ is the greatest.

Henry is making a tally chart and a bar graph.
The data are the different books that he has.

1 **Complete a copy of the tally chart and bar graph.**

ⓐ

Kinds of Books	Tally	Number of Books
Comic Book	‖‖‖	
Puzzle Book	‖‖	
Storybook	‖‖‖ ‖‖	

ⓑ

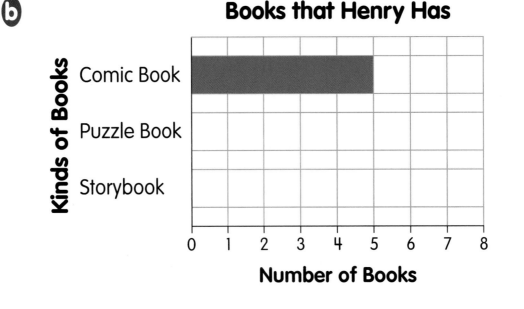

Books that Henry Has

2 Henry has ⬜ more storybooks than puzzle books.

3 He has ⬜ fewer comic books than storybooks.

ON YOUR OWN

Go to Workbook B:
Practice 3, pages 35–38

PROBLEM SOLVING

Read the sentences.
Then draw a graph.
It should start out like the picture below.

It rains on Monday and Tuesday.

It is sunny on Wednesday and Thursday.

There is heavy rain on Friday.

It is hot and does not rain on Saturday or Sunday.

Use ▲ to stand for 1 day.

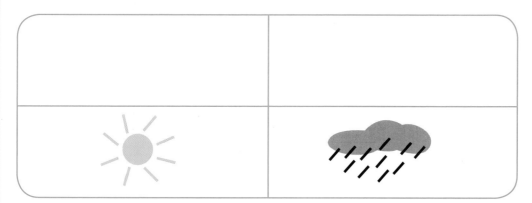

Sunny Days and Rainy Days

Are there more sunny days or rainy days?
How many more?

ON YOUR OWN

Go to Workbook B:
Put on Your Thinking Cap!
pages 39–42

Chapter Wrap Up

You have learned...

to collect and count data.

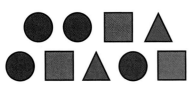

There are 4 circles.
There are 3 squares.
There are 2 triangles.

to draw and read picture graphs.

Shapes	
Circle	● ● ● ●
Square	■ ■ ■
Triangle	▲ ▲

Shapes

● ● ● ●	■ ■ ■	▲ ▲
Circle	Square	Triangle

....

to use a picture to represent 1 thing.
to understand the data shown in picture graphs using symbols.

Fruit I Ate This Week

Apple	★ ★ ★ ★
Banana	★ ★ ★
Pear	★ ★
Each ★ stands for 1 fruit.	

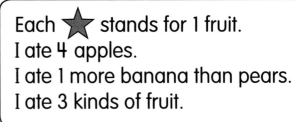

Each ★ stands for 1 fruit.
I ate 4 apples.
I ate 1 more banana than pears.
I ate 3 kinds of fruit.

Picture graphs, tally charts, and bar graphs can be used to show data.

to make a tally chart.

Kinds of Fruit	Tally
Apple	////
Banana	///
Pear	//

to show data in a bar graph.

a bar graph uses the lengths of bars and a scale to show data.

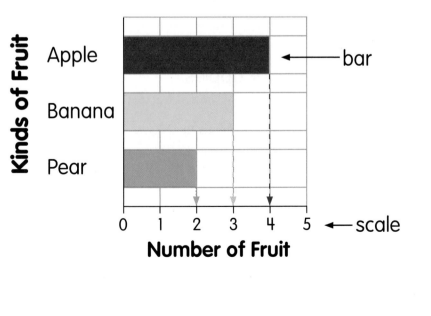

Fruit I Ate This Week

Kinds of Fruit — Apple, Banana, Pear

bar

Number of Fruit — 0 1 2 3 4 5

scale

I ate 4 apples. The lengths of the bars show the number of fruits. Use the scale to find the number of fruits.

ON YOUR OWN

Go to Workbook B: Chapter Review/Test, pages 43–44

BIG IDEA

Count, compare, and order numbers from 1 to 40.

Recall Prior Knowledge

Counting on from 10 to 20

10, ... 11, 12, 13, 14, 15, 16, 17, 18, 19, 20

13
thirteen

Making a ten, and then counting

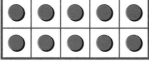

14 is 10 and 4.
14 = 10 + 4

Ten and four make fourteen.

Reading place-value charts

14 is 1 ten 4 ones
14 = 10 + 4

Tens	Ones
1	4

Comparing and ordering numbers

Compare 17, 14, and 19.

Compare the tens.
They are the same.

Compare the ones.
7 ones is greater than 4 ones.
So, 17 is greater than 14.

9 ones is greater than 7 ones
and greater than 4 ones.
19 is the greatest number.
14 is the least number.

Order the numbers from greatest to least.
19, 17, 14

Order the numbers from least to greatest.
14, 17, 19

Tens	Ones
1	7
1	4
1	9

Making number patterns

12, 14, 16, 18...

The numbers are arranged in a pattern.

Each number is 2 more than the number before it.

The next number is 2 more than 18.

It is 20.

Count on.

1 14, 15, 16, ⬜ , ⬜

2 10, 11, 12, ⬜ , ⬜

Find the missing numbers or words.

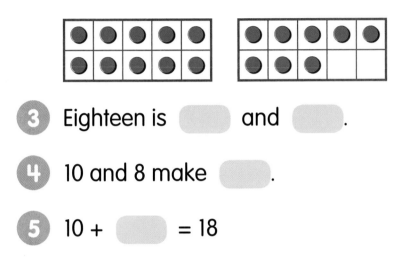

3 Eighteen is ⬜ and ⬜ .

4 10 and 8 make ⬜ .

5 10 + ⬜ = 18

Read the place value chart.
Find the missing numbers.

6

Tens	Ones
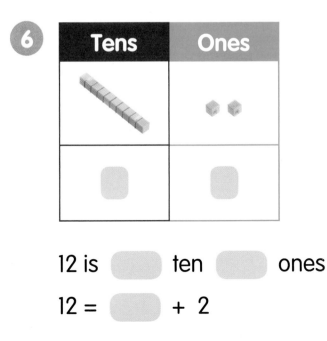	
⬜	⬜

12 is ⬜ ten ⬜ ones

12 = ⬜ + 2

Compare and order.

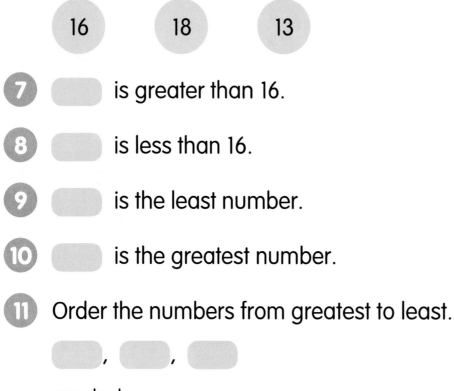

7 ⬭ is greater than 16.

8 ⬭ is less than 16.

9 ⬭ is the least number.

10 ⬭ is the greatest number.

11 Order the numbers from greatest to least.

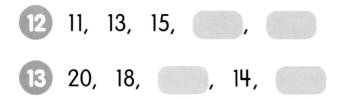

⬭ , ⬭ , ⬭

greatest

Complete the number patterns.

12 11, 13, 15, ⬭ , ⬭

13 20, 18, ⬭ , 14, ⬭

Counting to 40

Lesson Objectives

- Count on from 21 to 40.
- Read and write 21 to 40 in numbers and words.

Vocabulary

twenty-one	twenty-two
twenty-three	twenty-four
twenty-five	twenty-six
twenty-seven	twenty-eight
twenty-nine	thirty
forty	

Learn

You can count numbers greater than 20 in ones.

Count the 🔲.

1, 2, 3, 4, 5, 6, 7, 8, 9, 10

... 11, 12, 13, 14, 15, 16, 17, 18, 19, 20, 21

Continued on next page

It is easy to make tens with 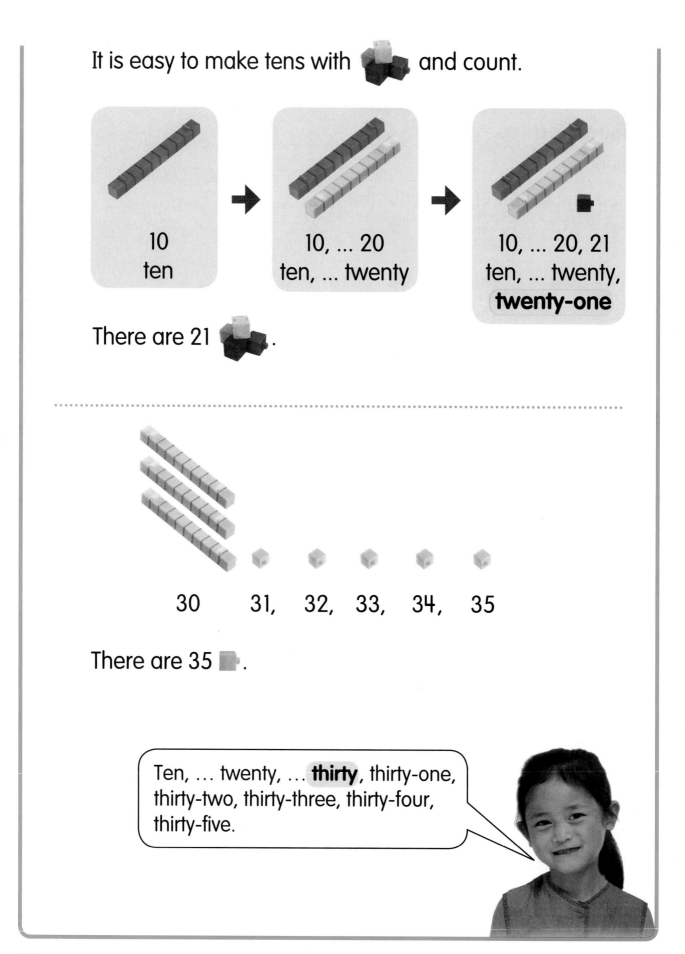 and count.

10
ten

10, ... 20
ten, ... twenty

10, ... 20, 21
ten, ... twenty,
twenty-one

There are 21 .

30   31,   32,   33,   34,   35

There are 35 .

Ten, ... twenty, ... **thirty**, thirty-one,
thirty-two, thirty-three, thirty-four,
thirty-five.

Guided Learning

Count in tens and ones.
Write the numbers and words.

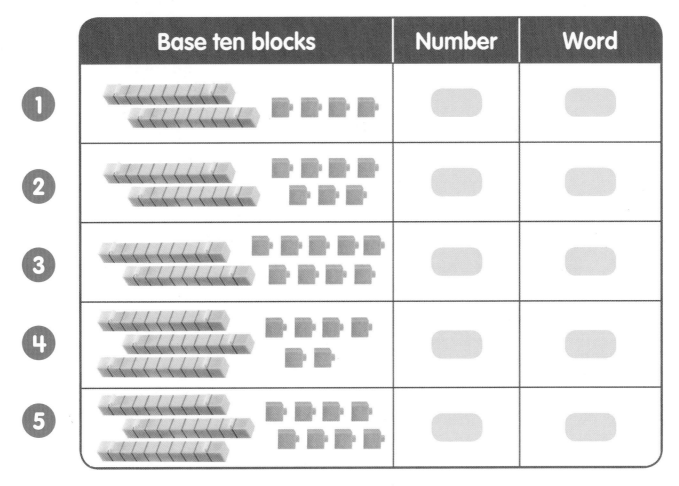

	Base ten blocks	Number	Word
1			
2			
3			
4			
5			

You can count by tens to 40.

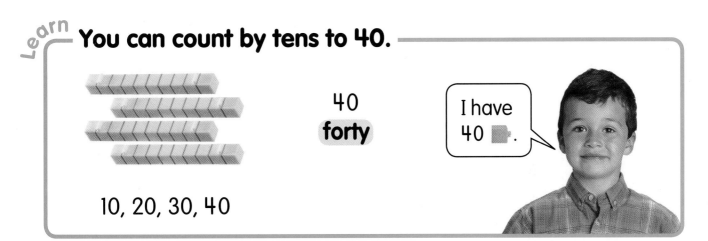

40
forty

I have 40 ▪.

10, 20, 30, 40

You can make numbers with tens and ones.

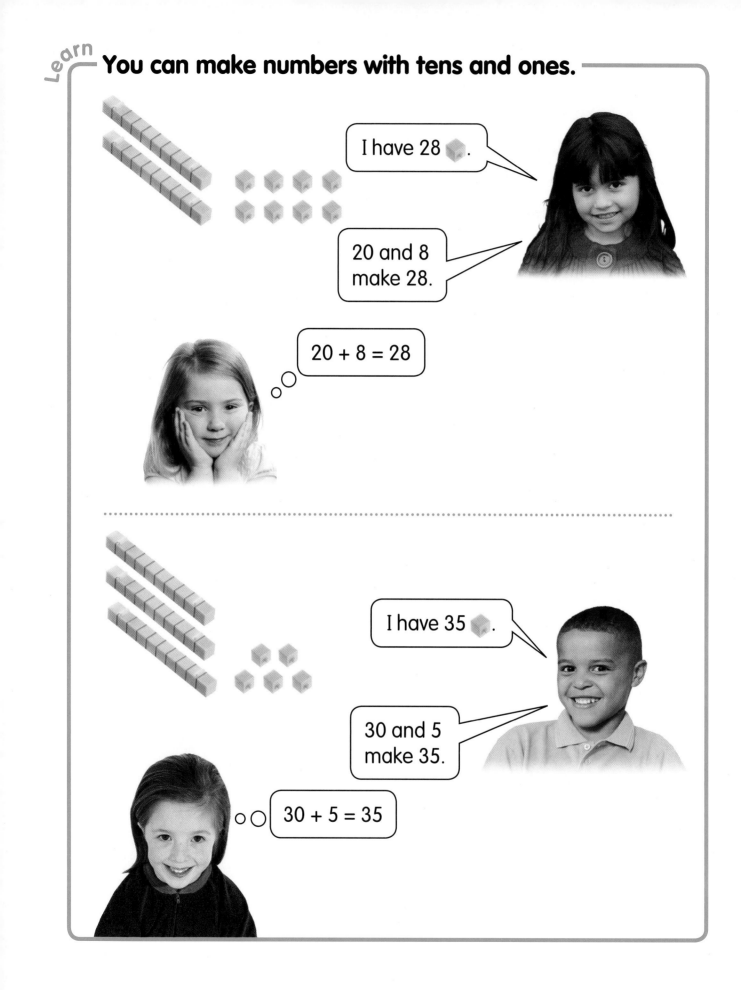

I have 28 🔲.

20 and 8 make 28.

20 + 8 = 28

I have 35 🔲.

30 and 5 make 35.

30 + 5 = 35

Find the missing number.

 20 and 6 make [ ].

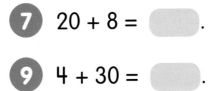 20 + 8 = [ ].

8 7 and 30 make [ ].

9 4 + 30 = [ ].

Let's Practice

Find the missing numbers.

1 First make tens.
Then count on.

10, 20, [ ], [ ], [ ], [ ]

2 Find how many . [ ]

Write the number.

3 thirty

4 forty

5 twenty-four

6 twenty-seven

7 thirty-two

8 thirty-six

Write the number in words.
Use the scrambled words to help you.

9 28   w t e n y t - t g e i h

10 30   r t y i t h

11 33   r t y i t h - r e e t h

12 40   y r t o f

Find the missing numbers.

13 20 and 9 make   .

14   is 9 and 30.

15 6 + 20 =

16 30 + 8 =

Find the missing numbers.

17 20 and   make 25.

18   and 30 make 34.

Can you think of other numbers that make 25 and 34?

ON YOUR OWN

Go to Workbook B:
Practice 1, pages 45–48

Place Value

Lesson Objectives

• Use a place-value chart to show numbers up to 40.

• Show objects up to 40 as tens and ones.

Learn **You can use place value to show numbers to 40.**

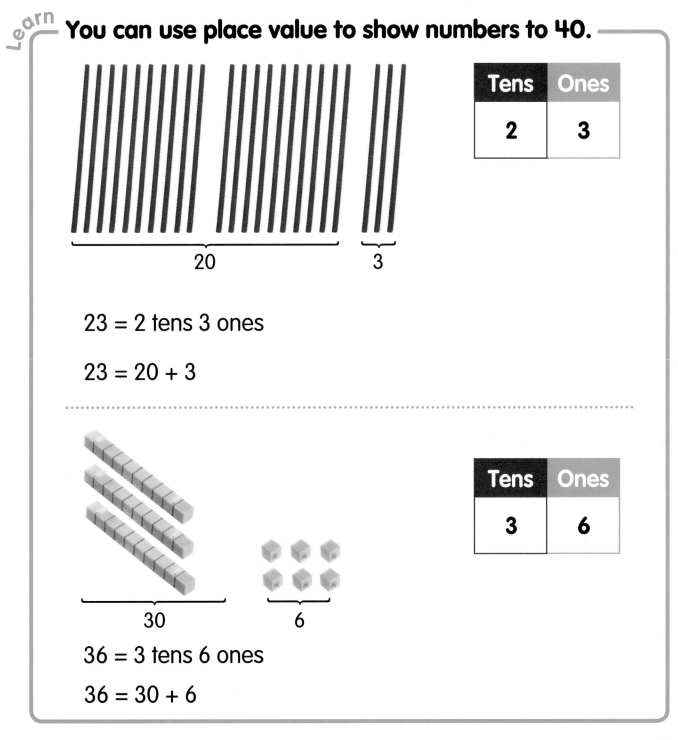

Tens	Ones
2	3

20   3

23 = 2 tens 3 ones

23 = 20 + 3

Tens	Ones
3	6

30   6

36 = 3 tens 6 ones

36 = 30 + 6

Guided Learning

Use place value to find the missing numbers.

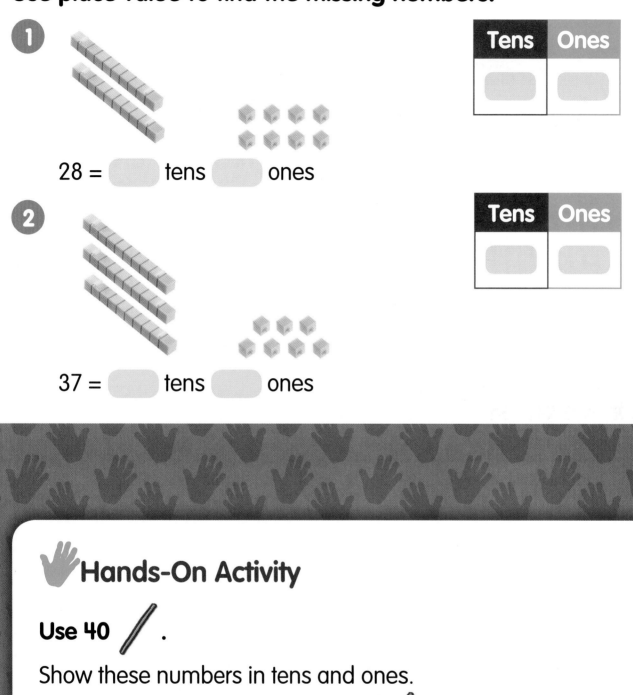

1 28 = ⬭ tens ⬭ ones

Tens	Ones

2 37 = ⬭ tens ⬭ ones

Tens	Ones

✋ Hands-On Activity

Use 40 ／ .

Show these numbers in tens and ones.

You can bundle each group of ten ／ together.

22 27 30 33 34 35

Let's Practice

Look at each place-value chart.
Find the number it shows.

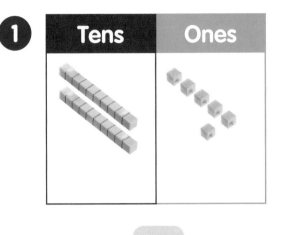

1

Tens	Ones

2

Tens	Ones

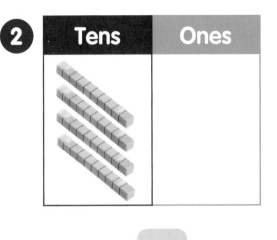

Count in tens and ones.
Fill in the blanks.

3

Tens	Ones

30 = [   ] tens [   ] ones

30 + 0 = [   ]

4

Tens	Ones

39 = [   ] tens [   ] ones

30 + 9 = [   ]

ON YOUR OWN

Go to Workbook B:
Practice 2, pages 49–50

LESSON 3 Comparing, Ordering, and Patterns

Lesson Objectives

• Use a strategy to compare numbers to 40.

• Compare numbers to 40.

• Order numbers to 40.

• Find the missing numbers in a number pattern.

Learn **You can count on and count back using a counting tape.**

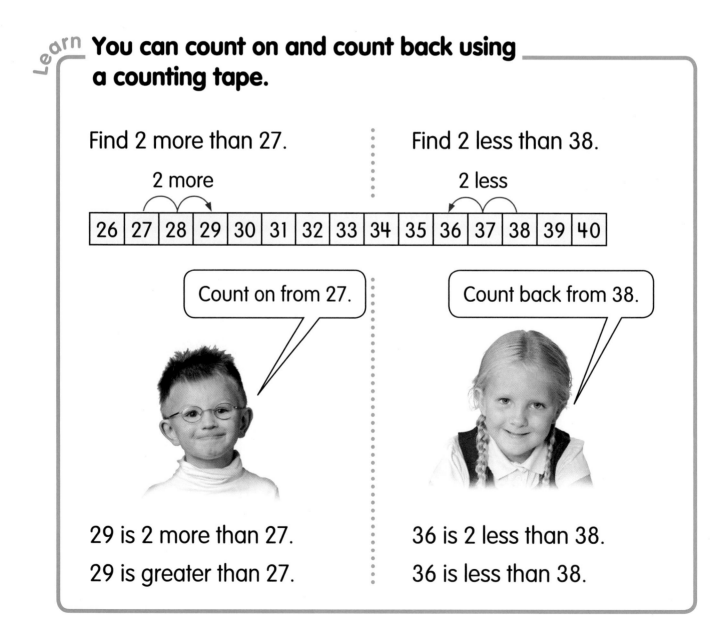

Find 2 more than 27.

Find 2 less than 38.

Count on from 27.

Count back from 38.

29 is 2 more than 27.

29 is greater than 27.

36 is 2 less than 38.

36 is less than 38.

Guided Learning

Find the missing numbers.

This picture shows part of a calendar.

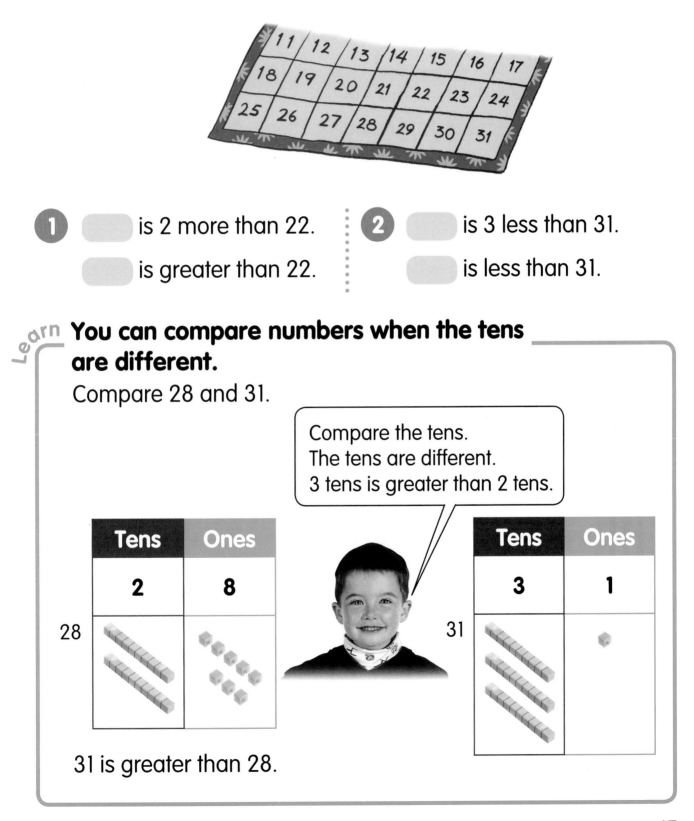

1 [ ] is 2 more than 22.

[ ] is greater than 22.

2 [ ] is 3 less than 31.

[ ] is less than 31.

Learn You can compare numbers when the tens are different.

Compare 28 and 31.

Compare the tens.
The tens are different.
3 tens is greater than 2 tens.

Tens	Ones
2	8

28

Tens	Ones
3	1

31

31 is greater than 28.

Guided Learning

3 **Compare the numbers.**

Which number is greater?
Which number is less?

26   32

Are the tens equal?

[   ] tens is greater than [   ] tens.

So, [   ] is greater than [   ].

[   ] is less than [   ].

Learn You can compare numbers when the tens are equal.

Compare 34 and 37.

The tens are equal.
So, compare the ones.
7 is greater than 4.

Tens	Ones
3	4

34

Tens	Ones
3	7

37

37 is greater than 34.

Guided Learning

Compare the numbers.

4 Which number is greater?
Which number is less?

35   34

So, _____ is greater than _____ .

_____ is less than _____ .

Are the tens equal?
Are the ones equal?
_____ ones is greater
than _____ ones.

Compare the numbers.

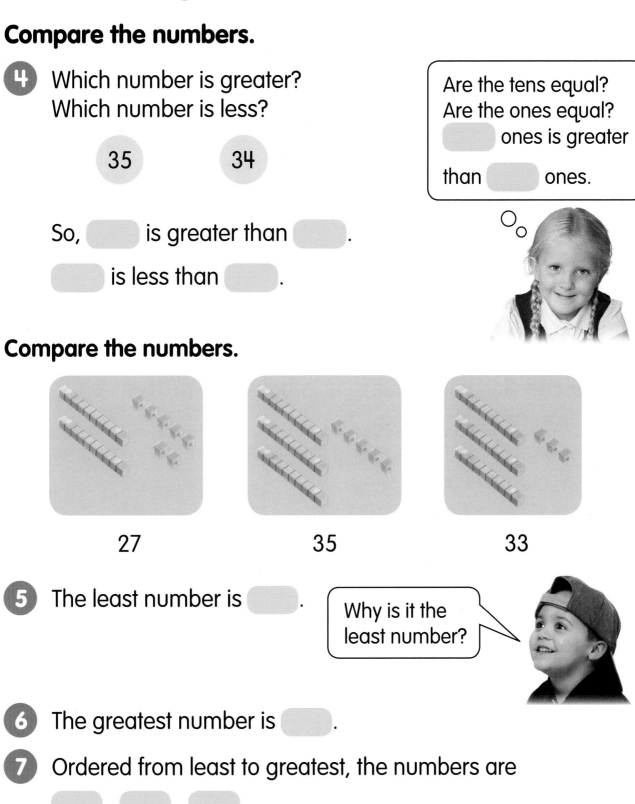

27   35   33

5 The least number is _____ .

Why is it the
least number?

6 The greatest number is _____ .

7 Ordered from least to greatest, the numbers are

_____ , _____ , _____ .

Order the numbers from least to greatest.

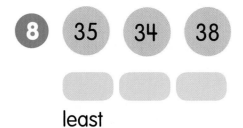

8 35 34 38

least

Order the numbers from greatest to least.

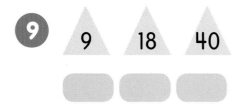

9 9 18 40

greatest

Learn **You can find the missing numbers in a pattern by adding or subtracting.**

The numbers on the counting tape are arranged in a pattern. Some numbers are missing.

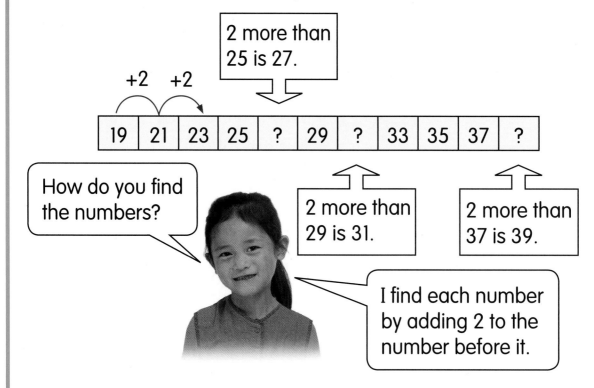

2 more than 25 is 27.

+2 +2

| 19 | 21 | 23 | 25 | ? | 29 | ? | 33 | 35 | 37 | ? |

How do you find the numbers?

2 more than 29 is 31.

2 more than 37 is 39.

I find each number by adding 2 to the number before it.

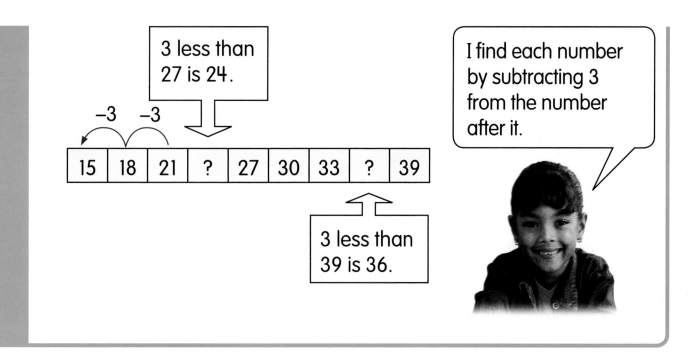

3 less than 27 is 24.

I find each number by subtracting 3 from the number after it.

−3 −3

| 15 | 18 | 21 | ? | 27 | 30 | 33 | ? | 39 |

3 less than 39 is 36.

Guided Learning

Find the missing numbers.

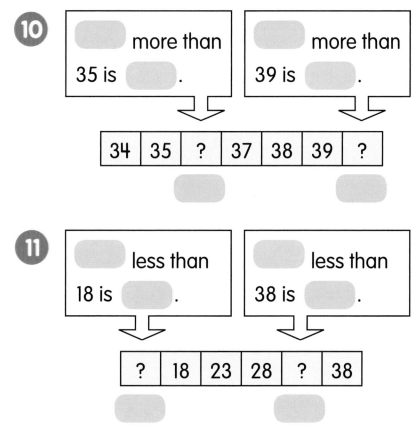

10

◻ more than 35 is ◻.

◻ more than 39 is ◻.

| 34 | 35 | ? | 37 | 38 | 39 | ? |

11

◻ less than 18 is ◻.

◻ less than 38 is ◻.

| ? | 18 | 23 | 28 | ? | 38 |

Let's Practice

Compare.

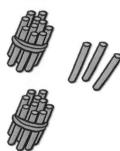

Set A   Set B

1 Set A has sticks.

2 Set B has ⬜ sticks.

3 Which set has more? ⬜

Set A   Set B

4 Set A has ⬜ sticks.

5 Set B has ⬜ sticks.

6 Which set has fewer? ⬜

Compare.
Which number is greater?

7 22   26   ⬜   **8** 35   29   ⬜

Compare.
Which number is less?

9 21 30 ⬚

10 38 24 ⬚

Order the numbers from least to greatest.

11 33 28 36

⬚ ⬚ ⬚

Solve.

12 ⬚ is 4 more than 33.

13 ⬚ is 5 less than 28.

14 2 more than 38 is ⬚.

15 ⬚ is 3 less than 40.

16 Name two numbers that are greater than 28 but less than 33.
⬚ ⬚

17 Name two numbers that are less than 36 but greater than 33.
⬚ ⬚

Find the missing numbers in each pattern.

18 25, 26, 27, 28, ⬚, ⬚, 31, ⬚, 33, 34

19 21, 23, 25, ⬚, 29, ⬚, ⬚, 35, 37

20 25, ⬚, 15, 10, 5, ⬚

ON YOUR OWN

Go to Workbook B:
Practice 3, pages 51–56

Tania completes this number pattern.

32, 33, 34, 35, 36, 37, 38, 39

She explains how she found each number in the pattern.

I added 1 to 32 to get 33.
I added 1 to 33 to get 34.

I just have to add 1 to get the next number.

33 is 1 more than 32.
34 is 1 more than 33.

$32 + 1 = 33$

$33 + 1 = 34$

How do you find the missing numbers in this pattern?

40, 30, [   ], 10, [   ]

In the pattern, is the next number more or less?

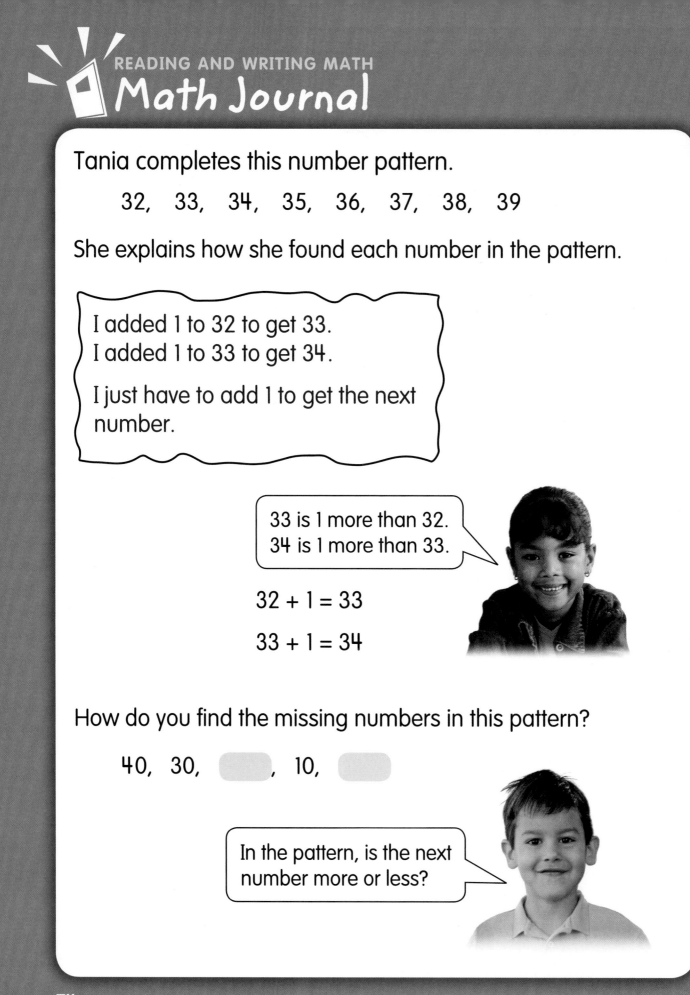

Complete the sentences below.
Choose from the helping words and numbers given.
Do not use other words or numbers.

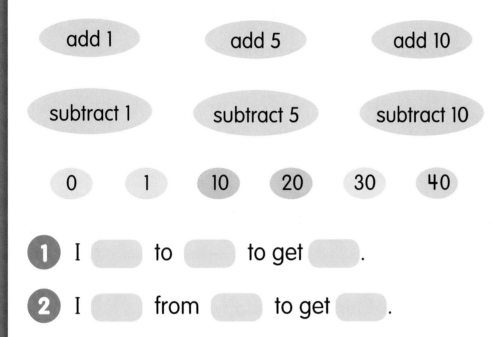

add 1   add 5   add 10

subtract 1   subtract 5   subtract 10

0   1   10   20   30   40

1 I ⬭ to ⬭ to get ⬭ .

2 I ⬭ from ⬭ to get ⬭ .

PROBLEM SOLVING

Solve.

1 Gary has five number cards that make a pattern.
He shows only three of the number cards to Eva.

Arrange the cards to make the pattern.
Which two number cards are not shown to Eva?

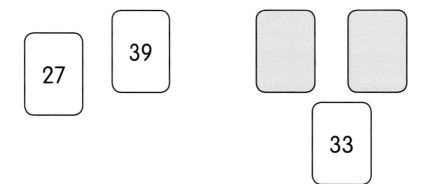

2 Gary has another five cards that make a pattern. Again, he shows only three of the number cards.

Which are the possible numbers not shown?

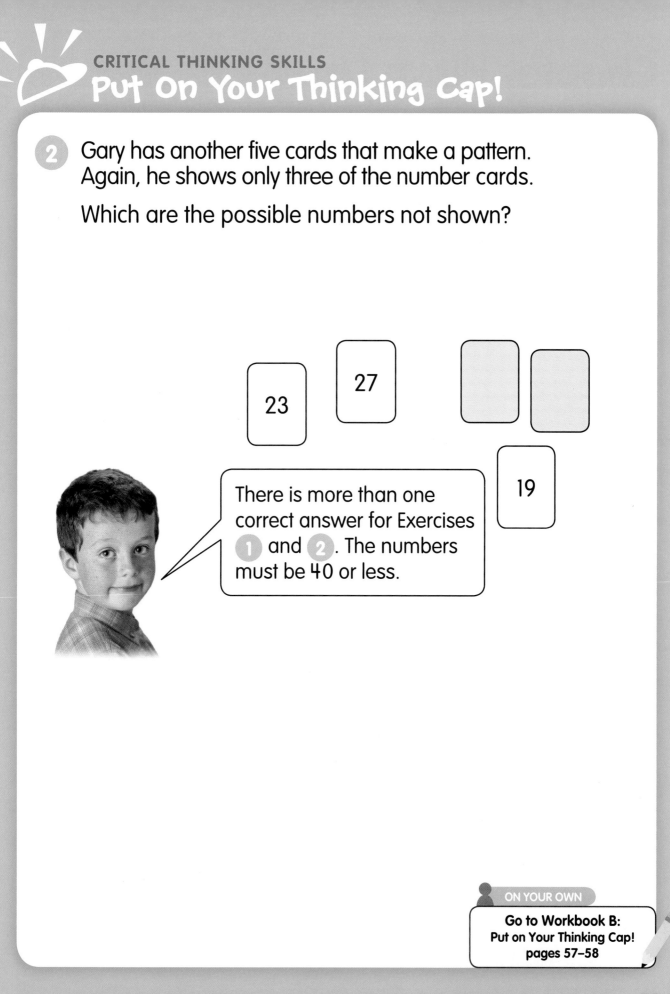

23

27

19

There is more than one correct answer for Exercises 1 and 2. The numbers must be 40 or less.

ON YOUR OWN

Go to Workbook B:
Put on Your Thinking Cap!
pages 57–58

Chapter Wrap Up

You have learned...

Numbers to 40

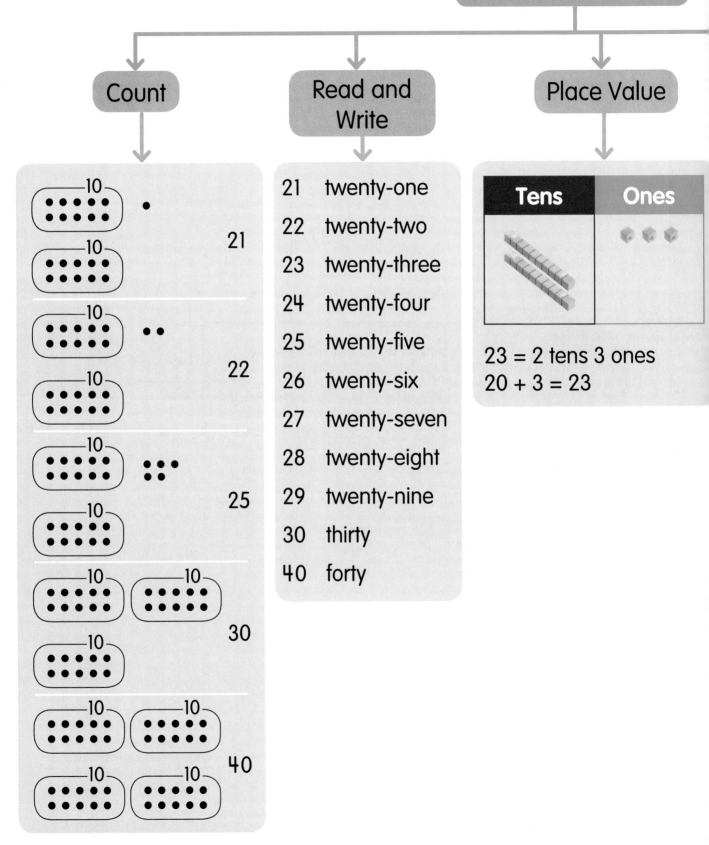

Count

21

22

25

30

40

Read and Write

21	twenty-one
22	twenty-two
23	twenty-three
24	twenty-four
25	twenty-five
26	twenty-six
27	twenty-seven
28	twenty-eight
29	twenty-nine
30	thirty
40	forty

Place Value

Tens	Ones

23 = 2 tens 3 ones
20 + 3 = 23

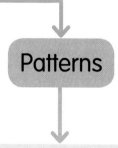

BIG IDEA

Count, compare, and order numbers from 1 to 40.

Compare and Order

38 **19** **25**

25 is greater than 19.
19 is less than 25.

25 is 6 more than 19.
19 is 6 less than 25.

Order the numbers from least to greatest.

19   25   38
least

Order the numbers from greatest to least.

38   25   19
greatest

The greatest number is 38.
The least number is 19.

Patterns

a 27, 28, 29, 30, 31

Add 1 to get the next number.

b 40, 36, 32, 28, 24

Subtract 4 to get the next number.

ON YOUR OWN

Go to Workbook B:
Chapter Review/Test,
pages 59–60

Addition and Subtraction to 40

6 🍎 + 1 🍎 = 7 🍎

4 🛍 + 1 🛍 = 5 🛍

Mom, we need 1 more bottle of apple juice and 1 more loaf of bread.

7 bottles of apple juice

5 loaves of bread

BIG IDEA

Whole numbers can be added and subtracted with and without regrouping.

Recall Prior Knowledge

Adding by making a 10

7 + 5 = ?

Step 1 7 + 5

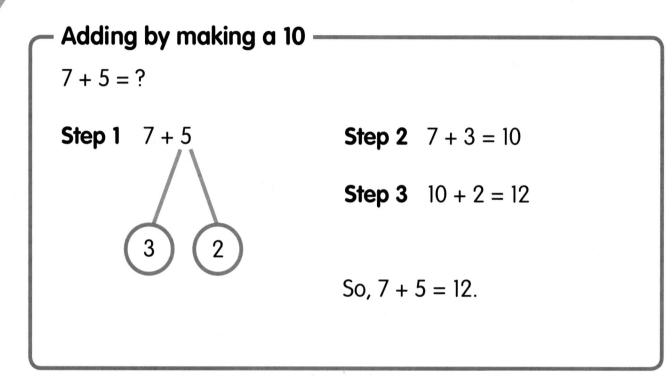

Step 2 7 + 3 = 10

Step 3 10 + 2 = 12

So, 7 + 5 = 12.

Adding by grouping into a 10 and ones

14 + 5 = ?

Step 1 14 + 5

Step 2 4 + 5 = 9

Step 3 10 + 9 = 19

So, 14 + 5 = 19.

Subtracting by grouping into a 10 and ones

$16 - 3 = ?$

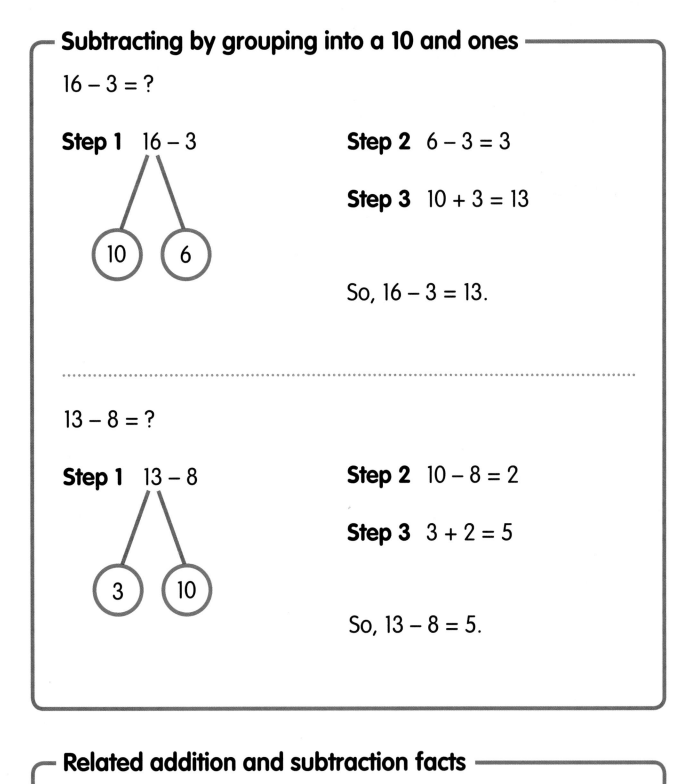

Step 1 $16 - 3$

10   6

Step 2 $6 - 3 = 3$

Step 3 $10 + 3 = 13$

So, $16 - 3 = 13$.

$13 - 8 = ?$

Step 1 $13 - 8$

3   10

Step 2 $10 - 8 = 2$

Step 3 $3 + 2 = 5$

So, $13 - 8 = 5$.

Related addition and subtraction facts

$4 + 3 = 7$ .... $7 - 4 = 3$

$7 - 3 = 4$ .... $3 + 4 = 7$

Complete the number bonds.
Add.

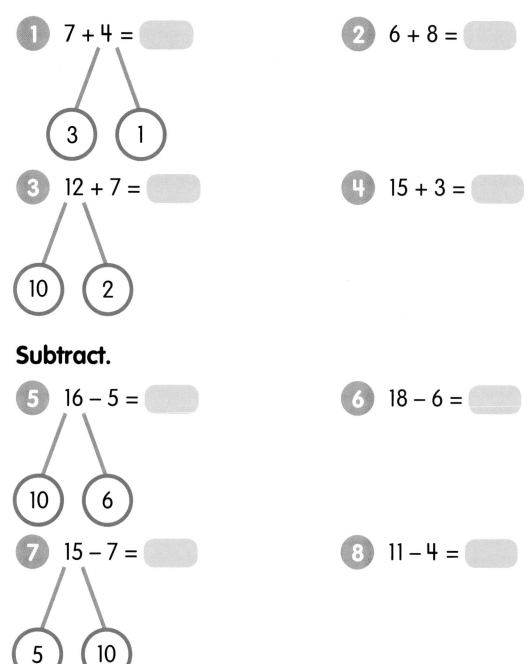

1 7 + 4 =

2 6 + 8 =

3 12 + 7 =

4 15 + 3 =

Subtract.

5 16 − 5 =

6 18 − 6 =

7 15 − 7 =

8 11 − 4 =

Find a related addition or subtraction sentence.

9 14 − 6 = 8

10 9 + 7 = 16

LESSON 1

Addition Without Regrouping

Lesson Objectives

- Add a 2-digit number and a 1-digit number without regrouping.

- Add two 2-digit numbers without regrouping.

Vocabulary
count on
place-value chart

Learn You can add ones to a number in different ways.

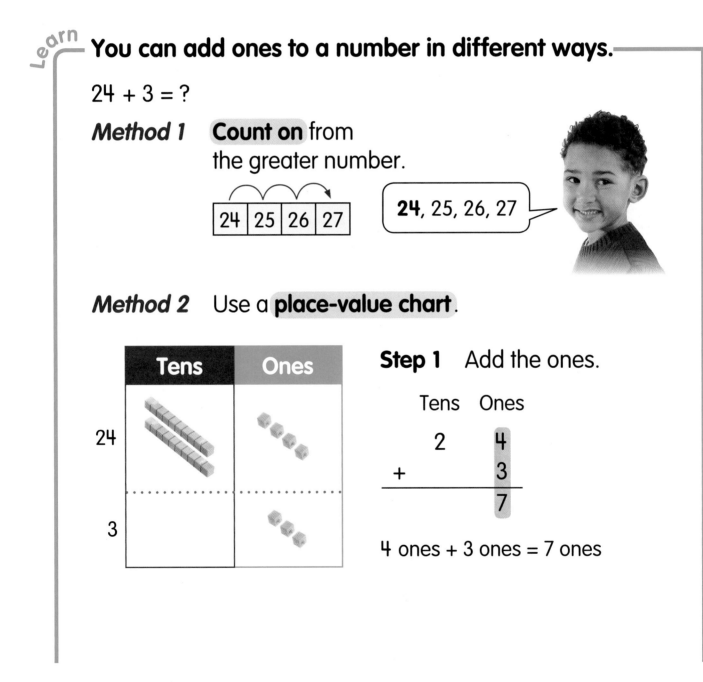

$24 + 3 = ?$

Method 1 **Count on** from the greater number.

| 24 | 25 | 26 | 27 |

24, 25, 26, 27

Method 2 Use a **place-value chart**.

Tens	Ones
24	
3	

Step 1 Add the ones.

```
  Tens  Ones
    2     4
  +       3
  ─────────
          7
```

4 ones + 3 ones = 7 ones

Step 2 Add the tens.

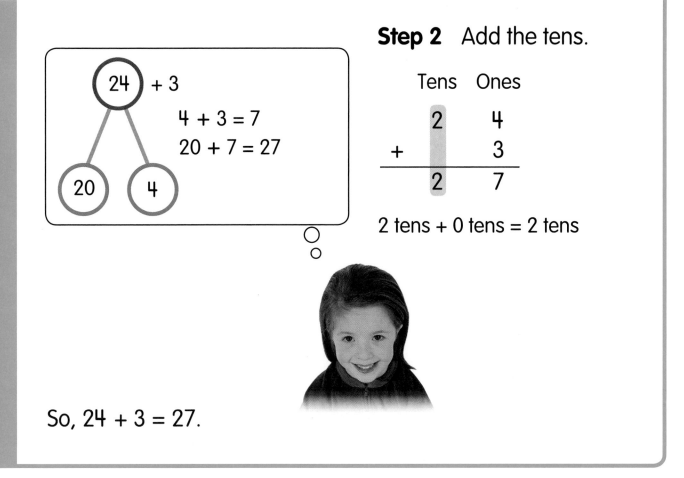

24 + 3

4 + 3 = 7

20 + 7 = 27

20   4

Tens	Ones
2	4
+	3
2	7

2 tens + 0 tens = 2 tens

So, 24 + 3 = 27.

Guided Learning

Add.

1 36 + 2 = ?

Method 1 Count on from the greater number.

36, ▢, ▢

Method 2   Use a place-value chart.

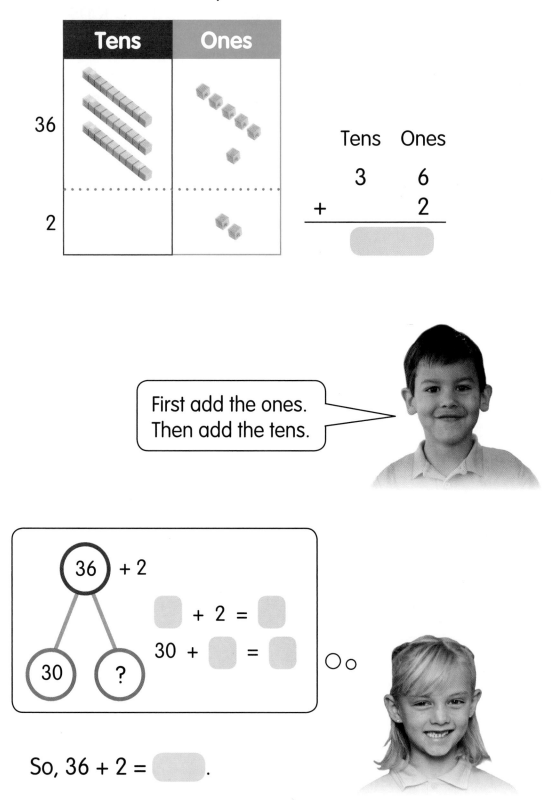

Tens	Ones
3	6
+	2

First add the ones.
Then add the tens.

36 + 2

30   ?

☐ + 2 = ☐

30 + ☐ = ☐

So, 36 + 2 = ☐ .

You can add tens in different ways.

20 + 20 = ?

Method 1 Count on from the greater number.

20, …30, …40

Method 2 Use a place-value chart.

Tens	Ones
20	
20	

Step 1 Add the ones.

Tens Ones

2   0
+ 2   0
———————
0

0 ones + 0 ones = 0 ones

Step 2 Add the tens.

Tens Ones

2   0
+ 2   0
———————
4   0

2 tens + 2 tens = 4 tens

2 tens + 2 tens = 4 tens
20 + 20 = 40

So, 20 + 20 = 40.

Guided Learning

Add.

2 20 + 10 = ?

Method 1 Count on from the greater number.

20, ...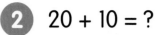

Method 2 Use a place-value chart.

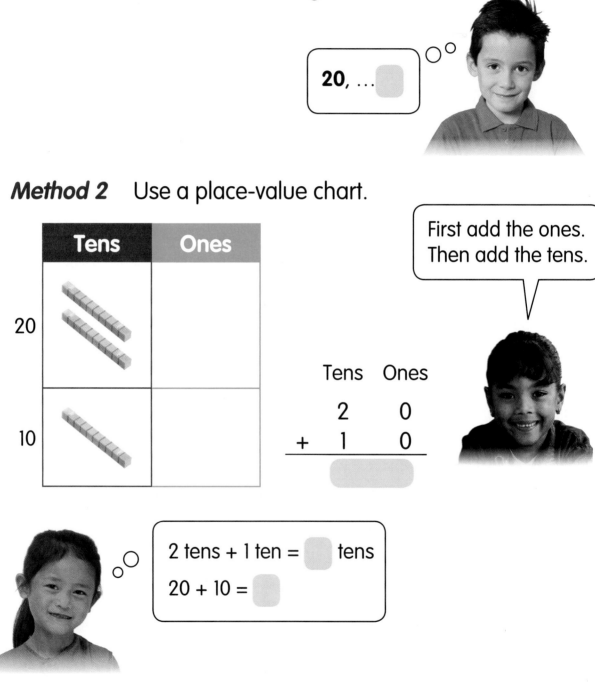

Tens	Ones
20	
10	

First add the ones.
Then add the tens.

	Tens	Ones
	2	0
+	1	0

2 tens + 1 ten = ▢ tens

20 + 10 = ▢

So, 20 + 10 = ▢ .

Learn

You can use place-value charts to add tens to a number.

17 + 20 = ?

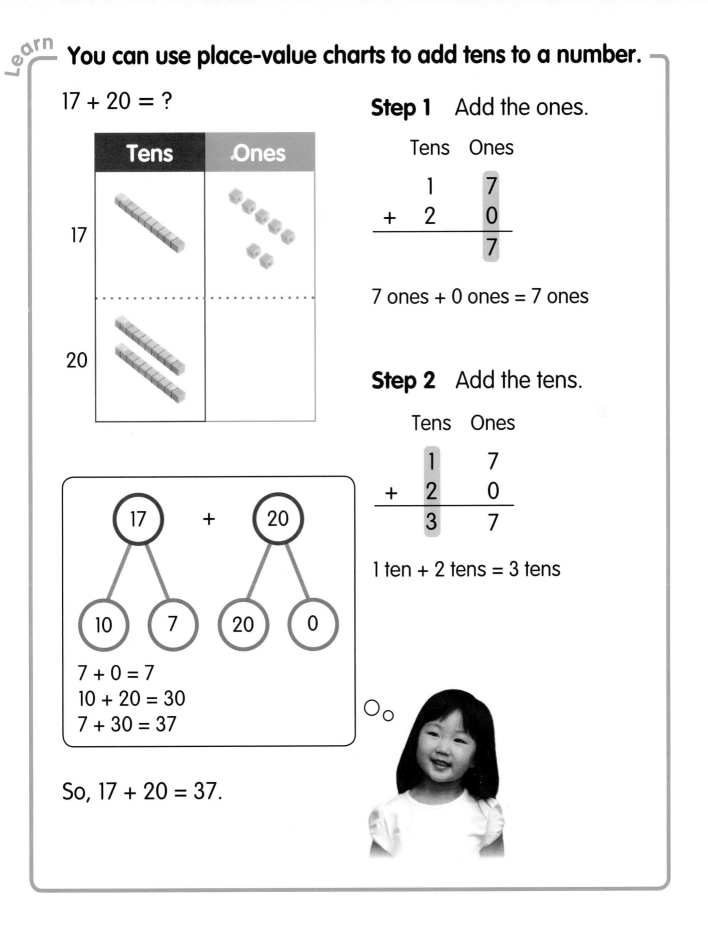

Tens	Ones
17	
20	

Step 1 Add the ones.

```
    Tens   Ones
      1      7
  +   2      0
  ───────────────
             7
```

7 ones + 0 ones = 7 ones

Step 2 Add the tens.

```
    Tens   Ones
      1      7
  +   2      0
  ───────────────
      3      7
```

1 ten + 2 tens = 3 tens

17 + 20

10   7   20   0

7 + 0 = 7
10 + 20 = 30
7 + 30 = 37

So, 17 + 20 = 37.

Guided Learning

Add.

3 20 + 13 = ?

Tens	Ones
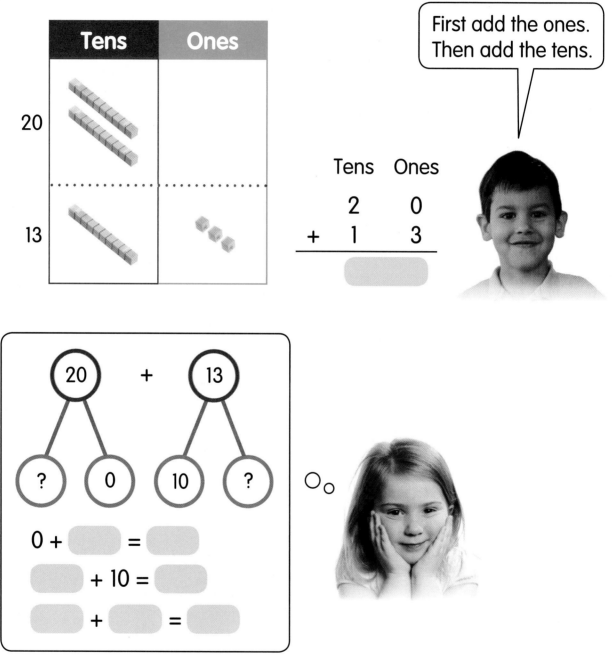	

First add the ones.
Then add the tens.

Tens Ones
  2   0
+ 1   3

```
      20        +        13
     /  \              /   \
   ?     0          10      ?
```

0 + ⬚ = ⬚

⬚ + 10 = ⬚

⬚ + ⬚ = ⬚

So, 20 + 13 = ⬚ .

You can use place-value charts to add two numbers.

14 + 25 = ?

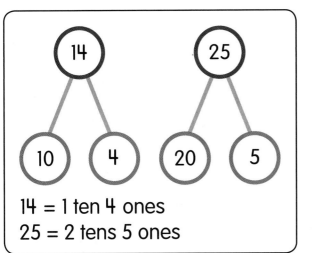

14 = 1 ten 4 ones
25 = 2 tens 5 ones

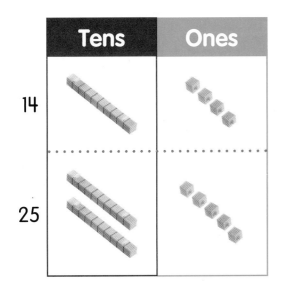

Tens	Ones
14	
25	

Step 1   Add the ones.

```
  Tens   Ones
    1      4
+   2      5
  ─────────────
           9
```

4 ones + 5 ones = 9 ones

Step 2   Add the tens.

```
  Tens   Ones
    1      4
+   2      5
  ─────────────
    3      9
```

1 ten + 2 tens = 3 tens

So, 14 + 25 = 39.

Guided Learning

Add.

4 13 + 14 = ?

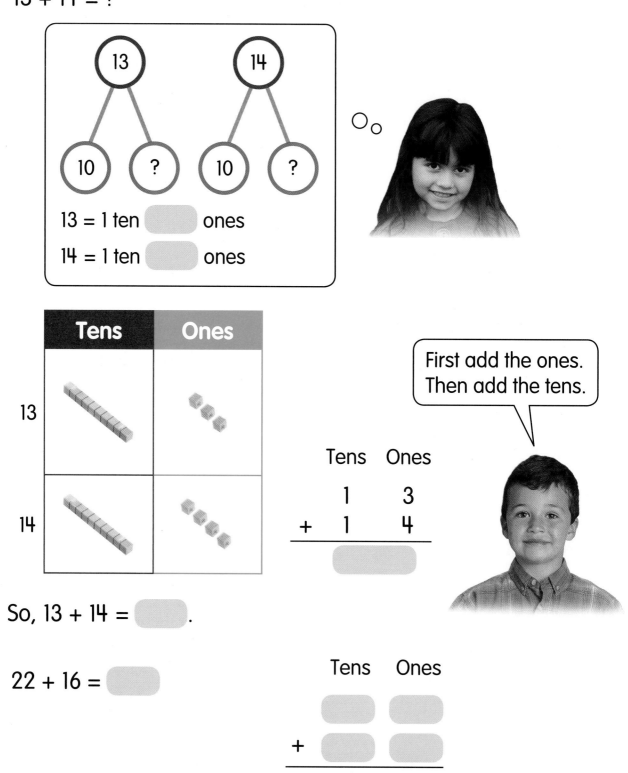

13 = 1 ten ___ ones

14 = 1 ten ___ ones

Tens	Ones
13	
14	

First add the ones.
Then add the tens.

```
    Tens   Ones
      1      3
+     1      4
   _____
```

So, 13 + 14 = ___ .

5 22 + 16 = ___

```
    Tens   Ones
     ___    ___
+    ___    ___
   _____
     ___
```

Add by counting on.

1 22 + 3 = _____

2 9 + 8 = _____

Add.

3
Tens	Ones
2	5
+	2

_____

4
Tens	Ones
1	9
+ 2	0

_____

5
Tens	Ones
2	7
+ 1	2

_____

6
Tens	Ones
1	4
+ 2	4

_____

7 6 + 33 = _____

Tens	Ones
+	

_____

8 21 + 18 = _____

Tens	Ones
+	

_____

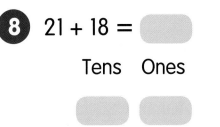

ON YOUR OWN

Go to Workbook B:
Practice 1, pages 61–64

LESSON 2 Addition with Regrouping

Lesson Objectives

- Add a 2-digit number and a 1-digit number with regrouping.

- Add two 2-digit numbers with regrouping.

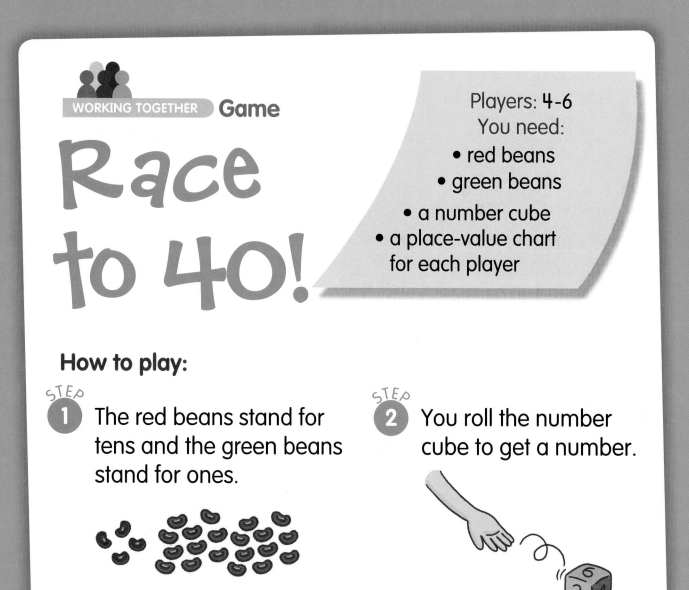

WORKING TOGETHER Game

Race to 40!

Players: 4-6
You need:
- red beans
- green beans
- a number cube
- a place-value chart for each player

How to play:

STEP 1 The red beans stand for tens and the green beans stand for ones.

STEP 2 You roll the number cube to get a number.

3 Put this number of green beans on your place-value chart.

STEP
4 The other players take turns to repeat **2** and **3**.

STEP
5 When it is your turn again, roll the number cube. Add to the number of beans on your chart.

You **regroup** when you change 10 ones for 1 ten.

STEP
6 If you get 10 or more green beans, exchange 10 of them for 1 red bean.

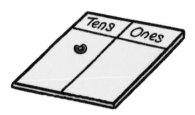

The first player to get 4 red beans or 4 tens wins!

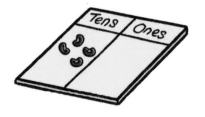

Guided Learning

Regroup the ones into tens and ones.
Then complete the place-value chart.

1.

Tens	Ones
	17

17 =

=

Tens	Ones
	7

Learn **You can use place-value charts to add ones to a number with regrouping.**

28 + 6 = ?

28 = 2 tens 8 ones

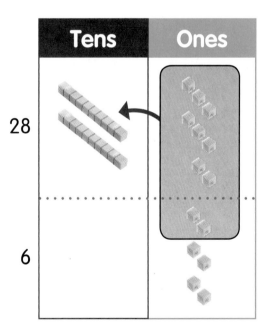

Step 1 Add the ones.

```
  Tens   Ones
   1
   2      8
+          6
_____
   3      4
```

8 ones + 6 ones = 14 ones

Regroup the ones.

14 ones = 1 ten 4 ones

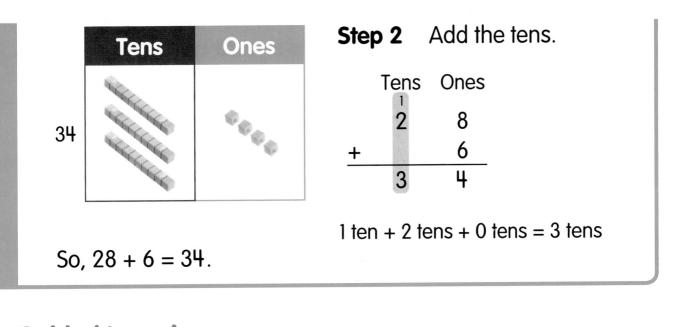

Tens	Ones

34

Step 2   Add the tens.

Tens	Ones
¹ 2	8
+	6
3	4

1 ten + 2 tens + 0 tens = 3 tens

So, 28 + 6 = 34.

Guided Learning

Add and regroup.

2

Tens	Ones
1	2
+	8

Step 1   Add the ones.

⬭ ones + ⬭ ones = ⬭ ones

Regroup the ones.

⬭ ones = ⬭ ten ⬭ ones

Step 2   Add the tens.

⬭ ten + ⬭ ten + 0 tens = ⬭ tens

3

Tens	Ones
3	1
+	9

4

Tens	Ones
2	5
+	7

5

Tens	Ones
2	9
+	6

6

Tens	Ones
3	5
+	8

You can use place-value charts to add numbers with regrouping.

14 + 18 = ?

14 = 1 ten 4 ones
18 = 1 ten 8 ones

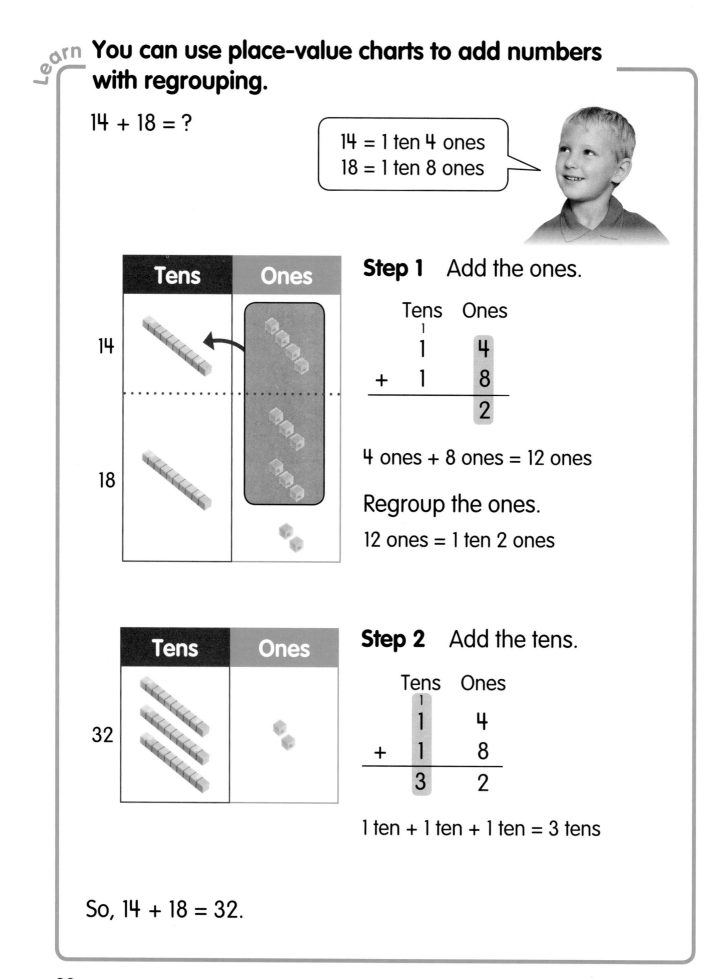

Tens	Ones
14	
18	

Step 1   Add the ones.

```
   Tens   Ones
     1
     1      4
+    1      8
   _____
            2
```

4 ones + 8 ones = 12 ones

Regroup the ones.

12 ones = 1 ten 2 ones

Tens	Ones
32	

Step 2   Add the tens.

```
   Tens   Ones
     1
     1      4
+    1      8
   _____
     3      2
```

1 ten + 1 ten + 1 ten = 3 tens

So, 14 + 18 = 32.

Guided Learning

Add and regroup.

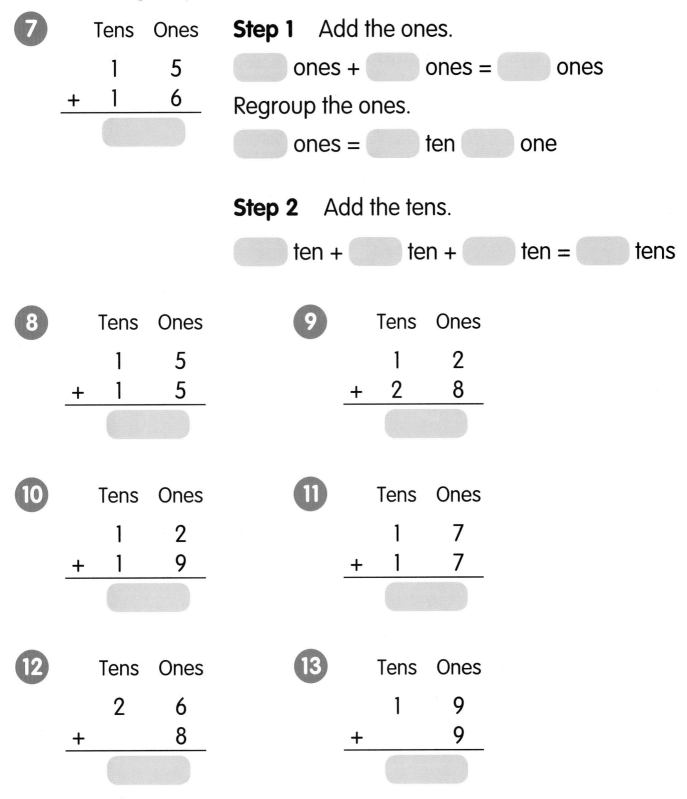

7

	Tens	Ones
	1	5
+	1	6

Step 1 Add the ones.

⬭ ones + ⬭ ones = ⬭ ones

Regroup the ones.

⬭ ones = ⬭ ten ⬭ one

Step 2 Add the tens.

⬭ ten + ⬭ ten + ⬭ ten = ⬭ tens

8

	Tens	Ones
	1	5
+	1	5

9

	Tens	Ones
	1	2
+	2	8

10

	Tens	Ones
	1	2
+	1	9

11

	Tens	Ones
	1	7
+	1	7

12

	Tens	Ones
	2	6
+		8

13

	Tens	Ones
	1	9
+		9

Let's Practice

Regroup the ones into tens and ones.
Then fill in the place-value chart.

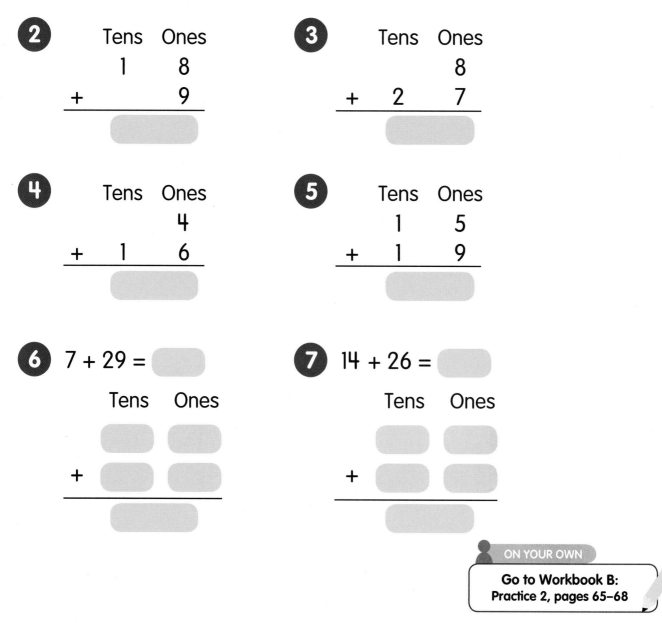

1

Tens	Ones
1	13

23 = =

Tens	Ones

Add and regroup.

2

Tens	Ones
1	8
+	9

3

Tens	Ones
	8
+ 2	7

4

Tens	Ones
	4
+ 1	6

5

Tens	Ones
1	5
+ 1	9

6 7 + 29 =

Tens	Ones
+	

7 14 + 26 =

Tens	Ones
+	

ON YOUR OWN

Go to Workbook B:
Practice 2, pages 65–68

LESSON 3 Subtraction Without Regrouping

Lesson Objectives

- Subtract a 1-digit number from a 2-digit number without regrouping.
- Subtract a 2-digit number from another 2-digit number without regrouping.

Vocabulary
count back

Learn **You can subtract ones from a number in different ways.**

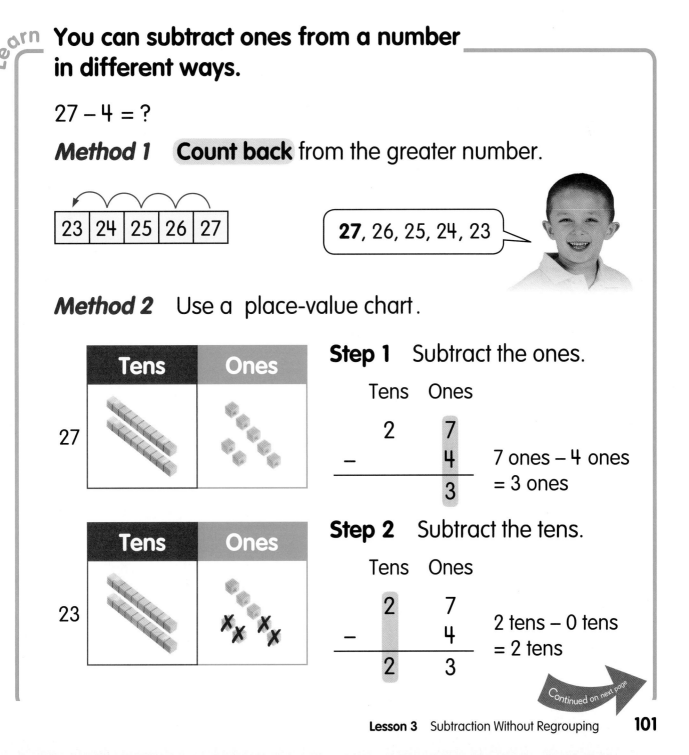

$27 - 4 = ?$

Method 1 **Count back** from the greater number.

| 23 | 24 | 25 | 26 | 27 |

27, 26, 25, 24, 23

Method 2 Use a place-value chart.

| Tens | Ones |

27

Step 1 Subtract the ones.

Tens Ones

```
    2    7
-        4
         3
```

7 ones − 4 ones
= 3 ones

| Tens | Ones |

23

Step 2 Subtract the tens.

Tens Ones

```
    2    7
-        4
    2    3
```

2 tens − 0 tens
= 2 tens

Continued on next page

Lesson 3 Subtraction Without Regrouping **101**

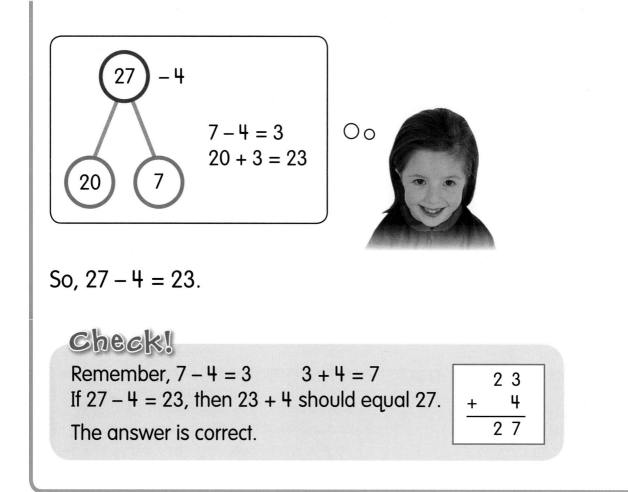

So, $27 - 4 = 23$.

Check!

Remember, $7 - 4 = 3$ $3 + 4 = 7$

If $27 - 4 = 23$, then $23 + 4$ should equal 27.

The answer is correct.

$$\begin{array}{r} 2\ 3 \\ +\quad 4 \\ \hline 2\ 7 \end{array}$$

Guided Learning

Subtract.

 $36 - 3 = ?$

Method 1   Count back from the greater number.

36, ☐ , ☐ , ☐

Method 2   Use a place-value chart.

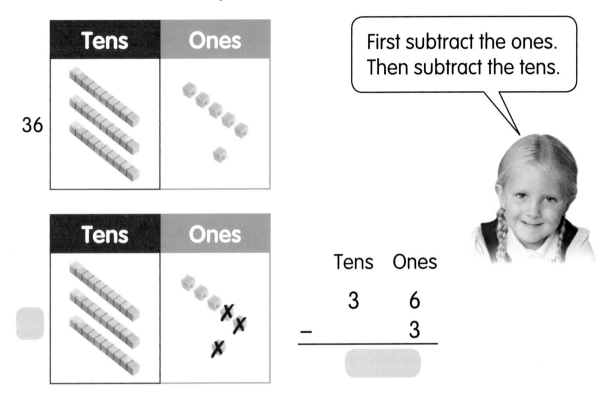

First subtract the ones.
Then subtract the tens.

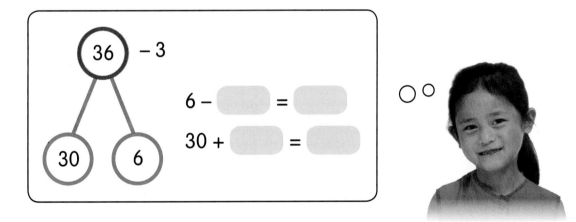

Tens	Ones
3	6
−	3

(36) − 3

30   6

6 − [ ] = [ ]

30 + [ ] = [ ]

So, 36 − 3 = [ ] .

Check!

[ ]
+   3
3 6

You can subtract tens in different ways.

20 − 10 = ?

Method 1   Count back from the greater number.

20, …10

Method 2   Use a place-value chart.

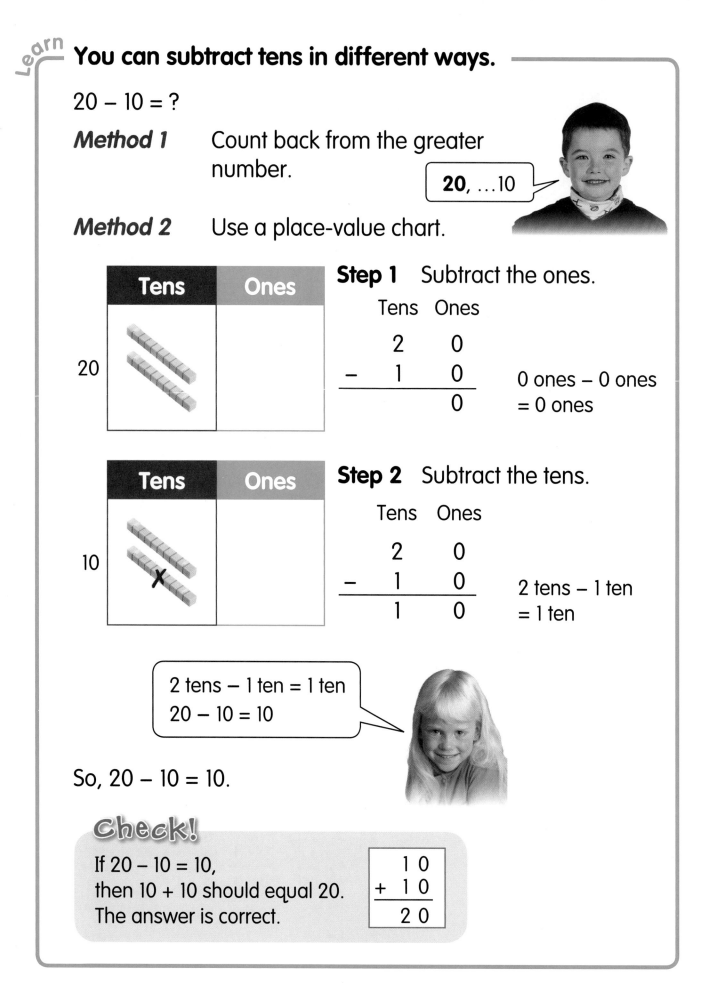

Tens	Ones
20	

Step 1   Subtract the ones.

$$
\begin{array}{cc}
\text{Tens} & \text{Ones} \\
2 & 0 \\
- \quad 1 & 0 \\
\hline
& 0 \\
\end{array}
$$

0 ones − 0 ones
= 0 ones

Tens	Ones
10	

Step 2   Subtract the tens.

$$
\begin{array}{cc}
\text{Tens} & \text{Ones} \\
2 & 0 \\
- \quad 1 & 0 \\
\hline
1 & 0 \\
\end{array}
$$

2 tens − 1 ten
= 1 ten

2 tens − 1 ten = 1 ten
20 − 10 = 10

So, 20 − 10 = 10.

Check!

If 20 − 10 = 10,
then 10 + 10 should equal 20.
The answer is correct.

$$
\begin{array}{r}
1\ 0 \\
+ \quad 1\ 0 \\
\hline
2\ 0 \\
\end{array}
$$

Guided Learning

Subtract.

2 30 − 20 = ?

30, … ⬜ , … ⬜

Method 1 Count back from the greater number.

Method 2 Use a place-value chart.

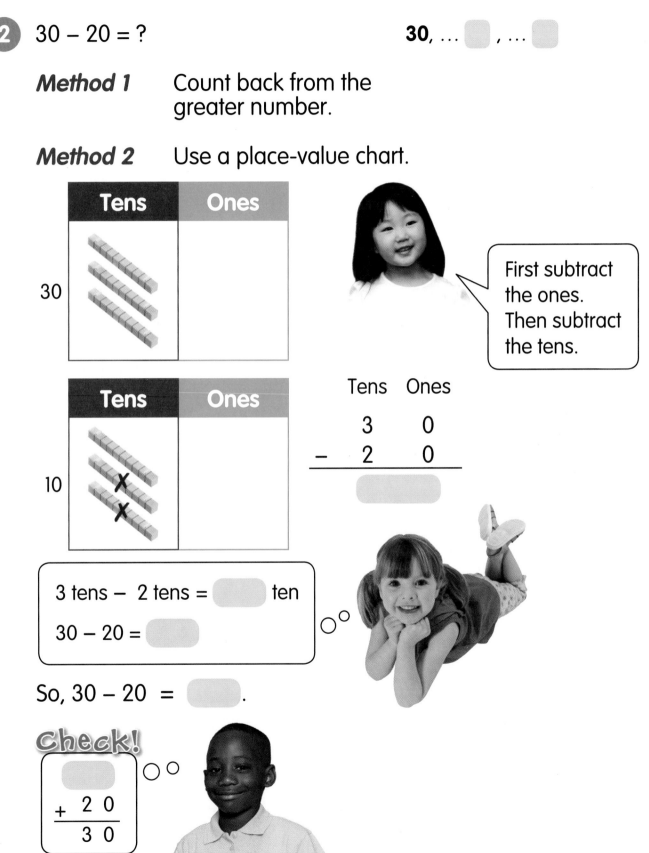

First subtract the ones. Then subtract the tens.

	Tens	Ones
	3	0
−	2	0

3 tens − 2 tens = ⬜ ten

30 − 20 = ⬜

So, 30 − 20 = ⬜ .

Check!

```
    ⬜
 +  2 0
 ──────
    3 0
```

Learn **You can use place-value charts to subtract tens and ones from a number.**

38 − 20 = ?

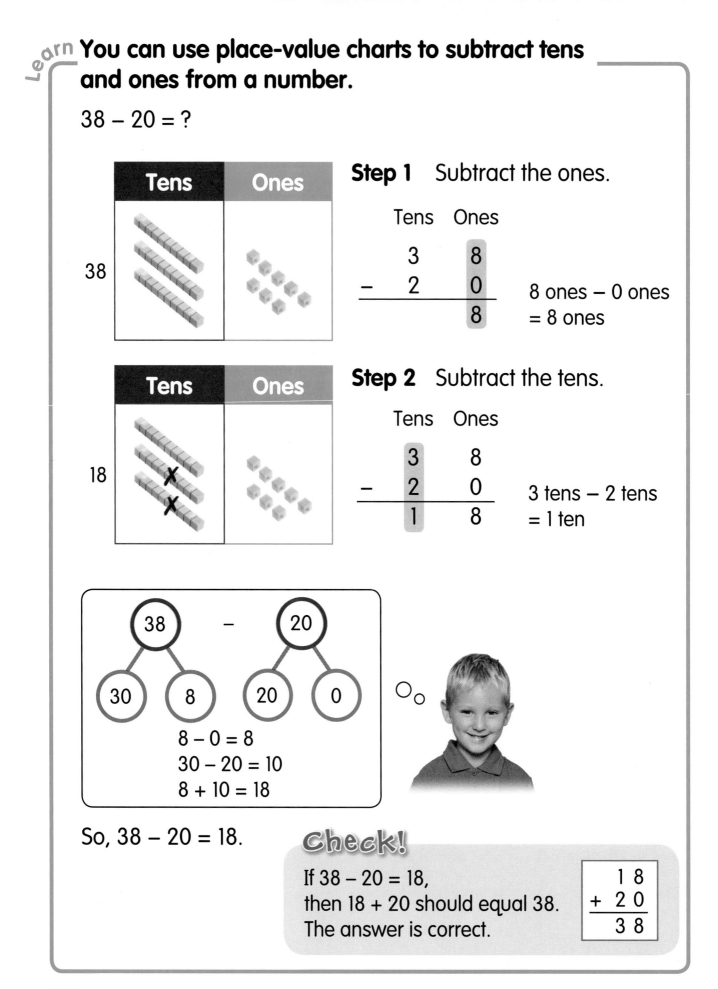

Tens	Ones
38	

Step 1 Subtract the ones.

	Tens	Ones
	3	8
−	2	0
		8

8 ones − 0 ones
= 8 ones

Tens	Ones
18	

Step 2 Subtract the tens.

	Tens	Ones
	3	8
−	2	0
	1	8

3 tens − 2 tens
= 1 ten

38 − 20

38 → 30, 8
20 → 20, 0

8 − 0 = 8
30 − 20 = 10
8 + 10 = 18

So, 38 − 20 = 18.

Check!

If 38 − 20 = 18,
then 18 + 20 should equal 38.
The answer is correct.

```
  1 8
+ 2 0
-----
  3 8
```

Guided Learning

Subtract.

3 35 − 20 = ?

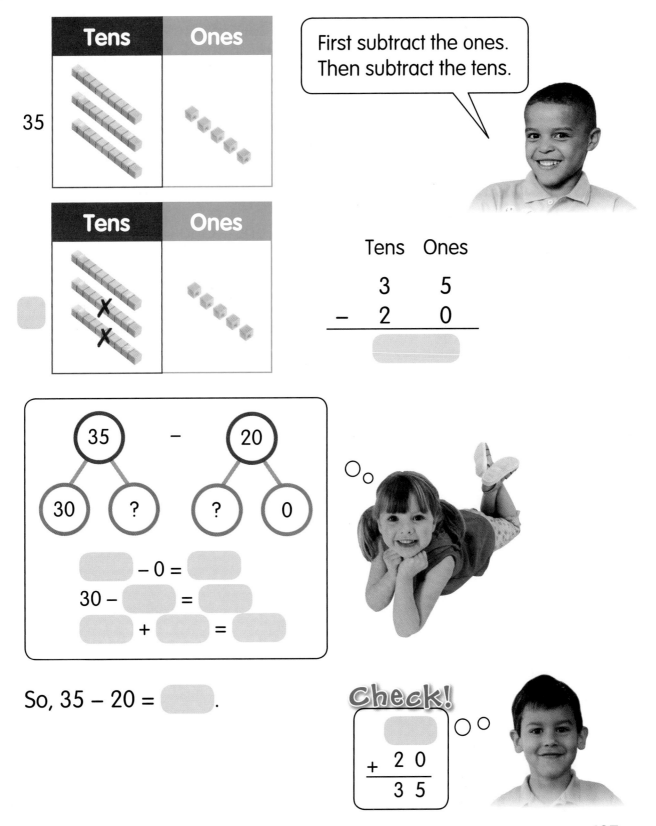

Tens	Ones

35

Tens	Ones

First subtract the ones.
Then subtract the tens.

Tens	Ones
3	5
− 2	0

35   −   20

30   ?   ?   0

[   ] − 0 = [   ]

30 − [   ] = [   ]

[   ] + [   ] = [   ]

So, 35 − 20 = [   ].

Check!

```
    [    ]
  +  2 0
  -------
    3 5
```

Learn **You can use place-value charts to subtract one number from another.**

28 – 14 = ?

28 = 2 tens 8 ones
14 = 1 ten 4 ones

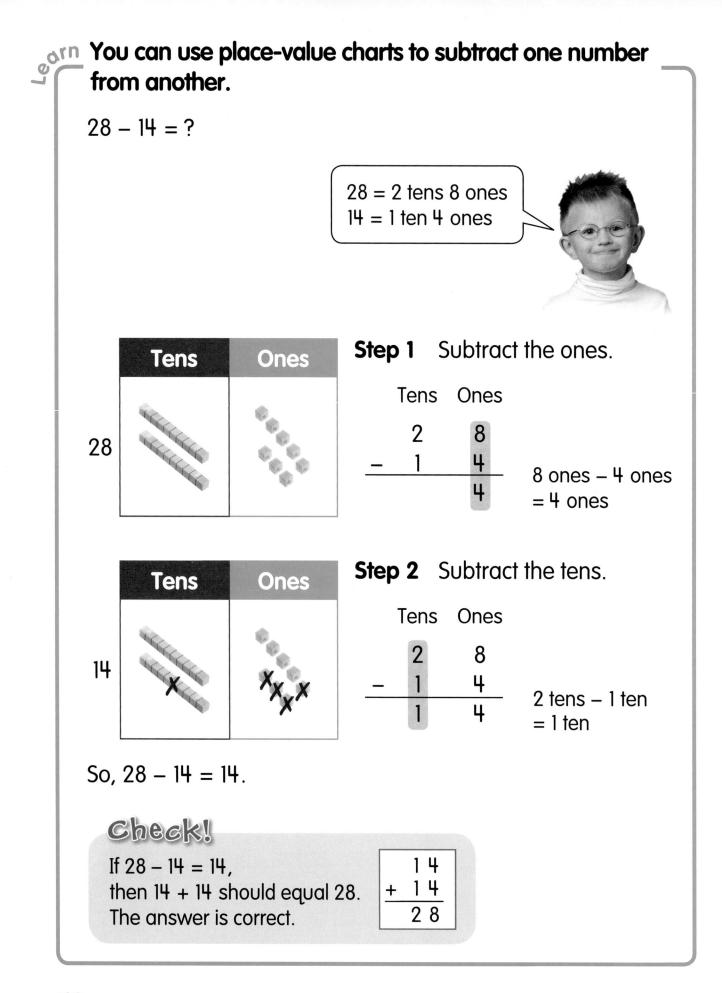

Tens	Ones

28

Step 1 Subtract the ones.

Tens   Ones

$$
\begin{array}{cc}
2 & 8 \\
-\ 1 & 4 \\
\hline
 & 4 \\
\end{array}
$$

8 ones – 4 ones
= 4 ones

Tens	Ones

14

Step 2 Subtract the tens.

Tens   Ones

$$
\begin{array}{cc}
2 & 8 \\
-\ 1 & 4 \\
\hline
1 & 4 \\
\end{array}
$$

2 tens – 1 ten
= 1 ten

So, 28 – 14 = 14.

Check!

If 28 – 14 = 14,
then 14 + 14 should equal 28.
The answer is correct.

$$
\begin{array}{r}
1\ 4 \\
+\ 1\ 4 \\
\hline
2\ 8 \\
\end{array}
$$

Guided Learning

Subtract.

4   39 − 22 = ?

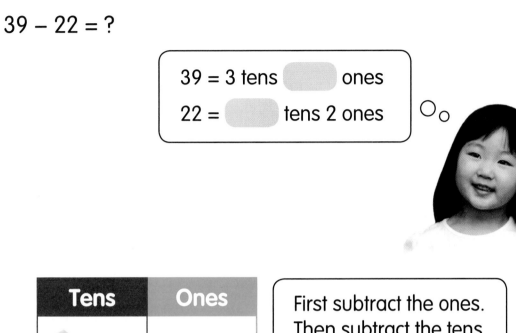

39 = 3 tens ◯ ones

22 = ◯ tens 2 ones

Tens	Ones
39	

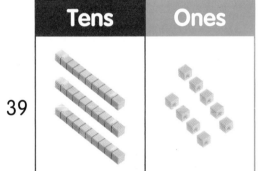

First subtract the ones.
Then subtract the tens.

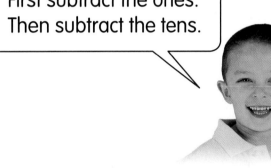

Tens	Ones

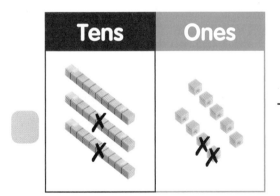

```
  Tens   Ones
    3      9
 −  2      2
 _____
```

So, 39 − 22 = ⬜ .

Check!

```
      ⬜
  +  2 2
  _____
     3 9
```

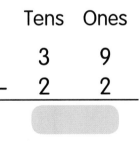

Let's Practice

Subtract by counting back.

1 28 − 3 = [ ]

2 40 − 20 = [ ]

Subtract.

3

Tens	Ones
2	6
−	5
[ ]	

4

Tens	Ones
3	6
− 1	0
[ ]	

5

Tens	Ones
2	9
− 1	3
[ ]	

6

Tens	Ones
3	8
− 2	5
[ ]	

7 34 − 3 = [ ]

Tens	Ones
[ ]	[ ]
− [ ]	[ ]
[ ]	

8 27 − 15 = [ ]

Tens	Ones
[ ]	[ ]
− [ ]	[ ]
[ ]	

ON YOUR OWN

Go to Workbook B:
Practice 3, pages 69–72

LESSON 4 Subtraction with Regrouping

Lesson Objectives

• Subtract a 1-digit number from a 2-digit number with regrouping.

• Subtract a 2-digit number from another 2-digit number with regrouping.

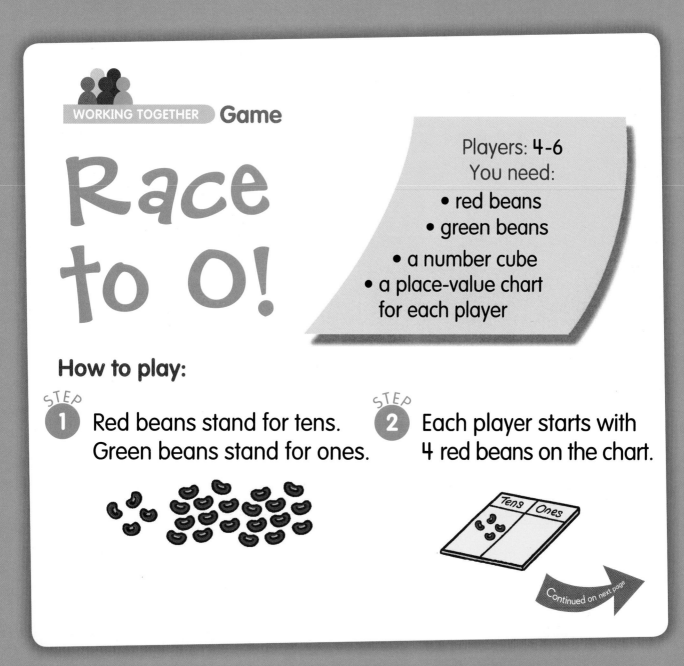

WORKING TOGETHER Game

Race to 0!

Players: 4-6
You need:
• red beans
• green beans
• a number cube
• a place-value chart for each player

How to play:

STEP 1 Red beans stand for tens. Green beans stand for ones.

STEP 2 Each player starts with 4 red beans on the chart.

Continued on next page

STEP
3
You exchange 1 red bean for 10 green beans. Then roll the number cube.

STEP
4
You take away this number of green beans from your chart.

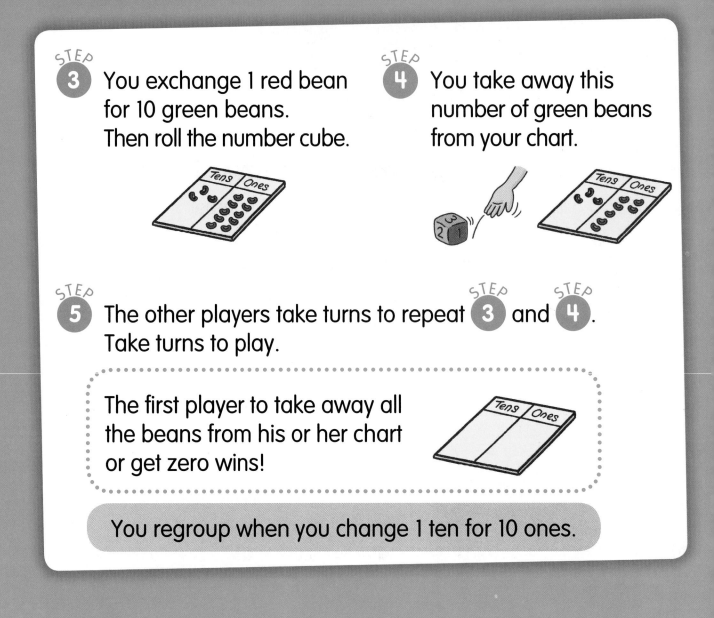

STEP
5
The other players take turns to repeat **3** and **4**.
Take turns to play.

The first player to take away all the beans from his or her chart or get zero wins!

You regroup when you change 1 ten for 10 ones.

Guided Learning

Regroup the tens and ones.
Then complete the place value chart.

1

Tens	Ones
2	5

$25 =$

Tens	Ones
1	

$=$

You can use place-value charts to subtract ones with regrouping.

$32 - 9 = ?$

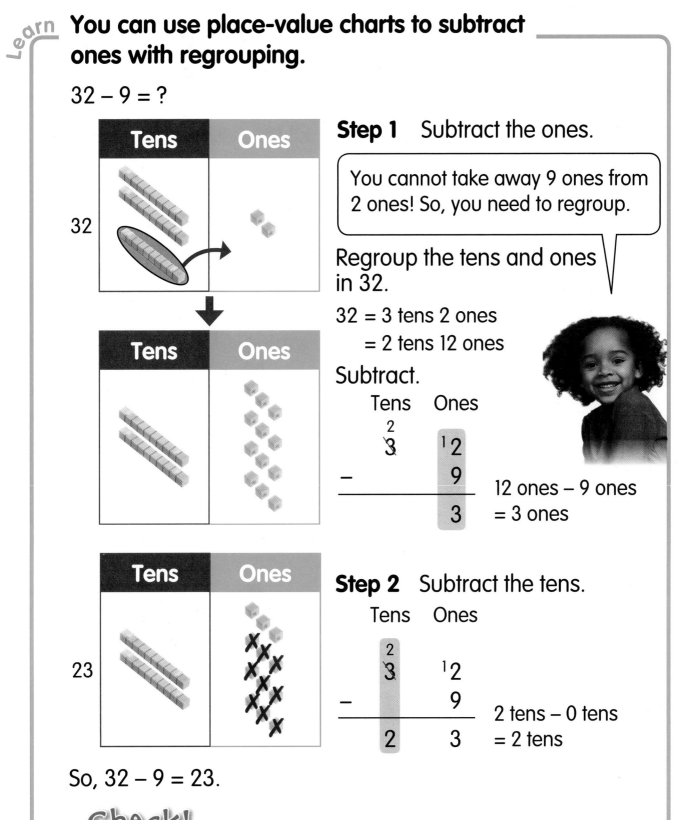

Step 1 Subtract the ones.

You cannot take away 9 ones from 2 ones! So, you need to regroup.

Regroup the tens and ones in 32.

$32 = 3 \text{ tens } 2 \text{ ones}$
$\quad\ = 2 \text{ tens } 12 \text{ ones}$

Subtract.

12 ones – 9 ones = 3 ones

Step 2 Subtract the tens.

2 tens – 0 tens = 2 tens

So, $32 - 9 = 23$.

Check!

If $32 - 9 = 23$,
then $23 + 9$ should equal 32.

The answer is correct.

$$\begin{array}{r} 2\ 3 \\ +\quad 9 \\ \hline 3\ 2 \end{array}$$

Guided Learning

Regroup and subtract.

2

Tens	Ones
2	6
−	7

Check!

+	7
2	6

Step 1 Subtract the ones.

Regroup the tens and ones in 26.

26 = 2 tens [____] ones

= 1 ten [____] ones

Subtract.

[____] ones − [____] ones = [____] ones

Step 2 Subtract the tens.

[____] ten − [____] tens = [____] ten

3

Tens	Ones
2	3
−	6

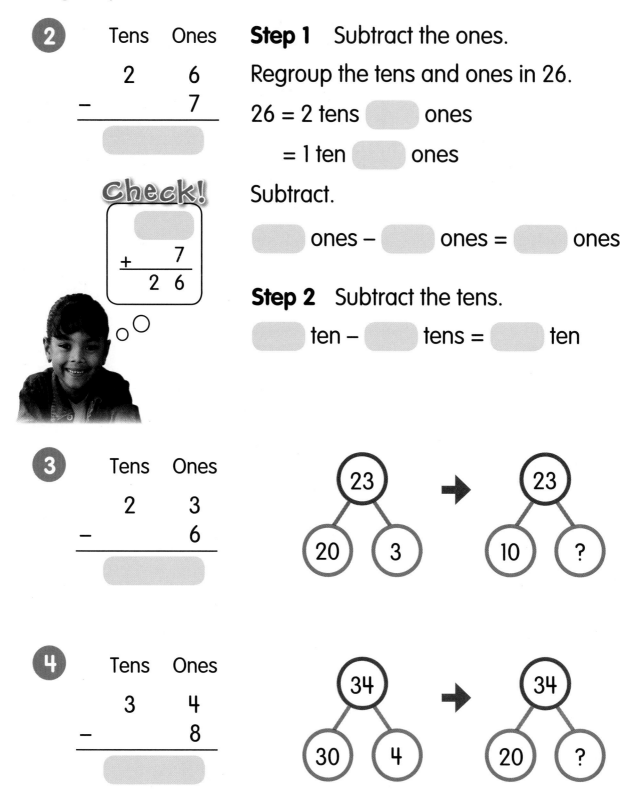

4

Tens	Ones
3	4
−	8

Learn You can use place-value charts to subtract numbers with regrouping.

41 − 29 = ?

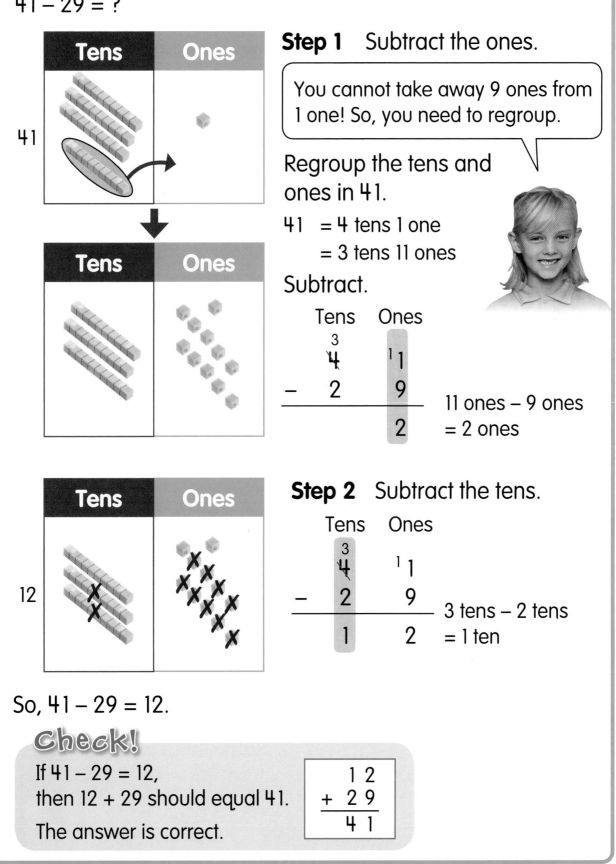

Step 1 Subtract the ones.

> You cannot take away 9 ones from 1 one! So, you need to regroup.

Regroup the tens and ones in 41.

41 = 4 tens 1 one
 = 3 tens 11 ones

Subtract.

Tens	Ones
³4̸	¹1
− 2	9
	2

11 ones − 9 ones
= 2 ones

Step 2 Subtract the tens.

Tens	Ones
³4̸	¹1
− 2	9
1	2

3 tens − 2 tens
= 1 ten

So, 41 − 29 = 12.

Check!

If 41 − 29 = 12,
then 12 + 29 should equal 41.
The answer is correct.

```
   1 2
 + 2 9
 -----
   4 1
```

Guided Learning

Regroup and subtract.

5

Tens	Ones
3	4
– 1	5

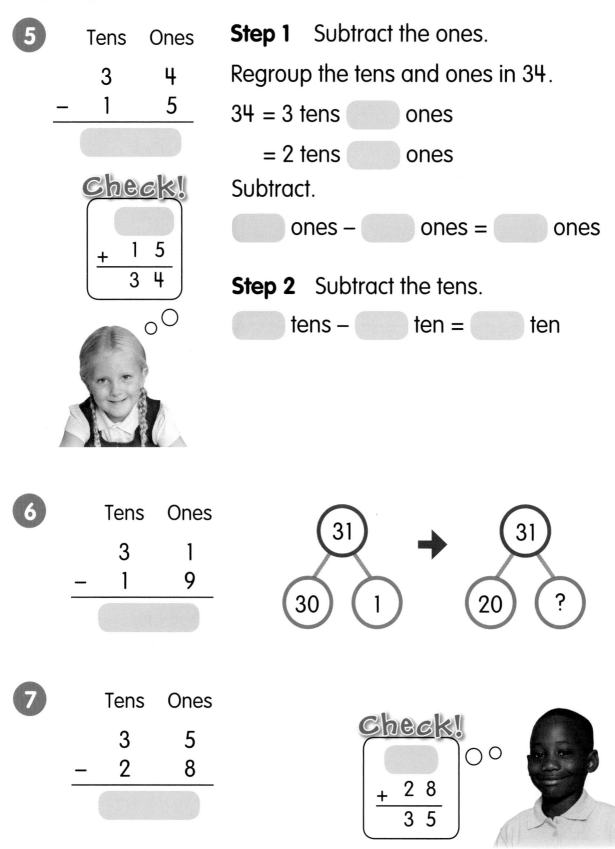

Check!

```
    1 5
  +
    3 4
```

Step 1 Subtract the ones.

Regroup the tens and ones in 34.

34 = 3 tens ⬭ ones

     = 2 tens ⬭ ones

Subtract.

⬭ ones – ⬭ ones = ⬭ ones

Step 2 Subtract the tens.

⬭ tens – ⬭ ten = ⬭ ten

6

Tens	Ones
3	1
– 1	9

31
30   1

→

31
20   ?

7

Tens	Ones
3	5
– 2	8

Check!

```
    2 8
  +
    3 5
```

Let's Practice

Regroup the tens and ones.
Then fill in the place-value chart.

1

25 =

Tens	Ones
2	**5**

=

Tens	Ones
1	

2

39 =

Tens	Ones
3	**9**

=

Tens	Ones
2	

Regroup and subtract.

3

Tens	Ones
2	4
−	7

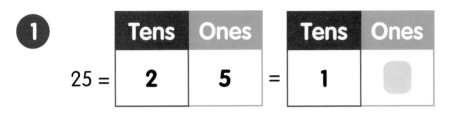

24 → 24
20 4   10 ?

4

Tens	Ones
3	1
− 1	4

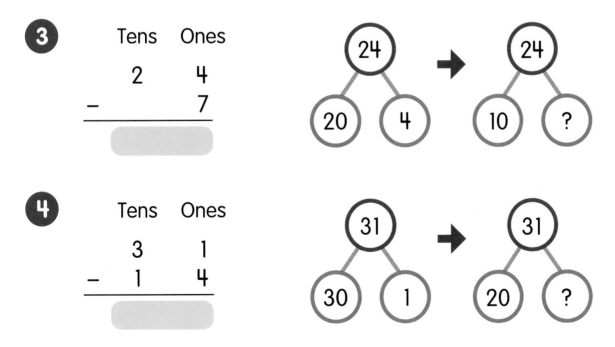

31 → 31
30 1   20 ?

5

Tens	Ones
3	3
−	8

6

Tens	Ones
3	5
− 1	9

7

Tens	Ones
3	7
− 1	9

8

Tens	Ones
2	6
− 1	8

9 40 − 18 =

Tens   Ones

−

10 28 − 19 =

Tens   Ones

−

11 34 − 26 =

Tens   Ones

−

12 23 − 6 =

Tens   Ones

−

ON YOUR OWN

**Go to Workbook B:
Practice 4, pages 73–76**

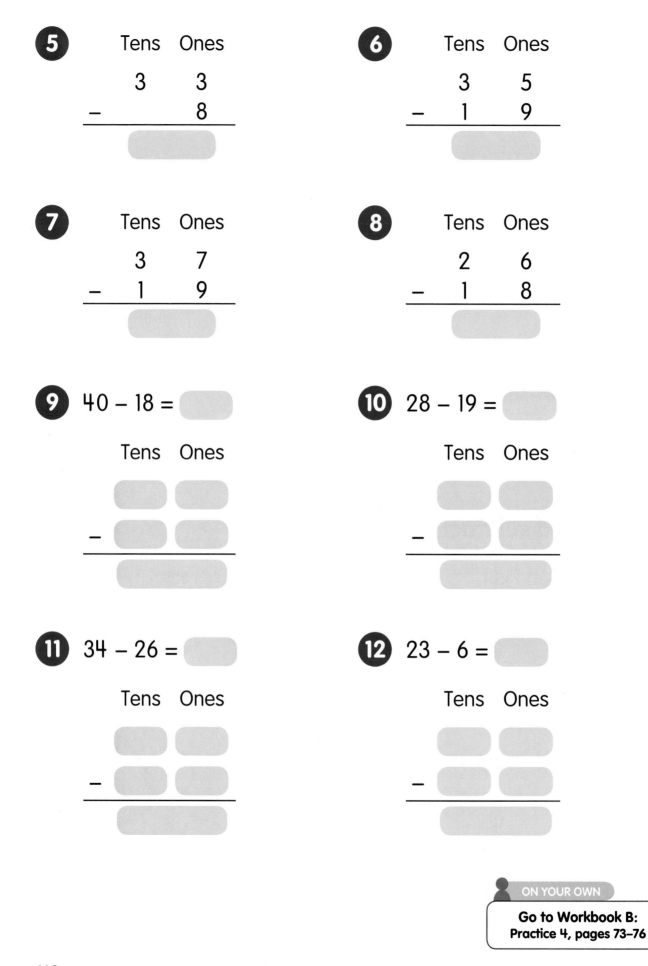

Adding Three Numbers

Lesson Objective

- Add three 1-digit numbers.

Learn **You can use number bonds to add three numbers.**

$5 + 7 + 6 = ?$

Method 1

Step 1 Make 10 first.

$5 + 5 = 10$

Step 2 $2 + 6 = 8$

Step 3 $10 + 8 = 18$

So, $5 + 7 + 6 = 18$.

$$5 \quad + \quad 7 \quad + \quad 6$$

5   2

10

Method 2

Step 1 Make 10 first.

$7 + 3 = 10$

Step 2 $5 + 3 = 8$

Step 3 $10 + 8 = 18$

So, $5 + 7 + 6 = 18$.

$$5 \quad + \quad 7 \quad + \quad 6$$

3   3

10

Guided Learning

Make ten.
Then add.

1 6 + 8 + 3 = ⬜

2 9 + 6 + 5 = ⬜

3 7 + 4 + 8 = ⬜

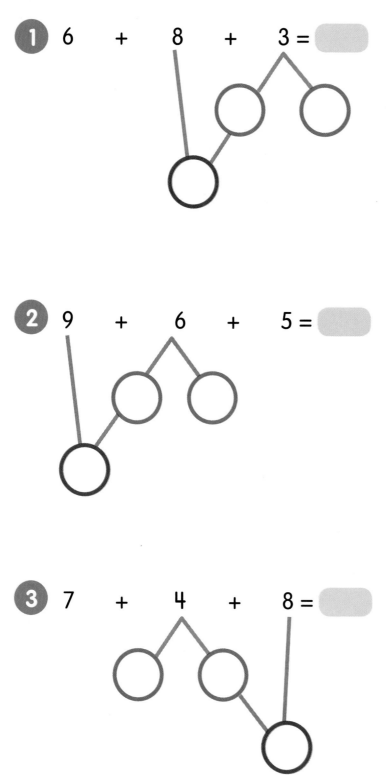

Let's Explore!

1 4 + 9 + 2 = ?

Method 1

Step 1   Add the first two numbers.

4 + 9 = ◻

Step 2   Add the result to the third number.

◻ + 2 = ◻

So, 4 + 9 + 2 = ◻

Method 2

Step 1   Add the last two numbers.

9 + 2 = ◻

Step 2   Add the first number to the result.

4 + ◻ = ◻

So, 4 + 9 + 2 = ◻

How are the methods alike?
How are they different?

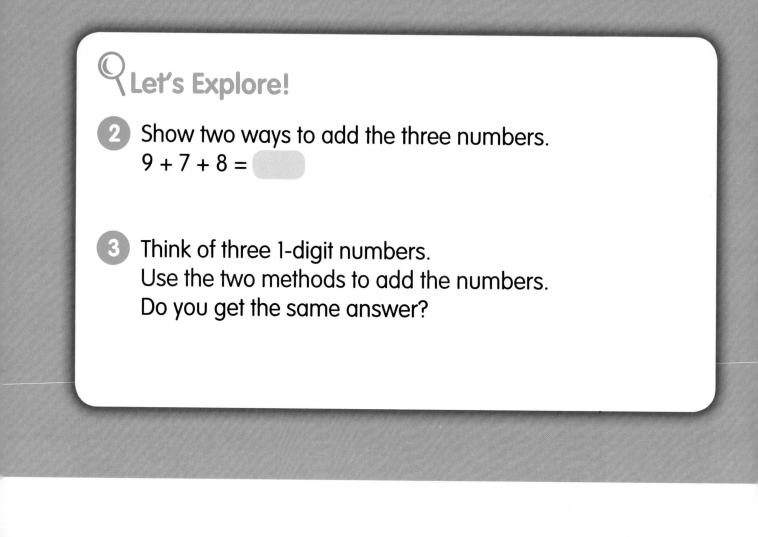

Let's Explore!

2 Show two ways to add the three numbers.
9 + 7 + 8 = [ ]

3 Think of three 1-digit numbers.
Use the two methods to add the numbers.
Do you get the same answer?

Let's Practice

Add.

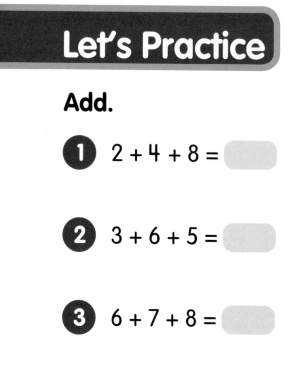

1 2 + 4 + 8 = [ ]

2 3 + 6 + 5 = [ ]

3 6 + 7 + 8 = [ ]

ON YOUR OWN

Go to Workbook B:
Practice 5, pages 77–78

LESSON 6 Real-World Problems: Addition and Subtraction

Lesson Objectives

- Solve real-world problems.
- Use related addition and subtraction facts to check the answers to real-world problems.

Learn You can solve real-world problems using addition.

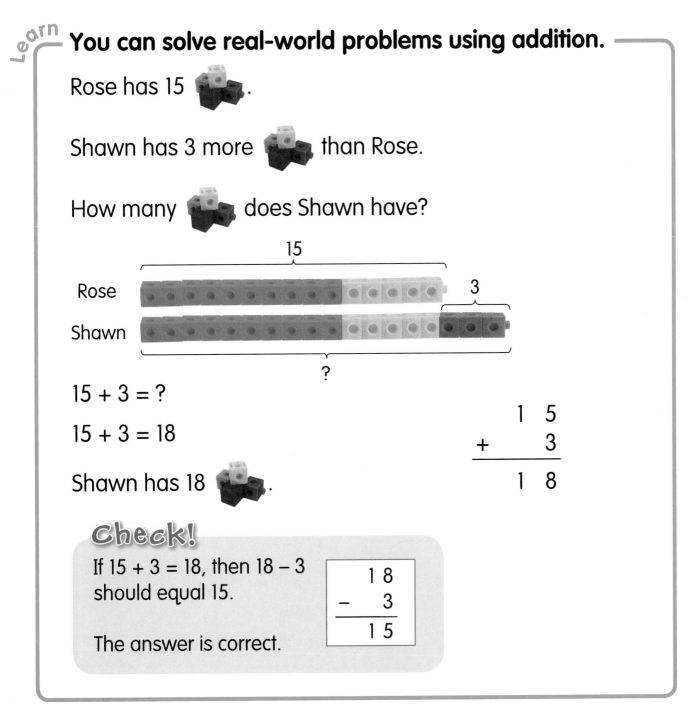

Rose has 15 .

Shawn has 3 more than Rose.

How many does Shawn have?

15 + 3 = ?

15 + 3 = 18

Shawn has 18 .

$$\begin{array}{r} 1\ 5 \\ +\quad 3 \\ \hline 1\ 8 \end{array}$$

Check!

If 15 + 3 = 18, then 18 – 3 should equal 15.

$$\begin{array}{r} 1\ 8 \\ -\quad 3 \\ \hline 1\ 5 \end{array}$$

The answer is correct.

Guided Learning

Solve. Check your answer.

1 Jake makes 10 glasses of orange juice.
Dave makes 8 more glasses of orange juice than Jake.
How many glasses of orange juice does Dave make?

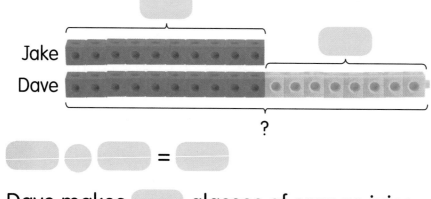

Jake

Dave

?

=

Dave makes ⬭ glasses of orange juice.

You can solve real-world problems using subtraction.

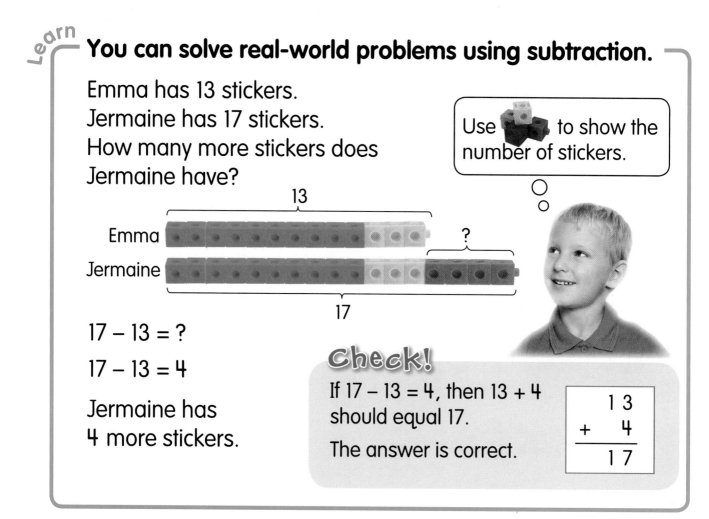

Emma has 13 stickers.
Jermaine has 17 stickers.
How many more stickers does
Jermaine have?

Use ▧ to show the
number of stickers.

13

Emma

Jermaine

?

17

$17 - 13 = ?$

$17 - 13 = 4$

Jermaine has
4 more stickers.

Check!

If $17 - 13 = 4$, then $13 + 4$
should equal 17.

The answer is correct.

$$\begin{array}{r} 1\ 3 \\ +\quad 4 \\ \hline 1\ 7 \end{array}$$

Guided Learning

Solve. Check your answer.

2 Raoul has 19 baseball cards.
Tyler has 11 baseball cards.
How many more baseball cards does Raoul have?

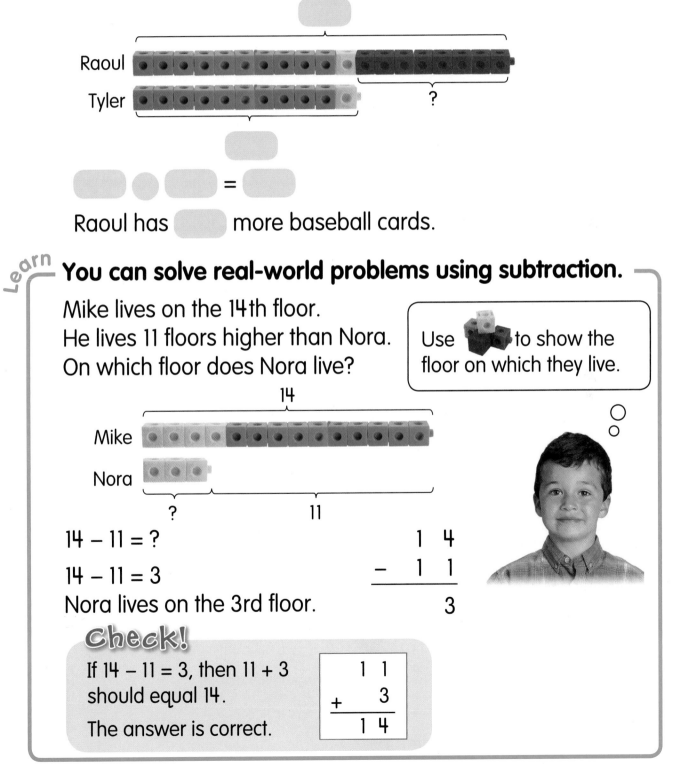

Raoul

Tyler

?

$\boxed{}$ $\boxed{}$ = $\boxed{}$

Raoul has $\boxed{}$ more baseball cards.

Learn You can solve real-world problems using subtraction.

Mike lives on the 14th floor.
He lives 11 floors higher than Nora.
On which floor does Nora live?

Use 🧊 to show the floor on which they live.

14

Mike

Nora

?   11

$14 - 11 = ?$

$14 - 11 = 3$

Nora lives on the 3rd floor.

$$\begin{array}{r} 1\ 4 \\ -\ 1\ 1 \\ \hline 3 \end{array}$$

Check!

If $14 - 11 = 3$, then $11 + 3$ should equal 14.

The answer is correct.

$$\begin{array}{r} 1\ 1 \\ +\ \ \ 3 \\ \hline 1\ 4 \end{array}$$

Guided Learning

Solve. Check your answer.

3 Sam makes 20 favors for a party.
He makes 6 more favors than Julia.
How many favors does Julia make?

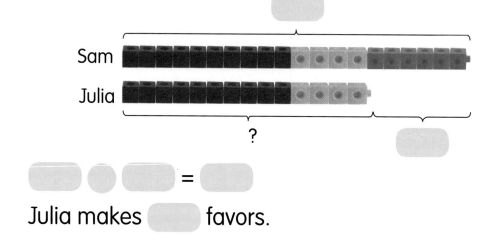

=

Julia makes ⬤ favors.

Learn **You can solve real-world problems using subtraction.**

Henry makes 19 valentines.
Beth makes 7 fewer valentines than Henry.
How many valentines does Beth make?

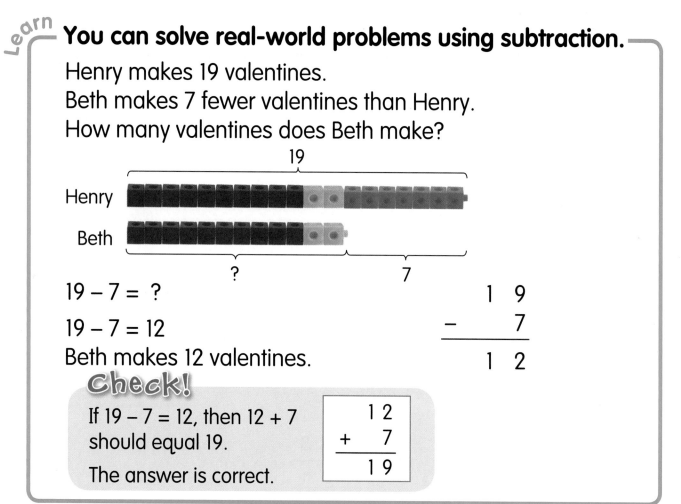

$19 - 7 = ?$

$19 - 7 = 12$

Beth makes 12 valentines.

$$\begin{array}{r} 1\ 9 \\ -\ 7 \\ \hline 1\ 2 \end{array}$$

Check!

If $19 - 7 = 12$, then $12 + 7$ should equal 19.

The answer is correct.

$$\begin{array}{r} 1\ 2 \\ +\ 7 \\ \hline 1\ 9 \end{array}$$

Guided Learning

Solve. Check your answer.

4 Amy has 16 beads.
Kevin has 7 fewer beads than Amy.
How many beads does Kevin have?

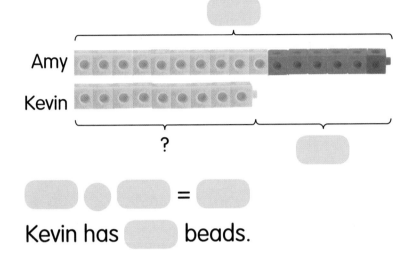

Kevin has [ ] beads.

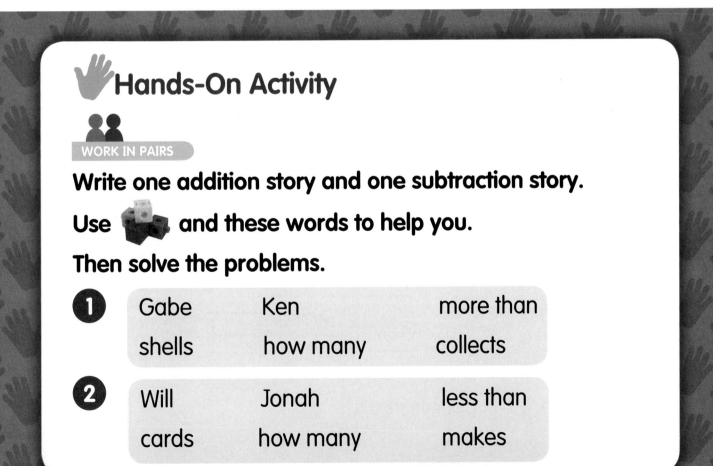

Hands-On Activity

WORK IN PAIRS

Write one addition story and one subtraction story.

Use [ ] and these words to help you.

Then solve the problems.

1

| Gabe | Ken | more than |
| shells | how many | collects |

2

| Will | Jonah | less than |
| cards | how many | makes |

Learn **You can solve real-world problems involving addition of three numbers.**

Mel bought 6 oranges and 5 pears.
She later bought 3 apples.
How many fruits did she buy in all?

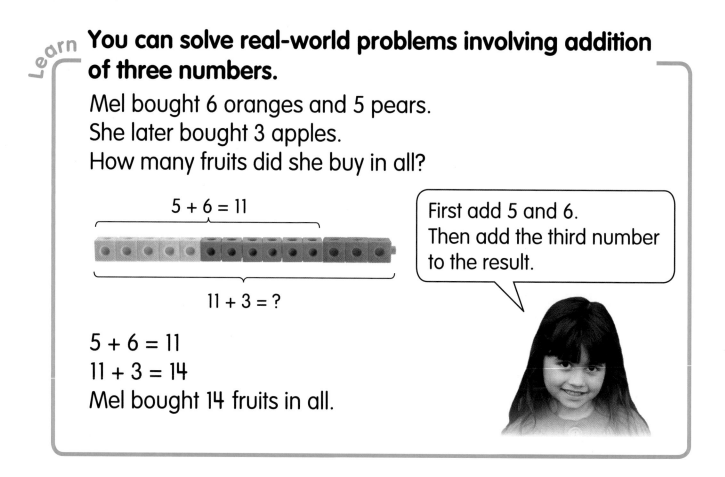

$5 + 6 = 11$

$11 + 3 = ?$

First add 5 and 6.
Then add the third number to the result.

$5 + 6 = 11$
$11 + 3 = 14$
Mel bought 14 fruits in all.

Guided Learning

Solve.

5 Jane has three bundles of pencils.
The first bundle has 4 pencils,
the second has 8 pencils,
and the third has 6 pencils.
How many pencils are there in all?

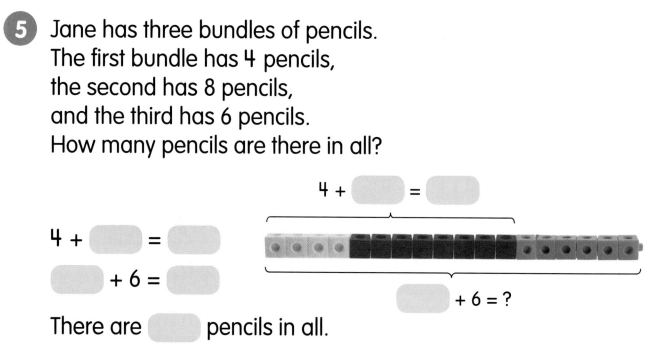

$4 + \boxed{} = \boxed{}$

$4 + \boxed{} = \boxed{}$

$\boxed{} + 6 = \boxed{}$

$\boxed{} + 6 = ?$

There are $\boxed{}$ pencils in all.

WORK IN PAIRS

1 Write a real-world problem using the words and numbers below. Use  or draw models to show your answer.

cherries	apricots	strawberries	
Will	Sean	Ben	
5	3	9	in all

2 Think of an addition story involving three numbers. Write a real-world problem involving addition of three numbers. Then solve the problem.

Choose three numbers from 0 to 9.

Let's Practice

Find the missing numbers.

1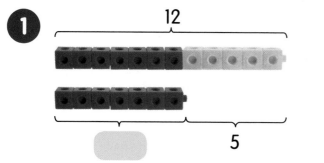

2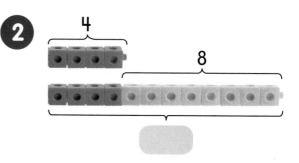

Solve. Check your answer.

3 Alexis has 18 bunnies.
Gabriella has 12 bunnies
How many more bunnies does Alexis have?

4 Devan buys 13 stickers.
Cara buys 7 more stickers than Devan.
How many stickers does Cara buy?

5 Sita picks up 13 bottles on the beach.
She picks up 8 fewer bottles than Tina.
How many bottles does Tina pick up?

Solve. Check your answer.

6 Ling counted 17 birds in a park.
She counted 9 more birds than butterflies.
How many butterflies did Ling count?

7 Lori makes 6 sandwiches.
Then she makes 2 more sandwiches.
Meg makes 5 sandwiches.
How many sandwiches are there in all?

ON YOUR OWN

Go to Workbook B:
Practice 6, pages 79–82

CRITICAL THINKING SKILLS
Put On Your Thinking Cap!

PROBLEM SOLVING

Pick any three numbers shown below and complete the addition sentence.
Use a number only once for each sentence.

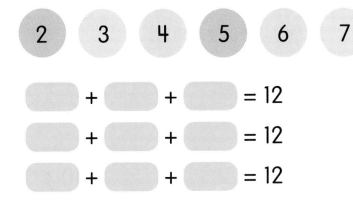

2   3   4   5   6   7

☐ + ☐ + ☐ = 12

☐ + ☐ + ☐ = 12

☐ + ☐ + ☐ = 12

ON YOUR OWN

Go to Workbook B:
Put on Your Thinking Cap!
pages 83–86

Chapter Wrap Up

You have learned...

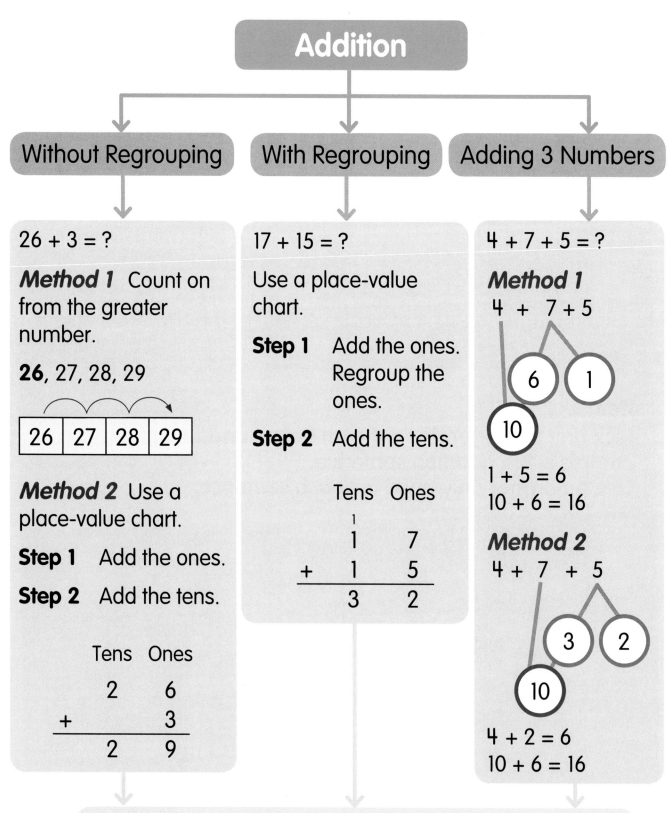

Addition

Without Regrouping

26 + 3 = ?

Method 1 Count on from the greater number.

26, 27, 28, 29

26	27	28	29

Method 2 Use a place-value chart.

Step 1 Add the ones.

Step 2 Add the tens.

```
  Tens  Ones
    2    6
 +       3
 ─────────
    2    9
```

With Regrouping

17 + 15 = ?

Use a place-value chart.

Step 1 Add the ones. Regroup the ones.

Step 2 Add the tens.

```
  Tens  Ones
    ¹
    1    7
 +  1    5
 ─────────
    3    2
```

Adding 3 Numbers

4 + 7 + 5 = ?

Method 1

4 + 7 + 5

⑥ ①

⑩

1 + 5 = 6
10 + 6 = 16

Method 2

4 + 7 + 5

③ ②

⑩

4 + 2 = 6
10 + 6 = 16

Solve real-world problems.

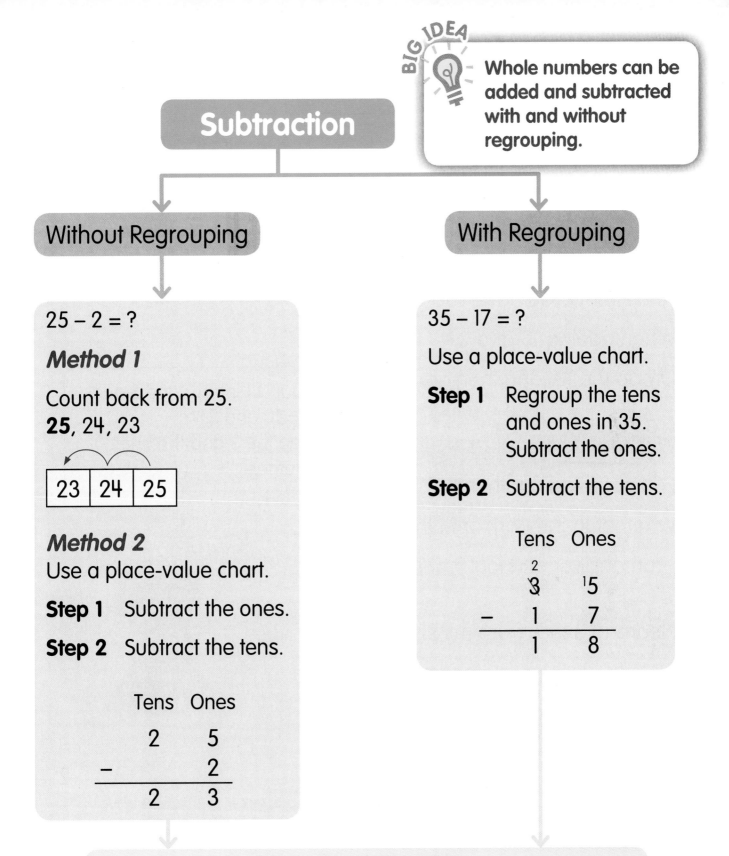

Subtraction

BIG IDEA
Whole numbers can be added and subtracted with and without regrouping.

Without Regrouping

25 − 2 = ?

Method 1

Count back from 25.
25, 24, 23

| 23 | 24 | 25 |

Method 2

Use a place-value chart.

Step 1 Subtract the ones.

Step 2 Subtract the tens.

	Tens	Ones
	2	5
−		2
	2	3

With Regrouping

35 − 17 = ?

Use a place-value chart.

Step 1 Regroup the tens and ones in 35. Subtract the ones.

Step 2 Subtract the tens.

	Tens	Ones
	²3̷	¹5
−	1	7
	1	8

Solve real-world problems.

ON YOUR OWN

Go to Workbook A:
Chapter Review/Test,
pages 87–88

I have learned what to do,

And I know you have, too.

When adding 13 and 2,

Group the 13, and then add 2.

With that as the rule,

I do not need another tool.

Whether in the park or in the pool,

I can answer and look cool.

I learned a trick from my sister,

So I can answer much faster.

I am still learning from her,

And I will soon outpace her.

Group 13 into 10 and 3 ones.
13 = 10 and 3.
Keep the 3 and the ones together.

BIG IDEA

Number bonds help you to add and subtract mentally.

Recall Prior Knowledge

Making some number bonds for 10

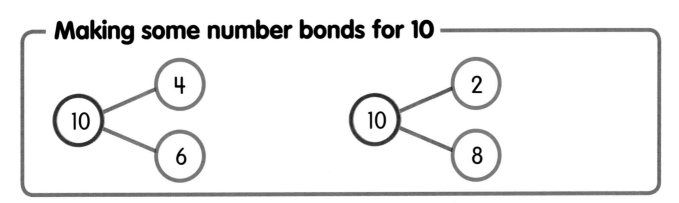

Making number bonds for other numbers

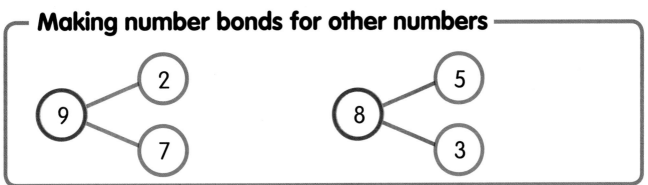

Making a fact family

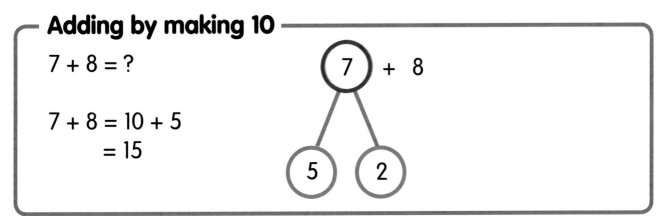

$4 + 5 = 9$
$5 + 4 = 9$
$9 - 4 = 5$
$9 - 5 = 4$

Adding by making 10

$7 + 8 = ?$

$7 + 8 = 10 + 5$
$\quad\quad = 15$

Knowing doubles facts

These are doubles facts.

$$2 + 2 = 4 \qquad 3 + 3 = 6 \qquad 4 + 4 = 8$$

What is double 3?
Double 3 is to add 3 more to 3. $3 + 3$
Double 3 is 6. $3 + 3 = 6$

Adding by using a doubles plus one fact

$3 + 4 = ?$

Step 1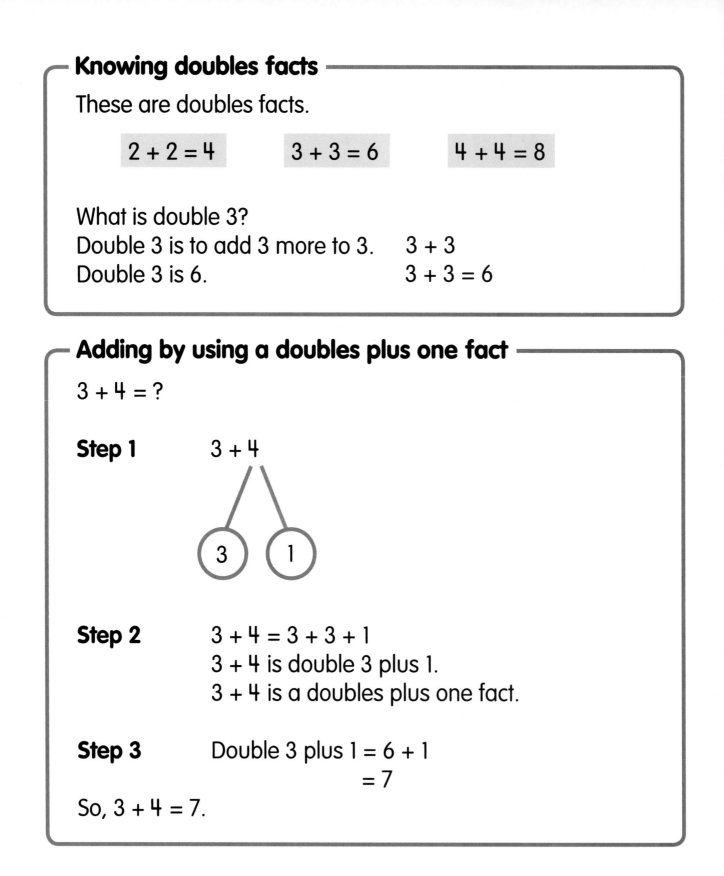

$3 + 4$

$3 \quad 1$

Step 2 $3 + 4 = 3 + 3 + 1$
$3 + 4$ is double 3 plus 1.
$3 + 4$ is a doubles plus one fact.

Step 3   Double 3 plus 1 = 6 + 1
$$= 7$$

So, $3 + 4 = 7$.

✔ Quick Check

Complete each number bond.

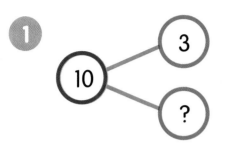

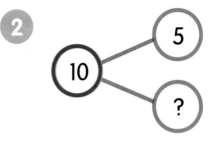

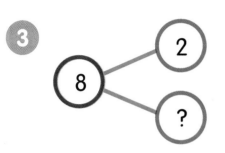

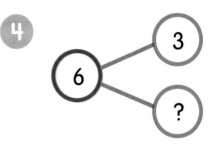

Complete the fact family.

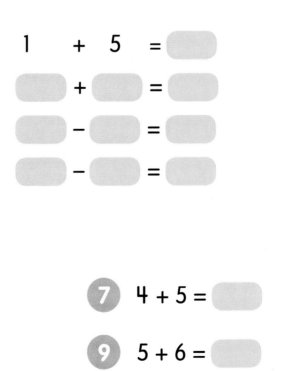

$$1 + 5 = \boxed{}$$

$$\boxed{} + \boxed{} = \boxed{}$$

$$\boxed{} - \boxed{} = \boxed{}$$

$$\boxed{} - \boxed{} = \boxed{}$$

Add.

6 $7 + 7 = \boxed{}$

7 $4 + 5 = \boxed{}$

8 $7 + 8 = \boxed{}$

9 $5 + 6 = \boxed{}$

LESSON 1 Mental Addition

Lesson Objectives

- Mentally add 1-digit numbers.
- Mentally add a 1-digit number to a 2-digit number.
- Mentally add a 2-digit number to tens.

Vocabulary
doubles fact
mentally

Learn **You can add ones mentally using a doubles fact.**

Find 5 + 5.

5 + 5 = 10

5 + 5 is
a doubles fact.

Guided Learning

**Add mentally.
Use doubles facts.**

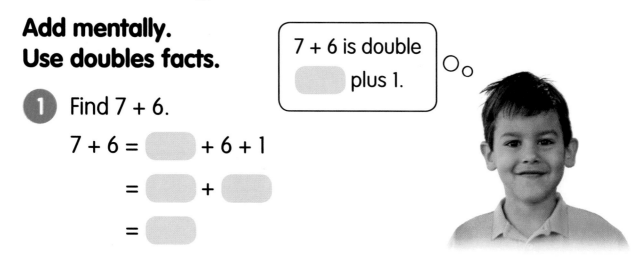

7 + 6 is double
⬚ plus 1.

1 Find 7 + 6.

7 + 6 = ⬚ + 6 + 1

    = ⬚ + ⬚

    = ⬚

You can add ones mentally using the 'add the ones' strategy.

Find 12 + 6.

Group 12 into tens and ones.

12	10
	2

Step 1 Add the ones.   2 + 6 = 8

Step 2 Add the result to the tens.   10 + 8 = 18

So, 12 + 6 = 18.

Guided Learning

Add mentally.

2 Find 23 + 4.

Group 23 into tens and ones.

23 → 20, ?

Step 1 Add the ones.   ▢ + 4 = ▢

Step 2 Add the result to the tens.   ▢ + ▢ = ▢

So, 23 + 4 = ▢.

3 Find 35 + 3.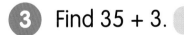

You can add tens mentally using the 'add the tens' strategy.

Find 23 + 10.

Group 23 into tens and ones.

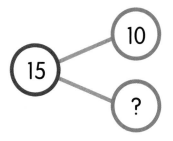

Step 1   Add the tens. $20 + 10 = 30$

Step 2   Add the result to the ones. $3 + 30 = 33$

So, $23 + 10 = 33$.

Guided Learning

Add mentally.

 Find 15 + 20.

Group 15 into tens and ones.

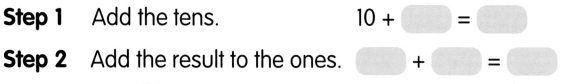

Step 1   Add the tens. $10 +$ ⬚ $=$ ⬚

Step 2   Add the result to the ones.   ⬚ $+$ ⬚ $=$ ⬚

So, $15 + 20 =$ ⬚ .

5 Find 29 + 10.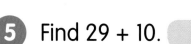

WORKING TOGETHER **Game**

Add Mentally!

Players: 2–5
You need:
• number cards
  (4, 5, 6, 7, 8, and 9)
• number cards
  (6, 7, 8, and 9)

How to play:

STEP 1 Player 1 draws a card from the first set.

STEP 2 Player 1 draws another card from the second set.

STEP 3 Player 1 adds the two numbers mentally.

$8 + 5 = ?$

STEP 4 The other players check Player 1's answer. Player 1 gets 1 point if the answer is correct. Take turns to play. End the game after ten rounds.

$8 + 5 = 13$

Correct!

The player with the most points wins!

Let's Practice

Add mentally.
Use doubles facts.

1 6 + 7 =

2 9 + 8 =

Add mentally.
First add the ones.
Then add the result to the tens.

3 14 + 2 =

4 31 + 8 =

Add mentally.
First add the tens.
Then add the result to the ones.

5 25 + 10 =

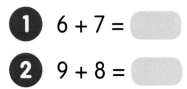

6 10 + 27 =

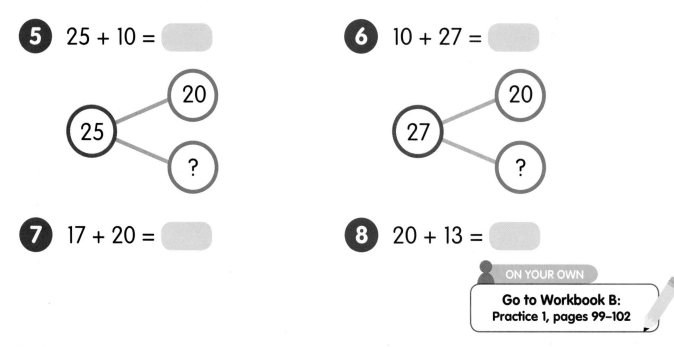

7 17 + 20 =

8 20 + 13 =

ON YOUR OWN

Go to Workbook B:
Practice 1, pages 99–102

LESSON 2 Mental Subtraction

Lesson Objectives

- Mentally subtract 1-digit numbers.
- Mentally subtract a 1-digit number from a 2-digit number.
- Mentally subtract tens from a 2-digit number.

Learn **You can subtract ones mentally by recalling number bonds.**

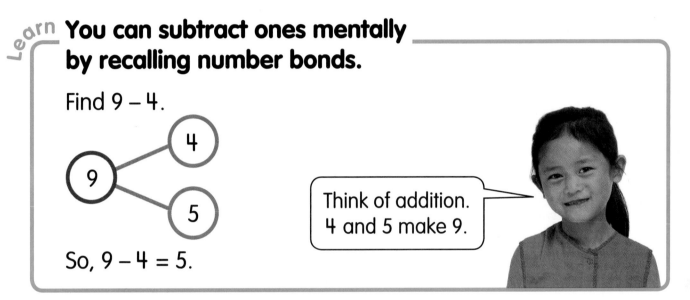

Find 9 – 4.

```
      4
  9 <
      5
```

Think of addition.
4 and 5 make 9.

So, 9 – 4 = 5.

Guided Learning

Subtract mentally.

1 Find 8 – 5.

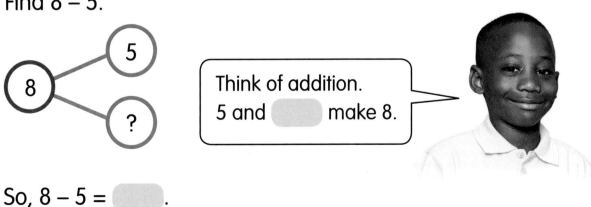

```
      5
  8 <
      ?
```

Think of addition.
5 and   make 8.

So, 8 – 5 =   .

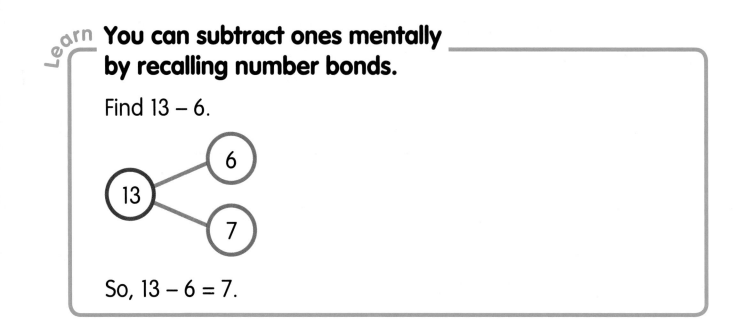

Learn **You can subtract ones mentally by recalling number bonds.**

Find 13 – 6.

So, 13 – 6 = 7.

Guided Learning

Subtract mentally.

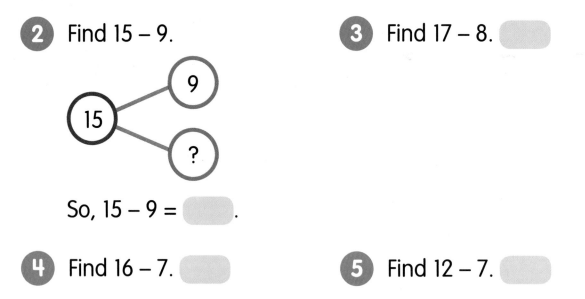

2 Find 15 – 9.

So, 15 – 9 = _____.

3 Find 17 – 8. _____

4 Find 16 – 7. _____

5 Find 12 – 7. _____

Learn **You can subtract ones mentally using 'subtract the ones' strategy.**

Find 28 – 3.

Group 28 into tens and ones.

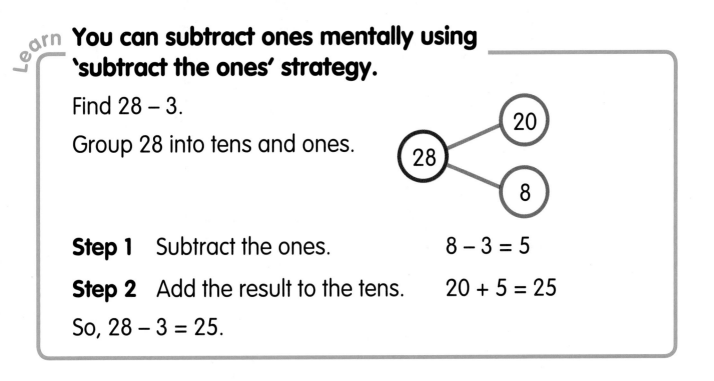

Step 1 Subtract the ones. $8 - 3 = 5$

Step 2 Add the result to the tens. $20 + 5 = 25$

So, 28 – 3 = 25.

Guided Learning

Subtract mentally.

6 Find 37 – 4.

Group 37 into tens and ones.

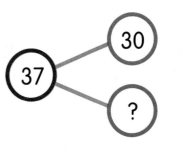

Step 1 Subtract the ones. ⬜ $- 4 =$ ⬜

Step 2 Add the result to the tens. ⬜ $+$ ⬜ $=$ ⬜

So, 37 – 4 = ⬜.

7 Find 36 – 5. ⬜

You can subtract tens mentally using 'subtract the tens' strategy.

Find 39 – 10.

Group 39 into tens and ones.

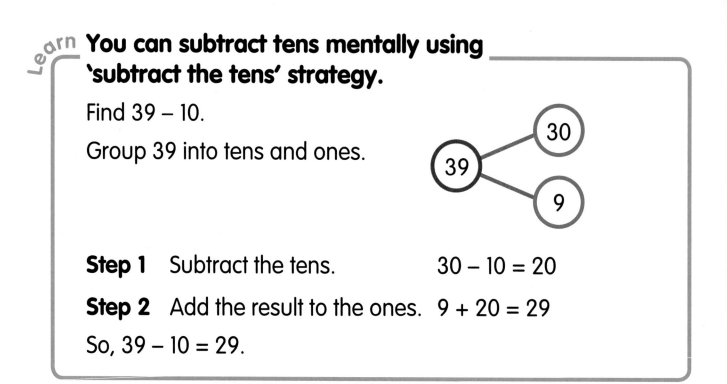

Step 1   Subtract the tens.   30 – 10 = 20

Step 2   Add the result to the ones.   9 + 20 = 29

So, 39 – 10 = 29.

Guided Learning

Subtract mentally.

8 Find 35 – 20.

Group 35 into tens and ones.

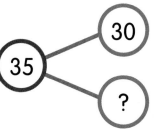

Step 1   Subtract the tens.   30 – [　　] = [　　]

Step 2   Add the result to the ones.   [　　] + [　　] = [　　]

So, 35 – 20 = [　　].

9 Find 29 – 20. [　　]

Subtract Mentally!

Players: 2–5
You need:
- spinner
- number cards (11–19)

How to play:

 STEP 1 Player 1 draws a card.

STEP 2 Player 1 spins the spinner once to get a number.

STEP 3 Player 1 subtracts the numbers mentally.

15 − 6 = 9

STEP 4 The other players check the answer.
Player 1 gets 1 point if the answer is correct. Take turns to play. End the game after ten rounds.

I win!

The player with the most points wins!

Let's Explore!

There are many ways to add two 1-digit numbers mentally.

Example

8 + 7 = ?

One way:

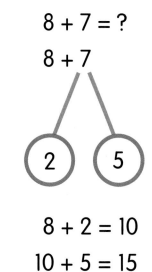

8 + 7 = ?

8 + 7

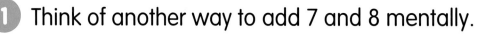

2   5

8 + 2 = 10

10 + 5 = 15

1 Think of another way to add 7 and 8 mentally.

2 Think of two different ways to add 6 and 7 mentally.

Let's Practice

Subtract mentally.
Think of addition.

1 $7 - 5 = $

2 $6 - 4 = $

3 $12 - 6 = $

4 $11 - 8 = $

Subtract mentally.
First subtract the ones.
Then add the result to the tens.

5 $27 - 6 = $

6 $39 - 4 = $

Subtract mentally.
First subtract the tens.
Then add the result to the ones.

7 $25 - 10 = $

8 $37 - 20 = $

9 $19 - 10 = $

ON YOUR OWN

Go to Workbook B:
Practice 2, pages 103–104

PROBLEM SOLVING

1   Tina adds two numbers mentally to get 24.
The ones digit of one of the numbers is 8.
What can the two numbers be?

There is more
than one correct
answer.

2   Jamal subtracts two numbers to get 17.
The ones digit of the greater number is 9.
What can the two numbers be?

ON YOUR OWN

Go to Workbook B:
Put on Your Thinking Cap!
pages 105–106

Chapter Wrap Up

You have learned...

BIG IDEA Number bonds help you to add and subtract mentally.

Mental Addition

Add ones

2 + 14 = ?

4   10

2 + 4 = 6
10 + 6 = 16

Add tens

12 + 20 = ?

2   10

10 + 20 = 30
2 + 30 = 32

Add ones using doubles facts

3 + 4 = ?

3   1

3 + 4 = 3 + 3 + 1
      = 6 + 1
      = 7

So, 3 + 4 is double 3 plus 1.

Mental Subtraction

Subtract by recalling number bonds

7 − 4 = ?

4   3

7 − 4 = 3

Subtract ones

27 − 3 = ?

20   7

7 − 3 = 4
20 + 4 = 24

Subtract tens

38 − 10 = ?

8   30

30 − 10 = 20
20 + 8 = 28

ON YOUR OWN

Go to Workbook B:
Chapter Review/Test,
pages 107–108

Calendar and Time

Thirty days have September,
April, June and November.
All the rest have thirty-one,
Except February alone,
Which has twenty-eight days clear,
And twenty-nine in each leap year.

Lesson 1 Using a Calendar

Lesson 2 Telling Time to the Hour

Lesson 3 Telling Time to the Half Hour

BIG IDEA

Calendars are used to show days, weeks, and months of a year. Clocks are used to read time of the day.

Recall Prior Knowledge

Using ordinal numbers and position

The children are running in a race.

James came in first.

Lily came in third.

Kurt was last.

The children are
running in a race.

Look at the picture. Complete the sentences.

1 _____ is fourth.

2 _____ is last.

3 _____ is 7th.

LESSON 1 Using a Calendar

Lesson Objectives

- Read a calendar.
- Know the days of the week and months of the year.
- Write the date.
- Know the seasons of the year.

Learn

You can read a calendar.

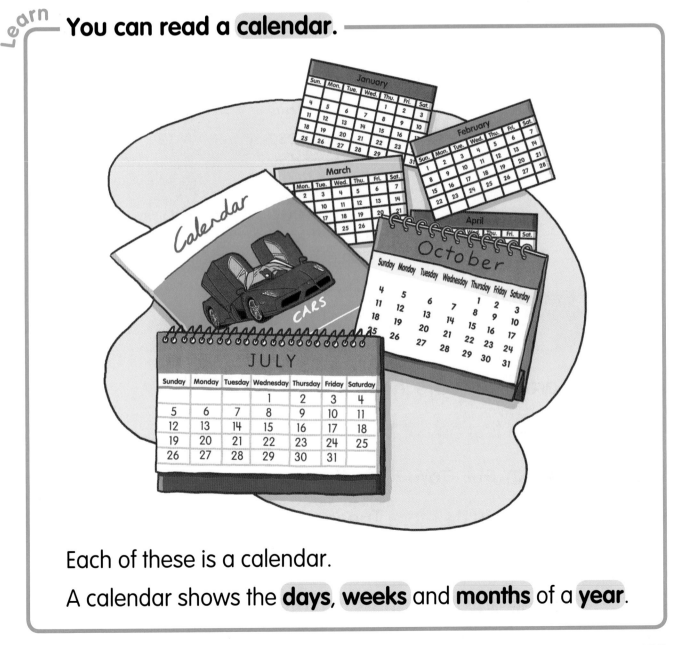

Each of these is a calendar.

A calendar shows the **days**, **weeks** and **months** of a **year**.

Learn **You can know the days of the week.**

There are 7 days in one week.
The first day of the week is Sunday.
The last day of the week is Saturday.

JULY

Sunday   Monday   Tuesday   Wednesday   Thursday   Friday   Saturday

Count the days of the week from Sunday through Saturday.

You can write Sunday as Sun.
Monday   → Mon.
Tuesday   → Tue.
Wednesday   → Wed.
Thursday   → Thu.
Friday   → Fri.
Saturday   → Sat.

Guided Learning

Complete.

1 There are ⬜ days in the week.

2 ⬜ is the first day of the week.

3 The last day of the week is ⬜ .

4 ⬜ comes just before Tuesday.

5 ⬜ is the day between Tuesday and Thursday.

6 ⬜ is the day that comes just after Thursday.

Hands-On Activity

Use seven index cards and write the names of the 7 days of the week in order.

Point to and say each day to your partner.

Your partner points to and says each day to you.

Mix up the cards and have your partner put them in order.

You can know the months of the year.

JANUARY						
Sun.	Mon.	Tue.	Wed.	Thu.	Fri.	Sat.
					1	2
3	4	5	6	7	8	9
10	11	12	13	14	15	16
17	18	19	20	21	22	23
24	25	26	27	28	29	30
31						

FEBRUARY						
Sun.	Mon.	Tue.	Wed.	Thu.	Fri.	Sat.
	1	2	3	4	5	6
7	8	9	10	11	12	13
14	15	16	17	18	19	20
21	22	23	24	25	26	27
28						

MARCH						
Sun.	Mon.	Tue.	Wed.	Thu.	Fri.	Sat.
	1	2	3	4	5	6
7	8	9	10	11	12	13
14	15	16	17	18	19	20
21	22	23	24	25	26	27
28	29	30	31			

APRIL						
Sun.	Mon.	Tue.	Wed.	Thu.	Fri.	Sat.
				1	2	3
4	5	6	7	8	9	10
11	12	13	14	15	16	17
18	19	20	21	22	23	24
25	26	27	28	29	30	

MAY						
Sun.	Mon.	Tue.	Wed.	Thu.	Fri.	Sat.
						1
2	3	4	5	6	7	8
9	10	11	12	13	14	15
16	17	18	19	20	21	22
23	24	25	26	27	28	29
30	31					

JUNE						
Sun.	Mon.	Tue.	Wed.	Thu.	Fri.	Sat.
		1	2	3	4	5
6	7	8	9	10	11	12
13	14	15	16	17	18	19
20	21	22	23	24	25	26
27	28	29	30			

JULY						
Sun.	Mon.	Tue.	Wed.	Thu.	Fri.	Sat.
				1	2	3
4	5	6	7	8	9	10
11	12	13	14	15	16	17
18	19	20	21	22	23	24
25	26	27	28	29	30	31

AUGUST						
Sun.	Mon.	Tue.	Wed.	Thu.	Fri.	Sat.
1	2	3	4	5	6	7
8	9	10	11	12	13	14
15	16	17	18	19	20	21
22	23	24	25	26	27	28
29	30	31				

SEPTEMBER						
Sun.	Mon.	Tue.	Wed.	Thu.	Fri.	Sat.
			1	2	3	4
5	6	7	8	9	10	11
12	13	14	15	16	17	18
19	20	21	22	23	24	25
26	27	28	29	30		

OCTOBER						
Sun.	Mon.	Tue.	Wed.	Thu.	Fri.	Sat.
					1	2
3	4	5	6	7	8	9
10	11	12	13	14	15	16
17	18	19	20	21	22	23
24	25	26	27	28	29	30
31						

NOVEMBER						
Sun.	Mon.	Tue.	Wed.	Thu.	Fri.	Sat.
	1	2	3	4	5	6
7	8	9	10	11	12	13
14	15	16	17	18	19	20
21	22	23	24	25	26	27
28	29	30				

DECEMBER						
Sun.	Mon.	Tue.	Wed.	Thu.	Fri.	Sat.
			1	2	3	4
5	6	7	8	9	10	11
12	13	14	15	16	17	18
19	20	21	22	23	24	25
26	27	28	29	30	31	

There are 12 months in one year.
The first month of the year is January.
The second month of the year is February.
The last month of the year is December.

Some months have 30 days.
Some months have 31 days.
How many days are there
in February?

Guided Learning

Complete.

7 There are ⬭ months in one year.

8 ⬭ is the third month of the year.

9 June is the ⬭ month of the year.

10 ⬭ is the month between April and June.

11 ⬭ comes just before August.

12 ⬭ is the month just after September.

13 April, June, ⬭ and ⬭ have only 30 days.

14 ⬭, ⬭, ⬭, ⬭, ⬭, ⬭, and ⬭, have 31 days.

15 February has ⬭ or ⬭ days.

16 School starts in the month of ⬭.

You can use a calendar to help you write the date.

March				2015		
Sunday	**Monday**	**Tuesday**	**Wednesday**	**Thursday**	**Friday**	**Saturday**
1	2	3	4	5	6	7
8	9	10	11	12	13	14
15	16	17	18	19	20	21
22	23	24	25	26	27	28
29	30	31				

This calendar shows the month of March in the year 2015.

The month begins on a Sunday.

The date is March 1, 2015.

The month ends on a Tuesday.

The date is March 31, 2015.

> If today is the second Wednesday of March 2015, what is the date?

Guided Learning

Use the calendar to complete.

17 The second day of the month falls on a _____ .

18 There are _____ Fridays in this month of March.

19 The date of the first Tuesday of the month is _____ .

20 If today is the last Wednesday of the month, the date is _____ .

21 The first day of the next month falls on a _____ .

22 A year after March 10, 2015 will be March 10, _____ .

You can know the months and seasons of the year.

January	February	March	April
May	June	July	August
September	October	November	December

These are the 12 months in one year.
Months help us to know the seasons of the year.

The Four Seasons

Spring

Summer

Fall

Winter

There are 4 seasons in one year.
They are spring, summer, fall and winter.
Some months are **warmer**.
Some are **colder**.

Guided Learning
Complete.

 23 Is December one of the colder months for you?
Explain your answer.

 # Hands-On Activity

Make your own calendar.

Show special days.

Birthdays, holidays, and school days are some special days.

Remember, the first day of a month can start on any day of the week.

Let's Practice

Fill in the blanks.
Use the calendar to help you.

2015

			JANUARY			
Sun.	Mon.	Tue.	Wed.	Thu.	Fri.	Sat.
				1	2	3
4	5	6	7	8	9	10
11	12	13	14	15	16	17
18	19	20	21	22	23	24
25	26	27	28	29	30	31

			FEBRUARY			
Sun.	Mon.	Tue.	Wed.	Thu.	Fri.	Sat.
1	2	3	4	5	6	7
8	9	10	11	12	13	14
15	16	17	18	19	20	21
22	23	24	25	26	27	28

			MARCH			
Sun.	Mon.	Tue.	Wed.	Thu.	Fri.	Sat.
1	2	3	4	5	6	7
8	9	10	11	12	13	14
15	16	17	18	19	20	21
22	23	24	25	26	27	28
29	30	31				

			APRIL			
Sun.	Mon.	Tue.	Wed.	Thu.	Fri.	Sat.
			1	2	3	4
5	6	7	8	9	10	11
12	13	14	15	16	17	18
19	20	21	22	23	24	25
26	27	28	29	30		

			MAY			
Sun.	Mon.	Tue.	Wed.	Thu.	Fri.	Sat.
					1	2
3	4	5	6	7	8	9
10	11	12	13	14	15	16
17	18	19	20	21	22	23
24	25	26	27	28	29	30
31						

			JUNE			
Sun.	Mon.	Tue.	Wed.	Thu.	Fri.	Sat.
	1	2	3	4	5	6
7	8	9	10	11	12	13
14	15	16	17	18	19	20
21	22	23	24	25	26	27
28	29	30				

			JULY			
Sun.	Mon.	Tue.	Wed.	Thu.	Fri.	Sat.
			1	2	3	4
5	6	7	8	9	10	11
12	13	14	15	16	17	18
19	20	21	22	23	24	25
26	27	28	29	30	31	

			AUGUST			
Sun.	Mon.	Tue.	Wed.	Thu.	Fri.	Sat.
						1
2	3	4	5	6	7	8
9	10	11	12	13	14	15
16	17	18	19	20	21	22
23	24	25	26	27	28	29
30	31					

			SEPTEMBER			
Sun.	Mon.	Tue.	Wed.	Thu.	Fri.	Sat.
		1	2	3	4	5
6	7	8	9	10	11	12
13	14	15	16	17	18	19
20	21	22	23	24	25	26
27	28	29	30			

			OCTOBER			
Sun.	Mon.	Tue.	Wed.	Thu.	Fri.	Sat.
				1	2	3
4	5	6	7	8	9	10
11	12	13	14	15	16	17
18	19	20	21	22	23	24
25	26	27	28	29	30	31

			NOVEMBER			
Sun.	Mon.	Tue.	Wed.	Thu.	Fri.	Sat.
1	2	3	4	5	6	7
8	9	10	11	12	13	14
15	16	17	18	19	20	21
22	23	24	25	26	27	28
29	30					

			DECEMBER			
Sun.	Mon.	Tue.	Wed.	Thu.	Fri.	Sat.
		1	2	3	4	5
6	7	8	9	10	11	12
13	14	15	16	17	18	19
20	21	22	23	24	25	26
27	28	29	30	31		

1 The fourth month of the year is ____ .

2 The date one week after May 8, 2015 is ____ .

3 The season for the month of January is ____ .

4 The date for the second Tuesday of March is ____ .

5 Independence Day, the Fourth of July, falls on a ____ .

6 ____ is the date two weeks before August 26, 2015.

7 Summer vacation starts in the month of ____ .

8 ____ is the only month with 28 days.

ON YOUR OWN

Go to Workbook B:
Practice 1, page 109–112

LESSON 2 Telling Time to the Hour

Lesson Objectives

- Use the term *o'clock* to tell the time to the hour.
- Read and show time to the hour on a clock.
- Read and show time to the hour on a digital clock.

Vocabulary

o'clock

minute hand

hour hand

digital clock

Learn **You can tell time to the hour.**

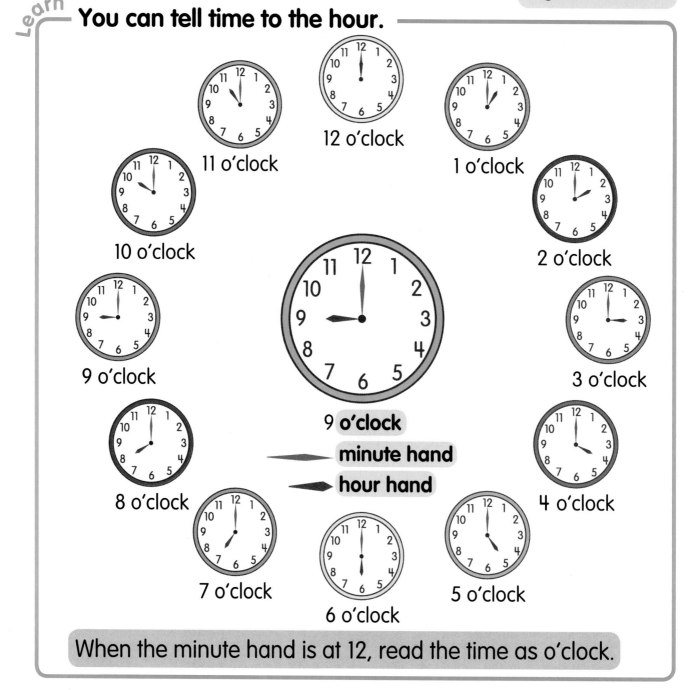

12 o'clock

11 o'clock

1 o'clock

10 o'clock

2 o'clock

9 o'clock

3 o'clock

9 **o'clock**

← **minute hand**

← **hour hand**

8 o'clock

4 o'clock

7 o'clock

6 o'clock

5 o'clock

When the minute hand is at 12, read the time as o'clock.

Guided Learning

Answer the question.

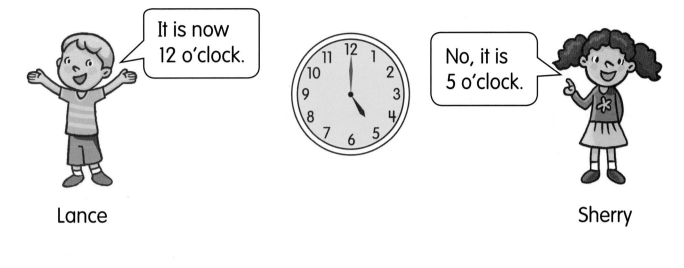

Lance

Sherry

1 Who is correct? _____ .

Tell the time.
Complete.

2

_____

3

_____

4

_____

5

_____

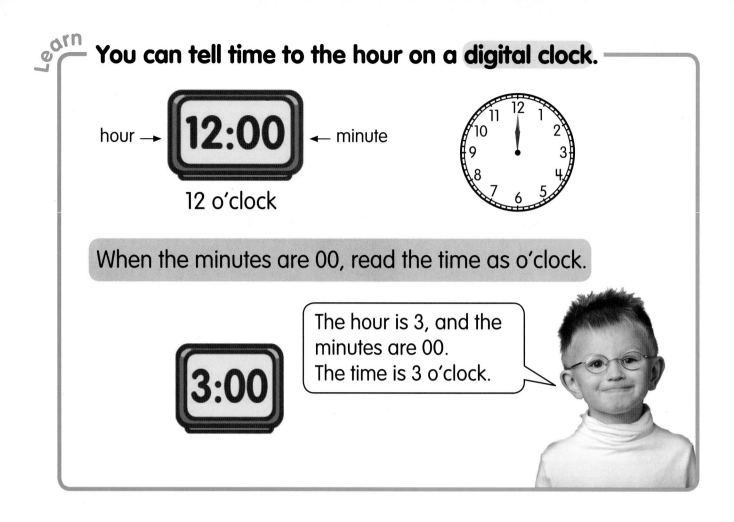

Learn **You can tell time to the hour on a digital clock.**

hour → **12:00** ← minute

12 o'clock

When the minutes are 00, read the time as o'clock.

3:00

The hour is 3, and the minutes are 00.
The time is 3 o'clock.

Guided Learning

Fill in the blank.

6 **10:00**   o'clock

7 **4:00**   o'clock

Write the time.

8 ____:____

9 ____:____

 # Hands-On Activity

WORK IN PAIRS

1 Use a paper plate, fastener and two clock hands to make your own clock.

Write the numbers on your clock.

Now use your clock to show these times.

2 o'clock   8 o'clock   12 o'clock

5 o'clock   9 o'clock

2 Use the clock to show the time when you do these activities.

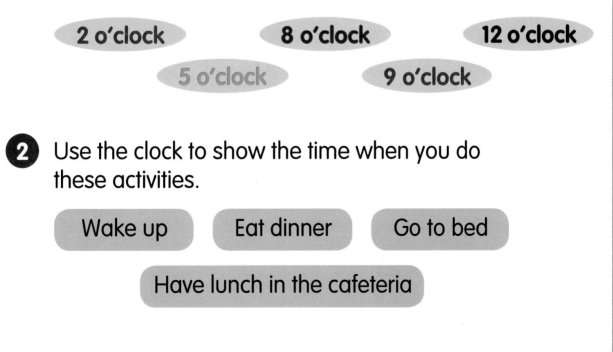

Wake up   Eat dinner   Go to bed

Have lunch in the cafeteria

Write the time.

1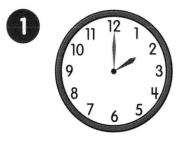

2

Match the picture to the time.
Choose the correct clock.

3

A

B

Math class starts in the morning.

4

A   B

Lunch time is at 12 o'clock.

Write the time.

5  1:00

6 11:00

7

8

ON YOUR OWN

Go to Workbook B:
Practice 2, pages 113–120

Telling Time to the Half Hour

Lesson Objectives

- Read time to the half hour.
- Use the term 'half past'.
- Relate time to daily activities.
- Read and show time to the half hour on a digital clock.

Vocabulary

half past

half hour

Learn — **You can tell time to the half hour.**

Leo wakes up at 7 o'clock in the morning.

Leo eats breakfast at **half past** 7.

When the minute hand is at 6, it is half past the hour.

The hour hand has moved too!

Guided Learning

Complete.
Use the clock to help you.

1

Pedro feeds his cat at 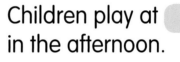 in the morning.

2

Children play at in the afternoon.

3

Maddie reads a story at at night.

Complete.
Use the clock to help you.

 4 Pa Lion and Baby Lion go to the carnival at _____ .

5 At _____ , Pa Lion plays a game.

6 Pa Lion wins the game and gets a toy chick at _____ .

7 At _____ , Pa Lion and Baby Lion take a ride on the Ferris wheel.

You can tell time to the half hour on a digital clock.

hour → **12:30** ← minute

half past 12

When the minutes are 30, read the time as half past the hour.

3:30

The hour is 3, and the minutes are 30.
The time is half past 3.

Guided Learning

Fill in the blank.

8   **6:30**   Half past ⬭

The hour is ⬭.

9   **8:30**   Half past ⬭

The minutes are ⬭.

Write the time.

10
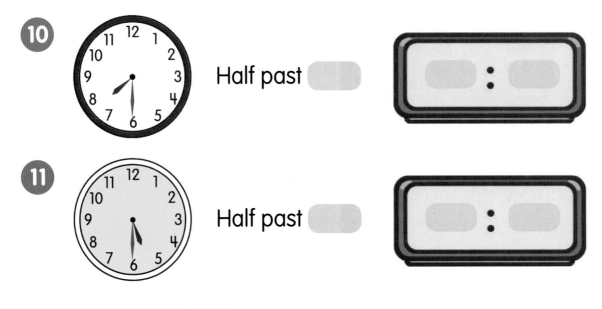

Half past [ ]

11

Half past [ ]

Let's Practice

Write the time.

1
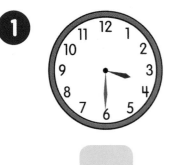

[ ]

2

[ ]

Match the picture to the time.
Choose the correct clock.

3

A   B

Dad watches TV at night before bedtime.

4

A

B

School starts in the morning.

Write the time.

5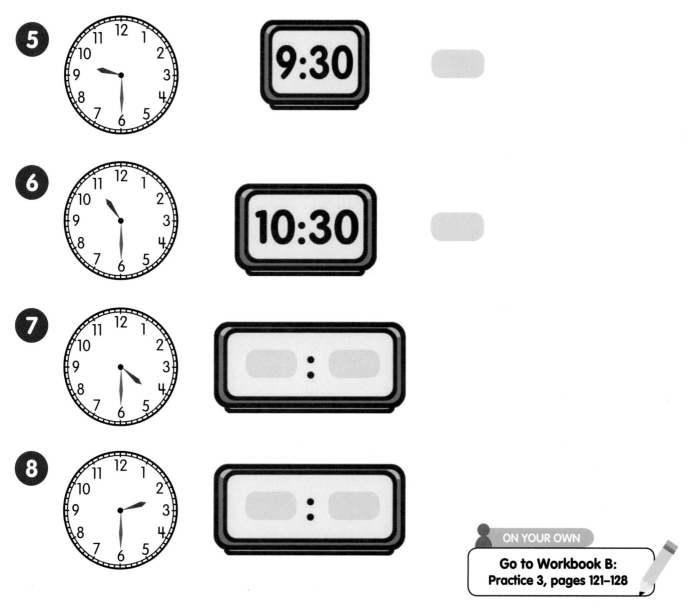

9:30

6

10:30

7

:

8

:

ON YOUR OWN

Go to Workbook B:
Practice 3, pages 121–128

PROBLEM SOLVING

1

At half past 6, the hour hand and the minute hand are pointing to the number 6.

Is this correct?
Explain your answer.

2 At what time of the day will the minute hand and the hour hand be on top of each other?

ON YOUR OWN

Go to Workbook B:
Put on Your Thinking Cap!
pages 129–130

Chapter Wrap Up

You have learned...

BIG IDEA

Calendars are used to show days, weeks, and months of a year. Clocks are used to read time of the day.

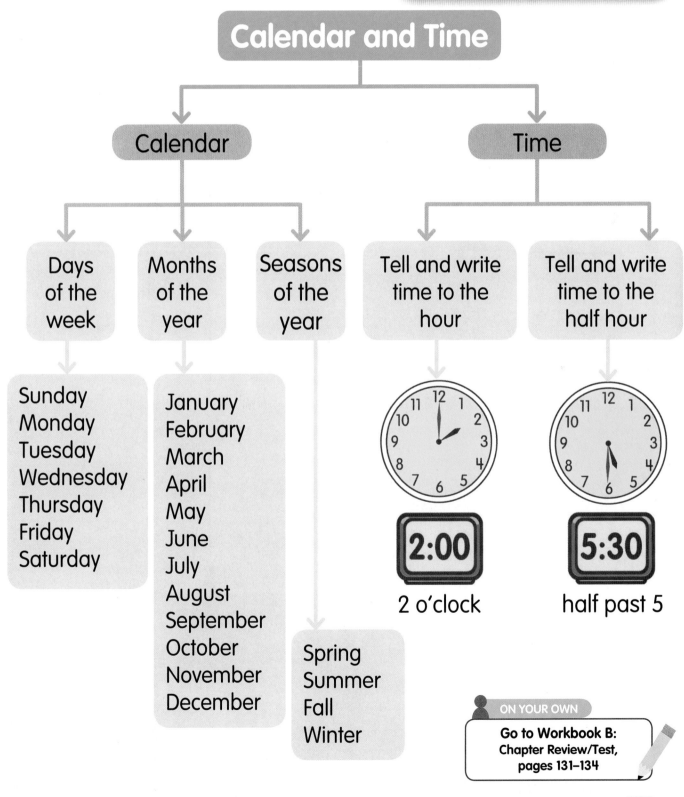

Calendar and Time

Calendar

Days of the week
Sunday
Monday
Tuesday
Wednesday
Thursday
Friday
Saturday

Months of the year
January
February
March
April
May
June
July
August
September
October
November
December

Seasons of the year
Spring
Summer
Fall
Winter

Time

Tell and write time to the hour
2:00
2 o'clock

Tell and write time to the half hour
5:30
half past 5

ON YOUR OWN

Go to Workbook B:
Chapter Review/Test,
pages 131–134

16 Numbers to 120

Lesson 1 Counting to 120

Lesson 2 Place Value

Lesson 3 Comparing, Ordering, and Patterns

BIG IDEA

Count, compare, and order numbers from 1 to 120.

Recall Prior Knowledge

Counting to 40

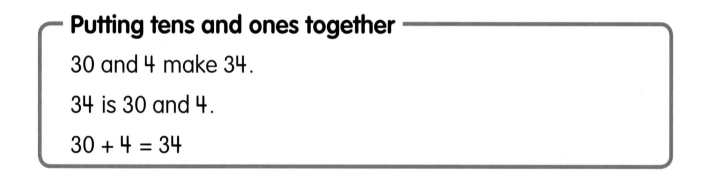

30
thirty

31, 32, 33, 34, 35, 36, 37, 38, 39, 40

forty

Putting tens and ones together

30 and 4 make 34.

34 is 30 and 4.

$30 + 4 = 34$

Using place value

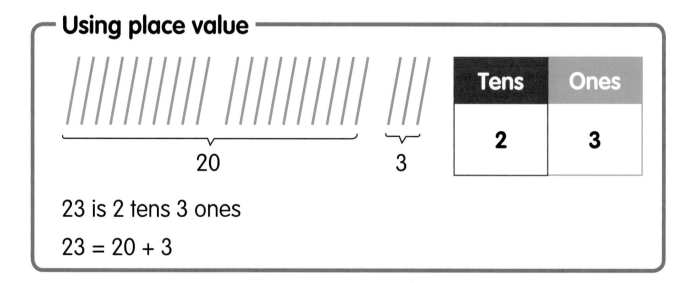

20

3

Tens	Ones
2	3

23 is 2 tens 3 ones

$23 = 20 + 3$

Comparing and ordering numbers

Compare 36, 39, and 40.

Compare the tens.
4 tens is greater than 3 tens.
40 is the greatest number.

In 36 and 39, the tens are the same.
So, compare the ones.

6 ones is less than 9 ones.
So, 36 is less than 39.
36 is the least number.

Order the numbers from greatest to least.
40, 39, 36

Tens	Ones
3	6
3	9
4	0

Making number patterns

24, 27, 30, 33, 36, 39

The numbers are arranged in a pattern.
Each number is 3 more than the number before it.

✔ Quick Check

Count on.

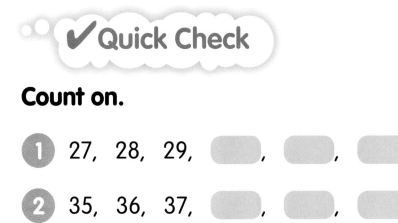

1 27, 28, 29, ____, ____, ____

2 35, 36, 37, ____, ____, ____

Find the missing numbers.

3 20 and 8 make ◯ .

4 35 is ◯ and 5.

5 $30 + $ ◯ $= 37$

6 $26 = $ ◯ tens ◯ ones

7 2 tens 9 ones = ◯

Compare and order.

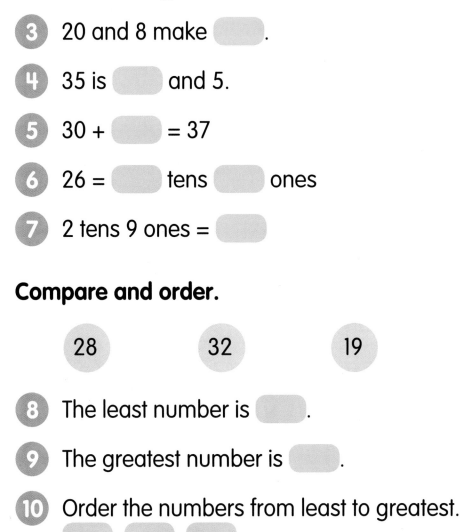

28   32   19

8 The least number is ◯ .

9 The greatest number is ◯ .

10 Order the numbers from least to greatest.

◯ , ◯ , ◯

least

Complete the number pattern.

11 31, 33, 35, ◯ , ◯ , 41

12 30, 27, 24, ◯ , ◯ , ◯ , 12

LESSON 1 Counting to 120

Lesson Objectives

- Count on from 41 to 120.
- Read and write 41 to 120 in numbers and words.

Vocabulary

fifty	ninety
sixty	one
seventy	hundred
eighty	estimate
one hundred twenty	

Learn **You can count numbers greater than 40.**

Count the sticks.

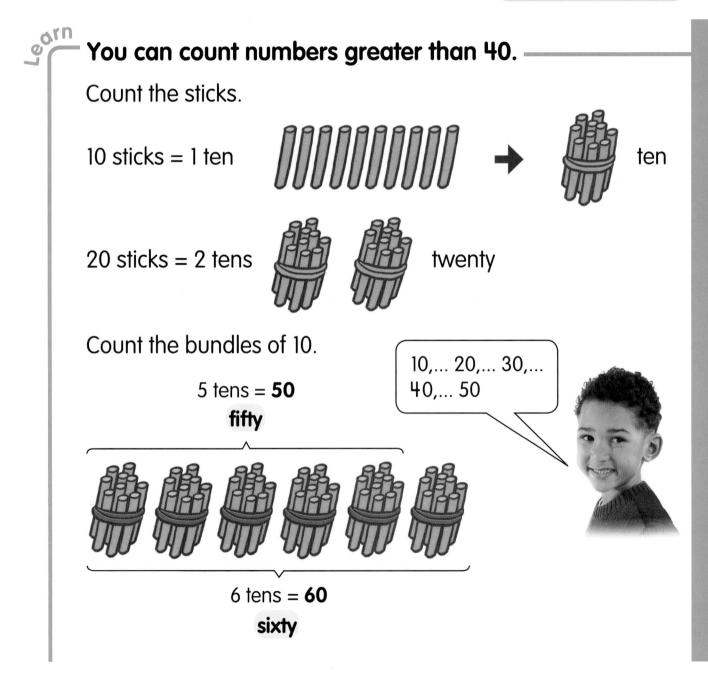

10 sticks = 1 ten   ten

20 sticks = 2 tens   twenty

Count the bundles of 10.

10,... 20,... 30,... 40,... 50

5 tens = **50**
fifty

6 tens = **60**
sixty

7 tens = **70**
seventy

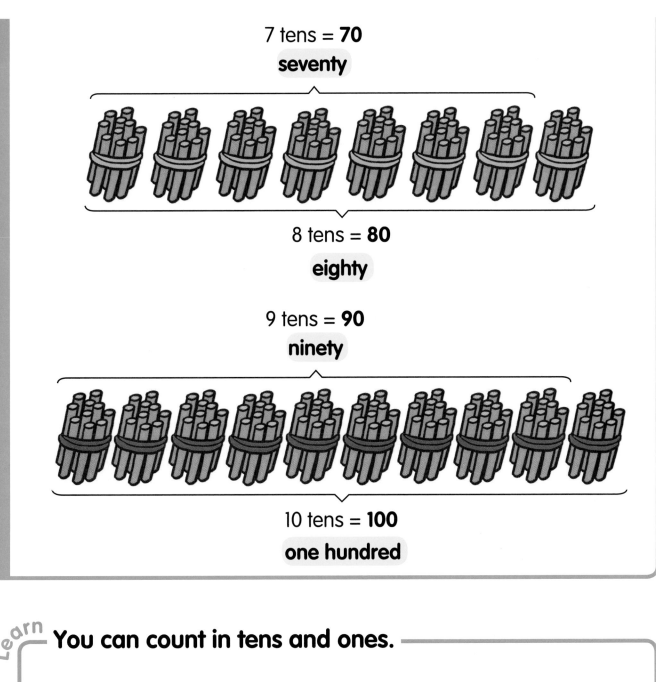

8 tens = **80**
eighty

9 tens = **90**
ninety

10 tens = **100**
one hundred

Learn

You can count in tens and ones.

40
forty

40, ... 50
forty, ... fifty

40, ... 50, 51, 52, 53
forty, ... fifty, fifty-one, fifty-two, fifty-three

There are 53 ▪.

Guided Learning

Count in tens and ones.
Then find the missing numbers.

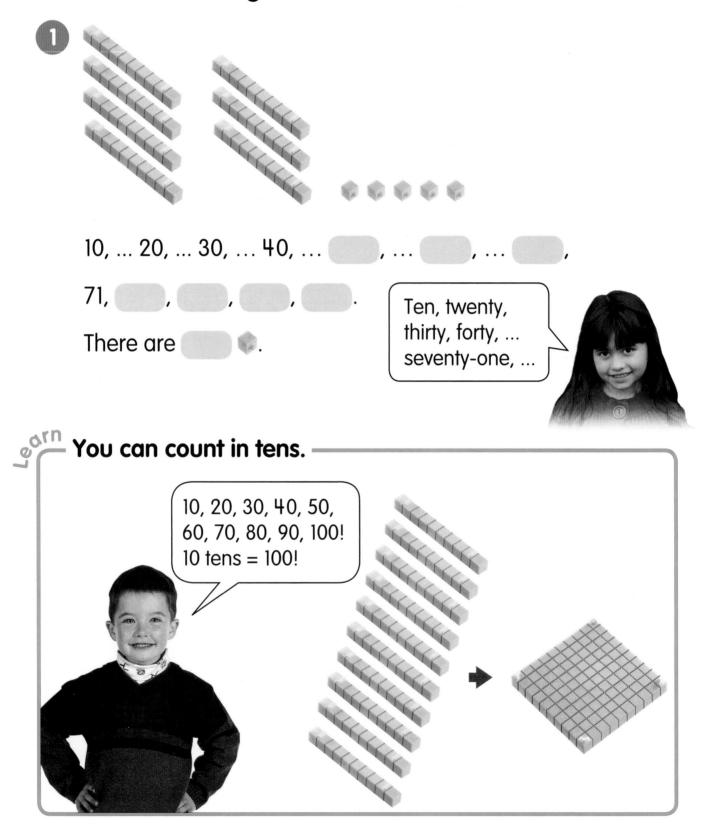

1

10, ... 20, ... 30, ... 40, ... [ ], ... [ ], ... [ ],

71, [ ], [ ], [ ], [ ].

There are [ ] ∎.

Ten, twenty, thirty, forty, ... seventy-one, ...

Learn You can count in tens.

10, 20, 30, 40, 50, 60, 70, 80, 90, 100! 10 tens = 100!

You can make numbers with tens and ones.

I have 74 🎲.

70 + 4 = 74

70 and 4 make 74.

Guided Learning

Find the missing number.

2 50 + 4 =

3 60 and 7 make .

4 7 and 70 make .

5 80 and 2 make .

6 3 and 90 make .

7 9 + 90 =

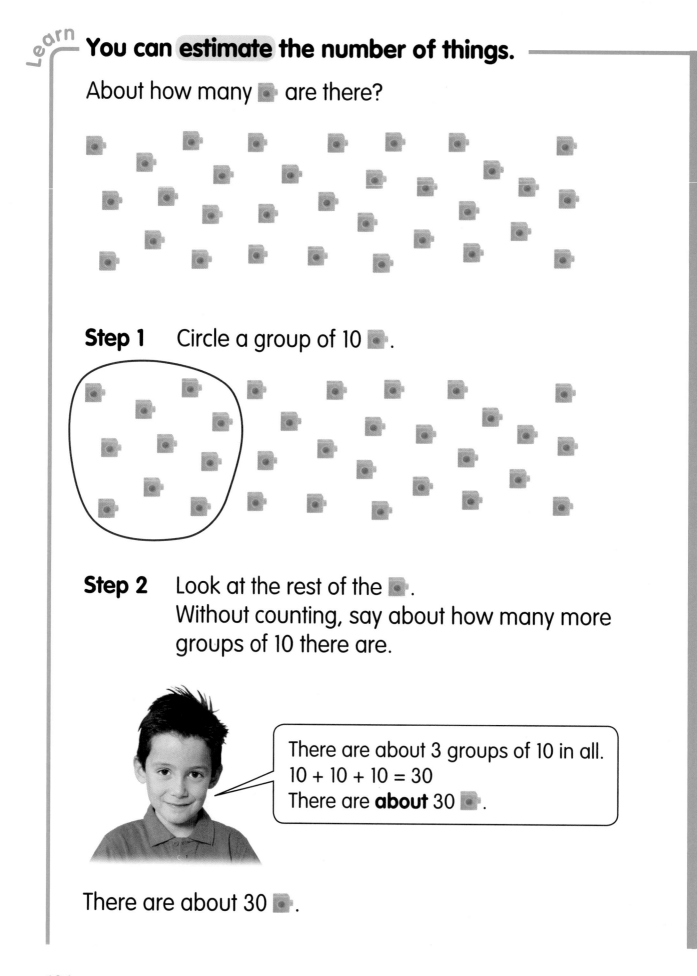

Learn

You can **estimate** the number of things.

About how many 🔲 are there?

Step 1   Circle a group of 10 🔲.

Step 2   Look at the rest of the 🔲.
Without counting, say about how many more groups of 10 there are.

> There are about 3 groups of 10 in all.
> 10 + 10 + 10 = 30
> There are **about** 30 🔲.

There are about 30 🔲.

Step 3   Count the 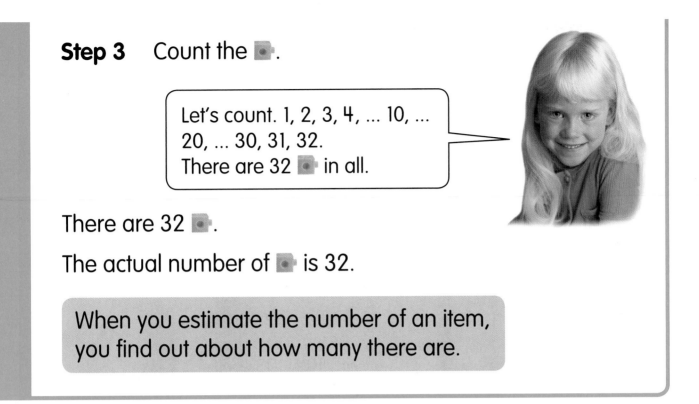.

> Let's count. 1, 2, 3, 4, ... 10, ...
> 20, ... 30, 31, 32.
> There are 32 ▪ in all.

There are 32 ▪.

The actual number of ▪ is 32.

> When you estimate the number of an item,
> you find out about how many there are.

Guided Learning

Circle a group of 10 ▪.
Estimate how many ▪ there are.
Then count.

8

Estimate:
Count:

9

Estimate:
Count:

Learn You can count numbers greater than 100.

Count the sticks.

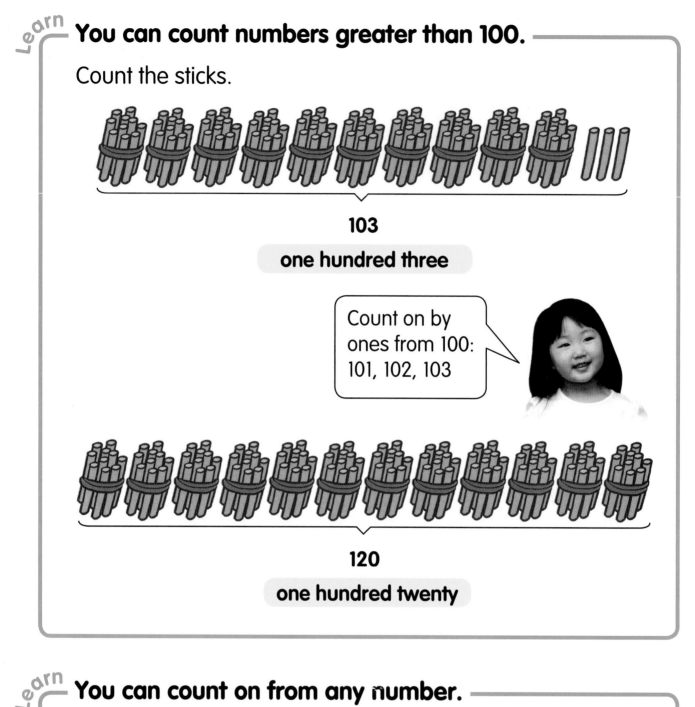

103

one hundred three

Count on by ones from 100: 101, 102, 103

120

one hundred twenty

Learn You can count on from any number.

97, 98, 99, 100, 101, ...

104, 105, 106, 107, 108, 109, ...

115, 116, 117, 118, 119, 120, ...

Guided Learning

**How many sticks are there?
Count. Write the number.**

10 Count on from 100.

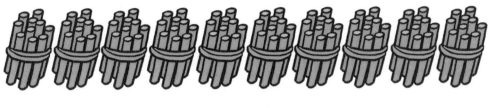

There are  sticks.

11 Count on from 108.

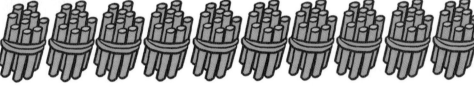

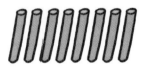 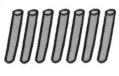

There are sticks.

Write the number.

12 one hundred twelve

Write the number in words.

13 119

Let's Practice

Count.

1

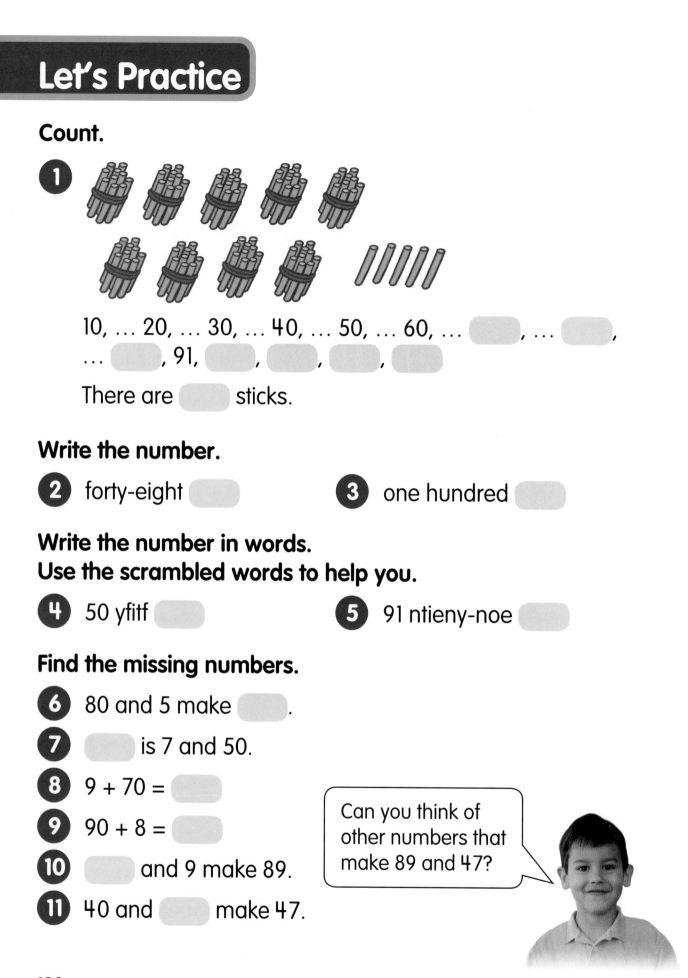

10, … 20, … 30, … 40, … 50, … 60, … ⬭, … ⬭,
… ⬭, 91, ⬭, ⬭, ⬭, ⬭

There are ⬭ sticks.

Write the number.

2 forty-eight ⬭

3 one hundred ⬭

Write the number in words.
Use the scrambled words to help you.

4 50 yfitf ⬭

5 91 ntieny-noe ⬭

Find the missing numbers.

6 80 and 5 make ⬭.

7 ⬭ is 7 and 50.

8 9 + 70 = ⬭

9 90 + 8 = ⬭

10 ⬭ and 9 make 89.

11 40 and ⬭ make 47.

> Can you think of other numbers that make 89 and 47?

Circle a group of 10.
Estimate how many there are.
Then count.

12

Estimate:

Count:

13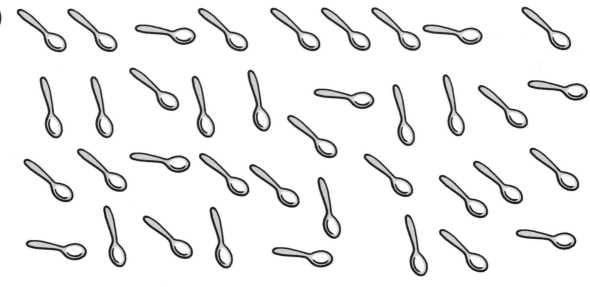

Estimate:

Count:

Count.

 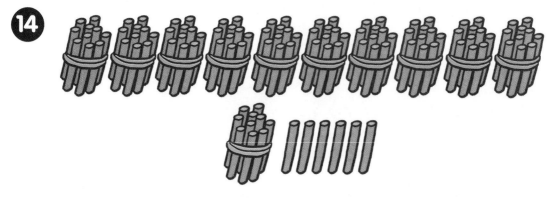

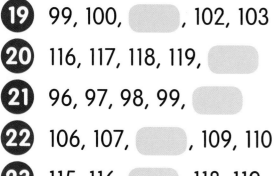

There are ____ sticks.

Write the number.

 15 one hundred six ____

16 one hundred twenty ____

Write the number in words.

17 108 ____

18 117 ____

Find the missing numbers.

19 99, 100, ____, 102, 103

20 116, 117, 118, 119, ____

21 96, 97, 98, 99, ____

22 106, 107, ____, 109, 110

23 115, 116, ____, 118, 119

ON YOUR OWN

Go to Workbook B:
Practice 1, pages 141–144

LESSON 2 Place Value

Lesson Objectives

- Use a place-value chart to show numbers up to 100.
- Show objects up to 100 as tens and ones.

Learn

You can use place value to show numbers to 100.

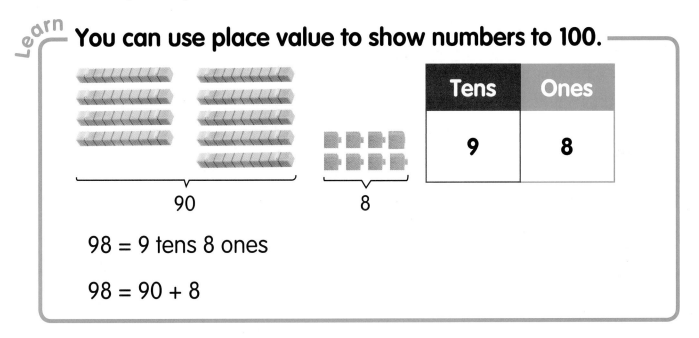

Tens	Ones
9	8

90   8

98 = 9 tens 8 ones

98 = 90 + 8

Guided Learning

Use place value to find the missing numbers.

1

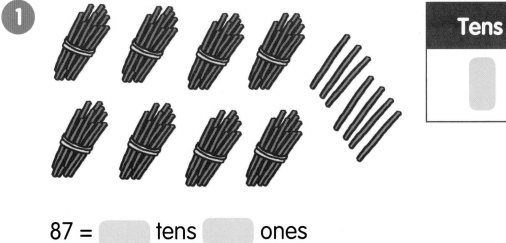

Tens	Ones

87 = [   ] tens [   ] ones

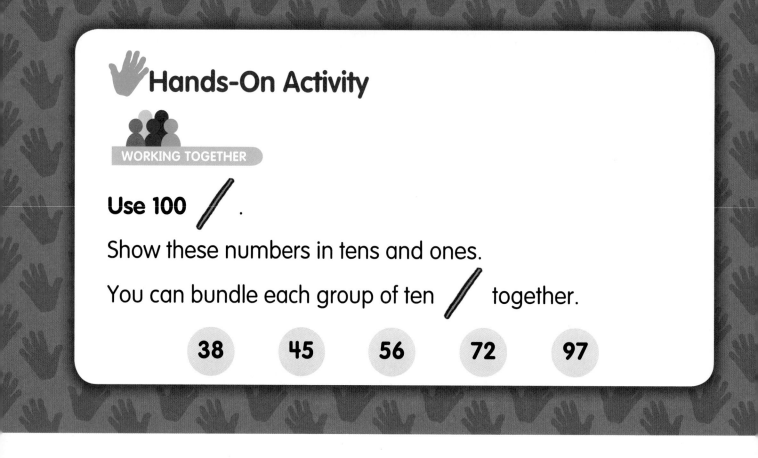

Hands-On Activity

WORKING TOGETHER

Use 100 .

Show these numbers in tens and ones.

You can bundle each group of ten together.

| 38 | 45 | 56 | 72 | 97 |

Let's Practice

Look at each place-value chart.
Find the number it shows.

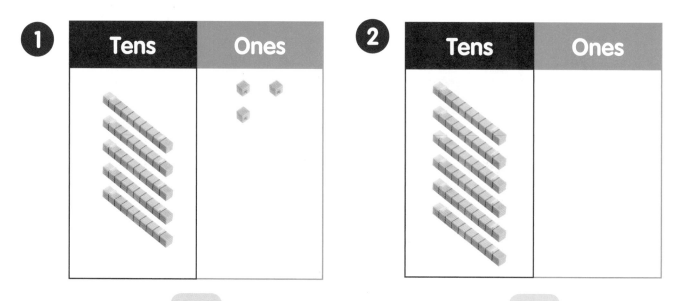

①	Tens	Ones

②	Tens	Ones

Count in tens and ones.
Find the missing numbers.

3

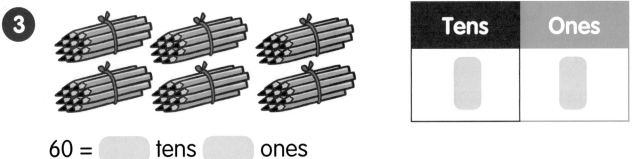

Tens	Ones

60 = ( ) tens ( ) ones

60 + 0 = ( )

4

Tens	Ones

54 = ( ) tens ( ) ones

50 + 4 = ( )

5

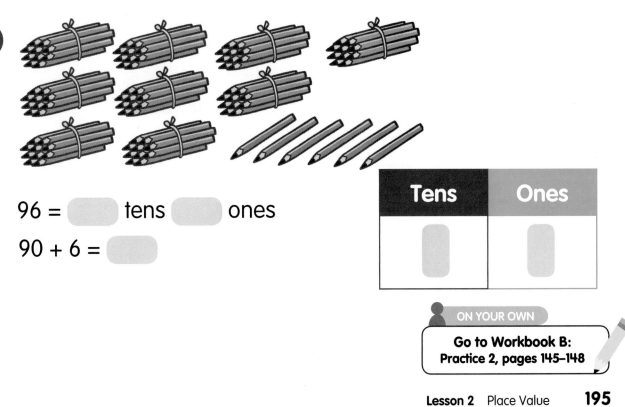

96 = ( ) tens ( ) ones

90 + 6 = ( )

Tens	Ones

ON YOUR OWN

Go to Workbook B:
Practice 2, pages 145–148

Comparing, Ordering, and Patterns

Lesson Objectives

- Use a strategy to compare numbers to 100.
- Compare numbers to 100 using the symbols >, <, and =.
- Compare and order numbers to 100.
- Find the missing numbers in a number pattern.

Learn **You can use a number line to count and compare numbers.**

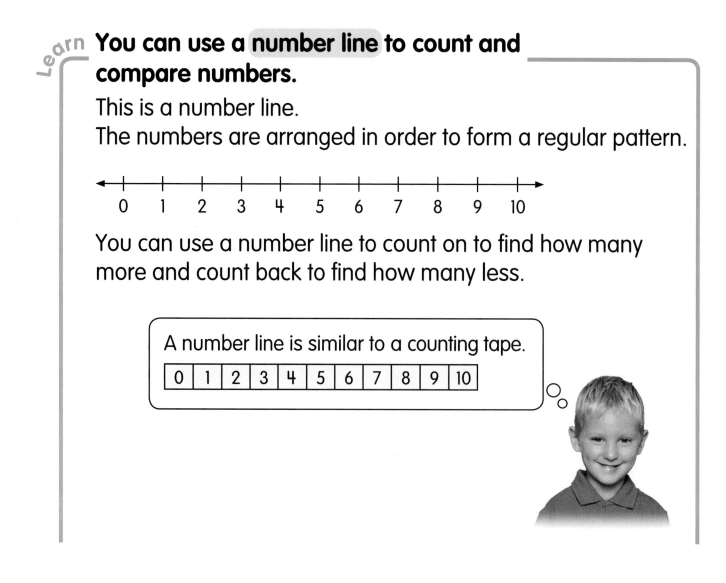

This is a number line.
The numbers are arranged in order to form a regular pattern.

0	1	2	3	4	5	6	7	8	9	10

You can use a number line to count on to find how many more and count back to find how many less.

A number line is similar to a counting tape.

0	1	2	3	4	5	6	7	8	9	10

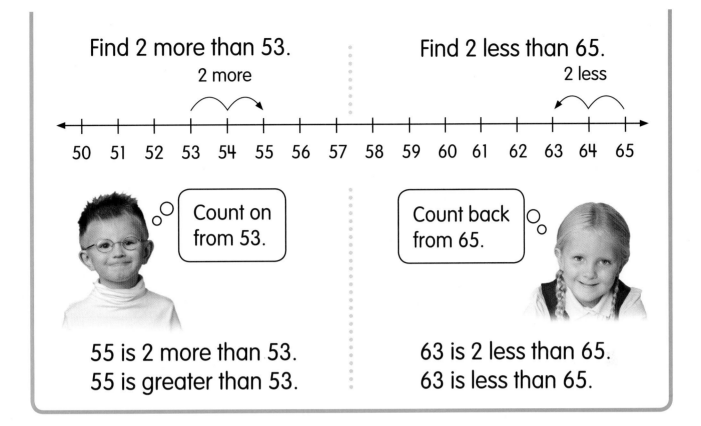

Find 2 more than 53.

2 more

Find 2 less than 65.

2 less

50 51 52 53 54 55 56 57 58 59 60 61 62 63 64 65

Count on from 53.

Count back from 65.

55 is 2 more than 53.
55 is greater than 53.

63 is 2 less than 65.
63 is less than 65.

Guided Learning

Find the missing numbers.
Use the number line to help you.

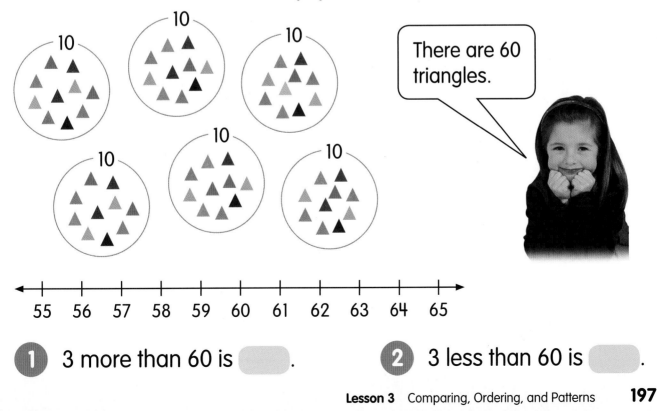

There are 60 triangles.

55 56 57 58 59 60 61 62 63 64 65

1 3 more than 60 is [   ].

2 3 less than 60 is [   ].

 **Hands-On Activity**

Use a hundred chart.

1	2	3	4	5	6	7	8	9	10
11	12	13	14	15	16	17	18	19	20
21	22	23	24	25	26	27	28	29	30
31	32	33	34	35	36	37	38	39	40
41	42	43	44	45	46	47	48	49	50
51	52	53	54	55	56	57	58	59	60
61	62	63	64	65	66	67	68	69	70
71	72	73	74	75	76	77	78	79	80
81	82	83	84	85	86	87	88	89	90
91	92	93	94	95	96	97	98	99	100

1 **STEP 1** Start at 50. Count on by 5.

 STEP 2 Circle the number in red.
Write the number on a piece of paper.

 STEP 3 Count on by 5 again. Then repeat **STEP 2**.
Do this six times.

 STEP 4 Write two sentences using the words **more than** and **less than**.

Example

65 is 5 more than 60.

70 is 5 less than 75.

2 **STEP 1** Start at 72. Count on by 2.

 STEP 2 Circle the number in yellow.
Write the number on a piece of paper.

 STEP 3 Count on by 2 again. Then repeat **STEP 2**.
Do this ten times.

 STEP 4 Look at the number line. Find the missing numbers.

72   ▢ ▢ ▢ ▢   82   ▢ ▢ ▢ ▢ ▢ ▢

 STEP 5 Write two sentences using the words **more than** and **less than**.

 3 **STEP 1** Start at 25. Count on by 10.

 STEP 2 Circle the number in green.
Write the number on a piece of paper.

 STEP 3 Count on by 10 again. Then repeat **STEP 2**.
Do this five times.

 STEP 4 Look at the number line. Find the missing numbers.

25   ▢ ▢ ▢   65   ▢ ▢

 STEP 5 Write two sentences using the words **more than** and **less than**.

Hands-On Activity

 STEP 1 Use two spinners.
Spin A to get a number less than 10.

 STEP 2 Spin B to get a number less than 100.

 STEP 3 Your partner uses the two numbers to complete the sentences.

1 ⬜ more than ⬜ is ⬜.

2 ⬜ less than ⬜ is ⬜.

Use a number line to help you.

Example

You spin the two spinners and get these numbers.

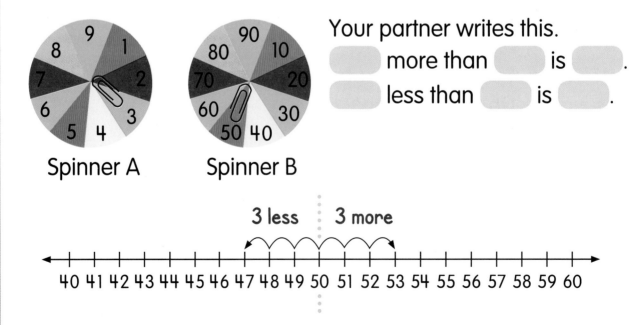

Your partner writes this.
⬜ more than ⬜ is ⬜.
⬜ less than ⬜ is ⬜.

Spinner A   Spinner B

3 less   3 more

40 41 42 43 44 45 46 47 48 49 50 51 52 53 54 55 56 57 58 59 60

Learn

You can compare numbers when the tens are different.

Compare 60 and 59.

Tens	Ones
6	0

Compare the tens. The tens are different. 6 tens is greater than 5 tens.

Tens	Ones
5	9

So, 60 is greater than 59.

Guided Learning

Compare the numbers.

3 Which number is greater?
Which number is less?

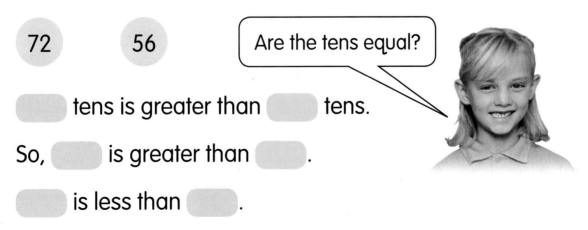

72   56

Are the tens equal?

☐ tens is greater than ☐ tens.

So, ☐ is greater than ☐ .

☐ is less than ☐ .

You can compare numbers when the tens are equal.

The tens are equal.
So, compare the ones.
7 is less than 9.

Tens	Ones
6	7

Tens	Ones
6	9

So, 67 is less than 69.

Guided Learning

Compare the numbers.

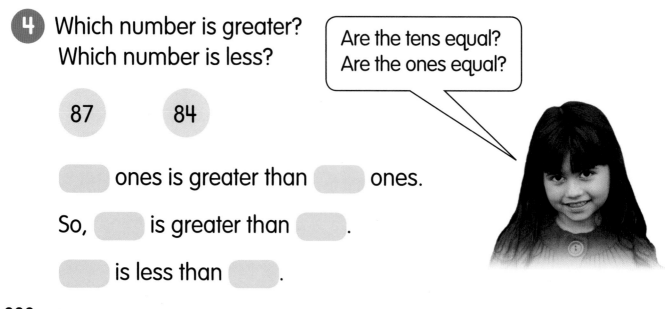

4 Which number is greater?
Which number is less?

Are the tens equal?
Are the ones equal?

87   84

⬭ ones is greater than ⬭ ones.

So, ⬭ is greater than ⬭ .

⬭ is less than ⬭ .

Compare the numbers.

5 Which is the least number?
Which is the greatest number?

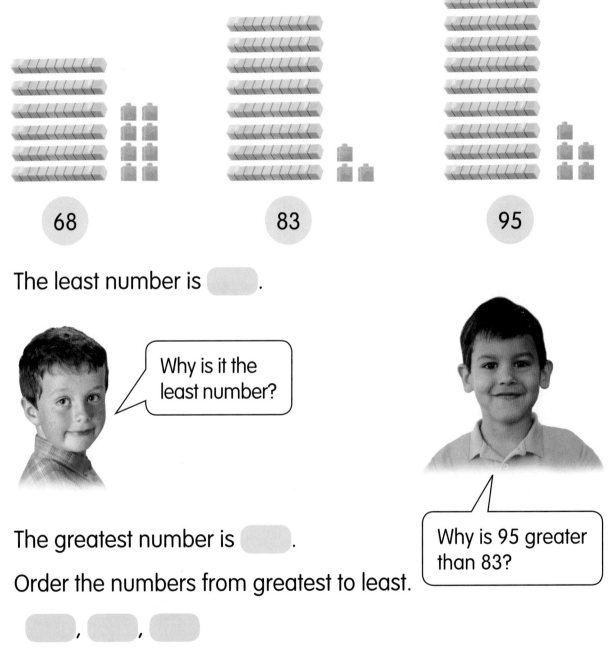

The least number is ⬭ .

Why is it the
least number?

The greatest number is ⬭ .

Why is 95 greater
than 83?

Order the numbers from greatest to least.

⬭ , ⬭ , ⬭

greatest

Order the numbers from least to greatest.

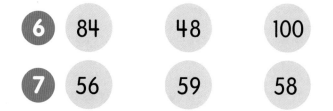

6 84　　48　　100

7 56　　59　　58

You can compare numbers with the symbols >, <, and =.

Tens	Ones
8	8

Tens	Ones
7	9

88 is greater than 79.
You can write 88 **>** 79.

79 is less than 88.
You can write 79 **<** 88.

> The symbol **>** means greater than.
> The symbol **<** means less than.

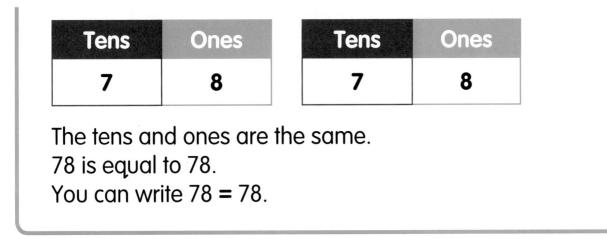

Tens	Ones
7	8

Tens	Ones
7	8

The tens and ones are the same.
78 is equal to 78.
You can write 78 = 78.

Guided Learning

Fill in the blanks with >, <, or =.

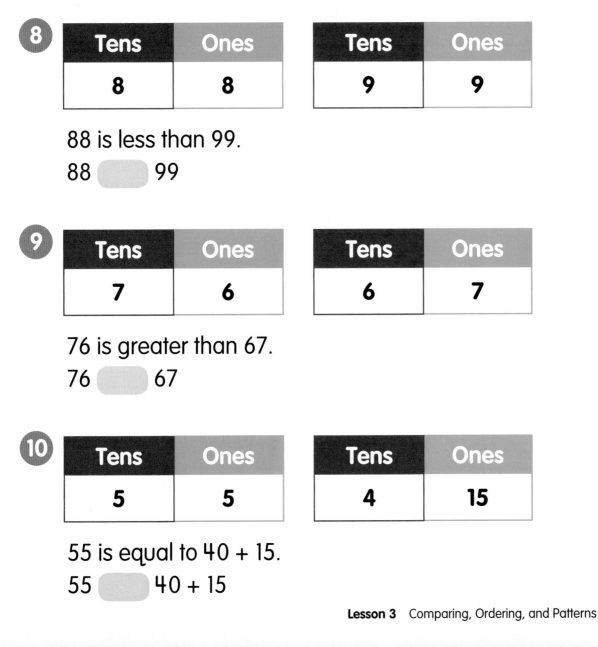

8

Tens	Ones
8	8

Tens	Ones
9	9

88 is less than 99.
88 _____ 99

9

Tens	Ones
7	6

Tens	Ones
6	7

76 is greater than 67.
76 _____ 67

10

Tens	Ones
5	5

Tens	Ones
4	15

55 is equal to 40 + 15.
55 _____ 40 + 15

You can find the missing numbers in a pattern by adding or subtracting.

The numbers on the number line make a pattern.
Some numbers are missing.

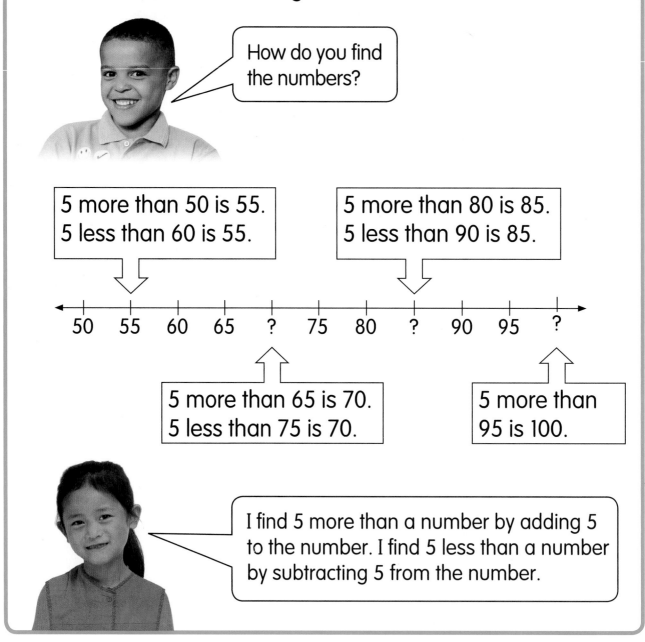

How do you find the numbers?

5 more than 50 is 55.
5 less than 60 is 55.

5 more than 80 is 85.
5 less than 90 is 85.

50 55 60 65 ? 75 80 ? 90 95 ?

5 more than 65 is 70.
5 less than 75 is 70.

5 more than 95 is 100.

I find 5 more than a number by adding 5 to the number. I find 5 less than a number by subtracting 5 from the number.

Guided Learning

The numbers on the number line make a pattern.
Find the missing numbers.

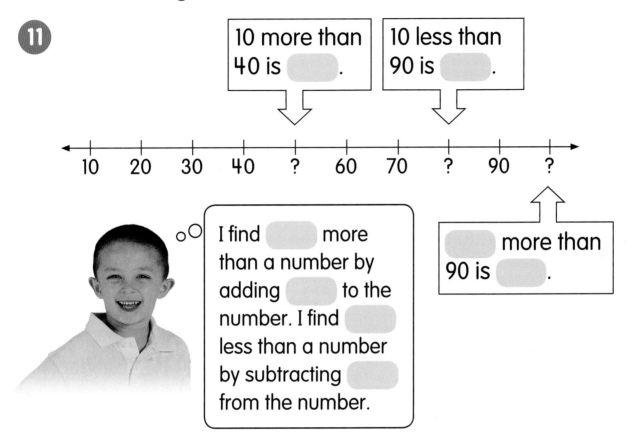

11

10 more than 40 is ____ .

10 less than 90 is ____ .

10 20 30 40 ? 60 70 ? 90 ?

I find ____ more than a number by adding ____ to the number. I find ____ less than a number by subtracting ____ from the number.

____ more than 90 is ____ .

Find the missing numbers.

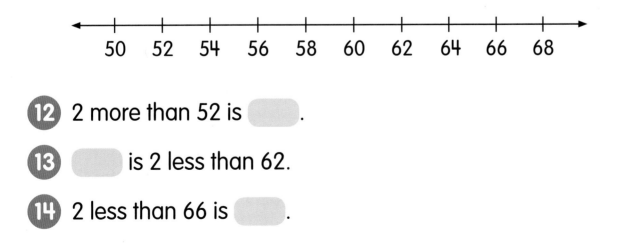

50 52 54 56 58 60 62 64 66 68

12 2 more than 52 is ____ .

13 ____ is 2 less than 62.

14 2 less than 66 is ____ .

What's My Number?

How to play:

STEP **1** Think of a number between 50 and 100.

STEP **2** Players take turns asking you questions to find the number.

STEP **3** You can answer only **Yes** or **No** to the questions.

STEP **4** See who gets the right number first!

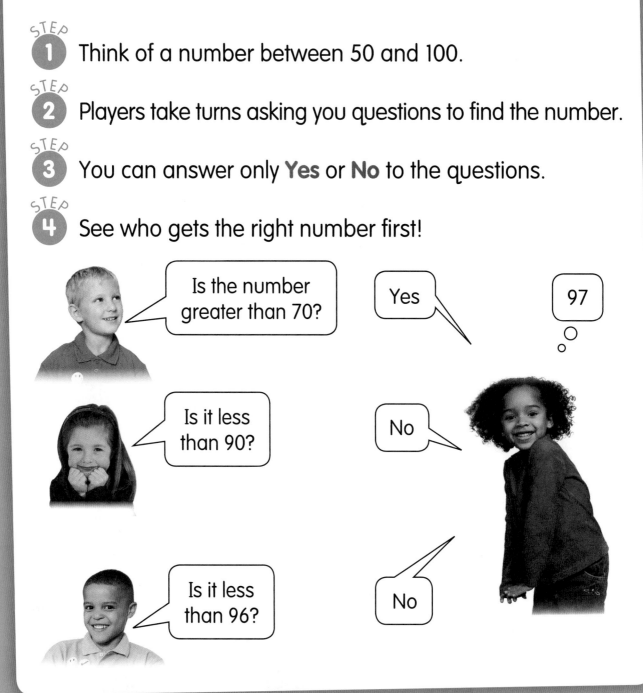

Is the number greater than 70?

Yes

97

Is it less than 90?

No

Is it less than 96?

No

Compare.

1 Which set has more? ◻
Which number is greater? ◻

Set A

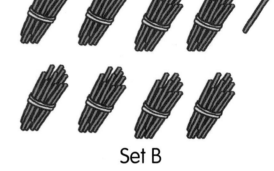

Set B

2 Which set has fewer? ◻
Which number is less? ◻

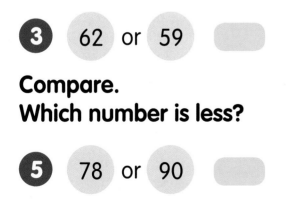

Set A

Set B

Compare.
Which number is greater?

3 62 or 59 ◻

4 79 or 84 ◻

Compare.
Which number is less?

5 78 or 90 ◻

6 68 or 52 ◻

Compare.

71   78   85

7 Which number is the least?

8 Which number is the greatest?

Complete.

82   53   95   60   79

9 Which number is the greatest?

10 Which number is the least?

11 Order the numbers from least to greatest.

_____ , _____ , _____ , _____ , _____

least

12 What is 5 more than 95?

13 What is 5 less than 95?

14 Name two numbers greater than 53 but less than 79.

_____ _____

15 Name two numbers less than 82 but greater than 79.

_____ _____

Find the missing numbers in each pattern.

16 56, 57, 58, 59, _____ , 61, 62, _____ , _____ , 65

17 81, 83, 85, _____ , 89, _____ , _____

18 _____ , _____ , 98, 97, 96, _____

19 95, 85, 75, _____ , _____ , _____ , 35

Fill in the blanks with >, <, or =.

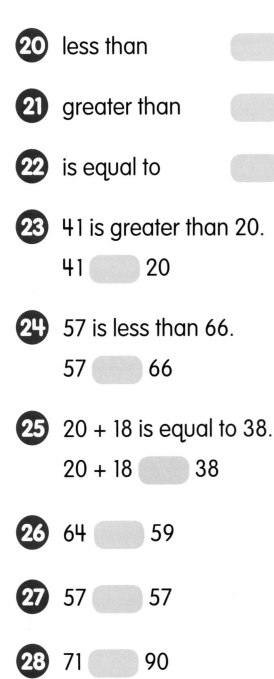

20 less than

21 greater than

22 is equal to

23 41 is greater than 20.

41 ___ 20

24 57 is less than 66.

57 ___ 66

25 20 + 18 is equal to 38.

20 + 18 ___ 38

26 64 ___ 59

27 57 ___ 57

28 71 ___ 90

ON YOUR OWN

Go to Workbook B:
Practice 3, pages 149-153

Let's Explore!

1	2	3	4	5	6	7	8	9	10
11	12	13	14	15	16	17	18	19	20
21	22	23	24	25	26	27	28	29	30
31	32	33	34	35	36	37	38	39	40
41	42	43	44	45	46	47	48	49	50
51	52	53	54	55	56	57	58	59	60
61	62	63	64	65	66	67	68	69	70
71	72	73	74	75	76	77	78	79	80
81	82	83	84	85	86	87	88	89	90
91	92	93	94	95	96	97	98	99	100

Write 5 different number patterns starting with 33.

Think of skip counting.

Example

33, 37, 41, 45, 49

READING AND WRITING MATH
Math Journal

Explain how you got the numbers in the patterns you wrote in the Let's Explore.

Example

33, 37, 41, 45, 49
I got each number by adding 4 to the number before it.

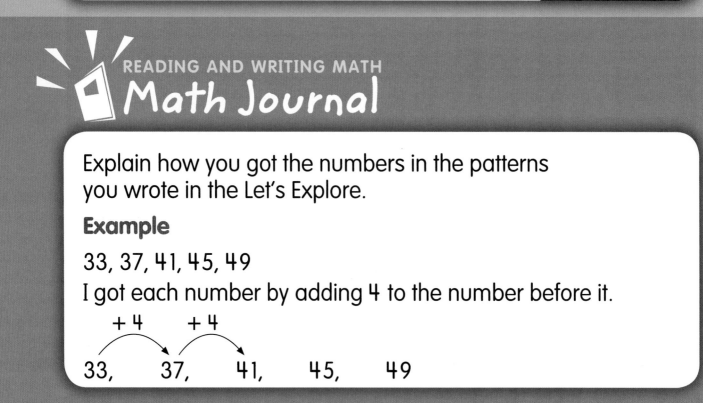

+4   +4

33,   37,   41,   45,   49

Put On Your Thinking Cap!

PROBLEM SOLVING

Put each number card into the number machine to make a pattern of 5 numbers.

For each card, the rule for the pattern is shown.

Example

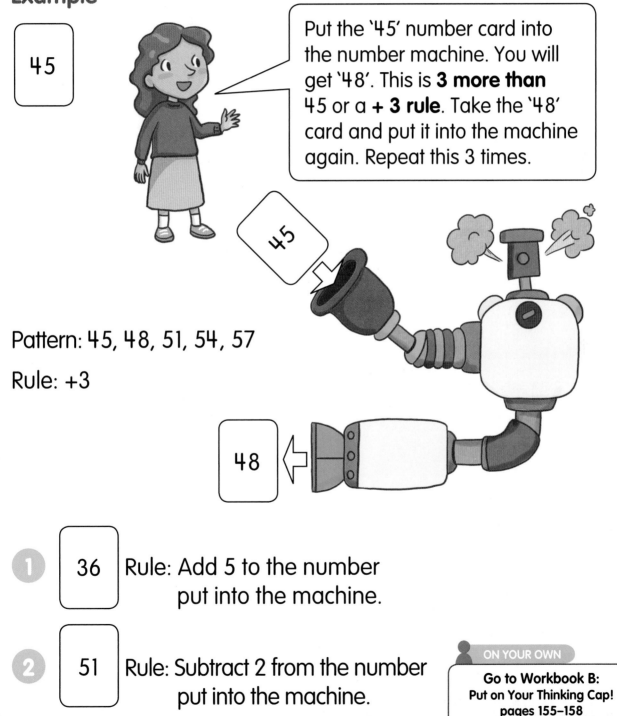

45

> Put the '45' number card into the number machine. You will get '48'. This is **3 more than** 45 or a **+ 3 rule**. Take the '48' card and put it into the machine again. Repeat this 3 times.

45

Pattern: 45, 48, 51, 54, 57

Rule: +3

48

1   36   Rule: Add 5 to the number put into the machine.

2   51   Rule: Subtract 2 from the number put into the machine.

ON YOUR OWN

Go to Workbook B: Put on Your Thinking Cap! pages 155–158

Chapter Wrap Up

You have learned...

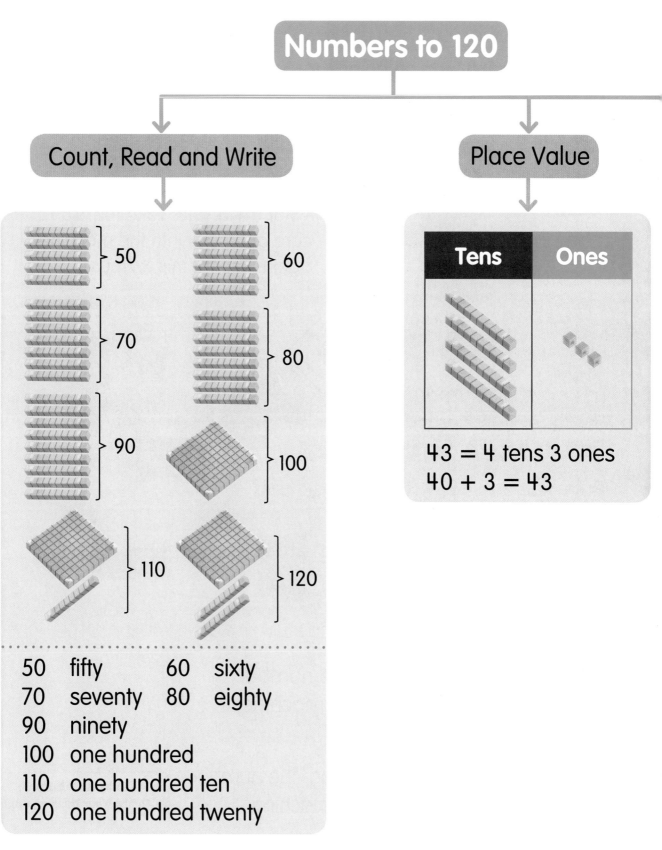

Numbers to 120

Count, Read and Write

50
60
70
80
90
100
110
120

50 fifty   60 sixty
70 seventy   80 eighty
90 ninety
100 one hundred
110 one hundred ten
120 one hundred twenty

Place Value

Tens	Ones

43 = 4 tens 3 ones
40 + 3 = 43

Count, compare, and order numbers from 1 to 120.

Compare and Order

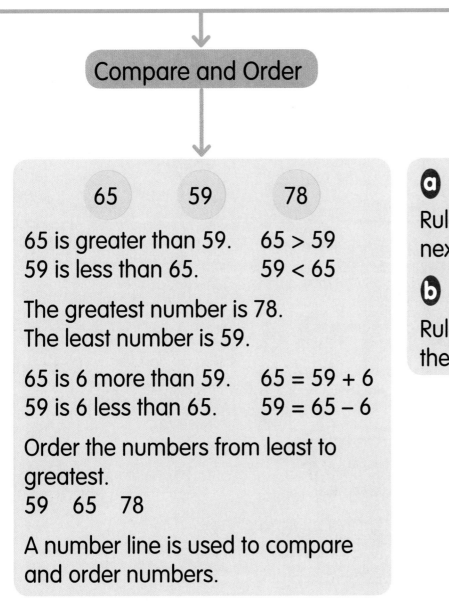

65   59   78

65 is greater than 59.   65 > 59
59 is less than 65.   59 < 65

The greatest number is 78.
The least number is 59.

65 is 6 more than 59.   65 = 59 + 6
59 is 6 less than 65.   59 = 65 − 6

Order the numbers from least to greatest.
59   65   78

A number line is used to compare and order numbers.

Patterns

ⓐ 67, 69, 71, 73, 75
Rule: Add 2 to get the next number.

ⓑ 100, 95, 90, 85, 80
Rule: Subtract 5 to get the next number.

ON YOUR OWN

Go to Workbook B:
Chapter Review/Test,
pages 159-160

Lesson 1 Addition Without Regrouping

Lesson 2 Addition with Regrouping

Lesson 3 Subtraction Without Regrouping

Lesson 4 Subtraction with Regrouping

BIG IDEA

Numbers to 100 can be added and subtracted with and without regrouping.

Recall Prior Knowledge

Making tens and ones

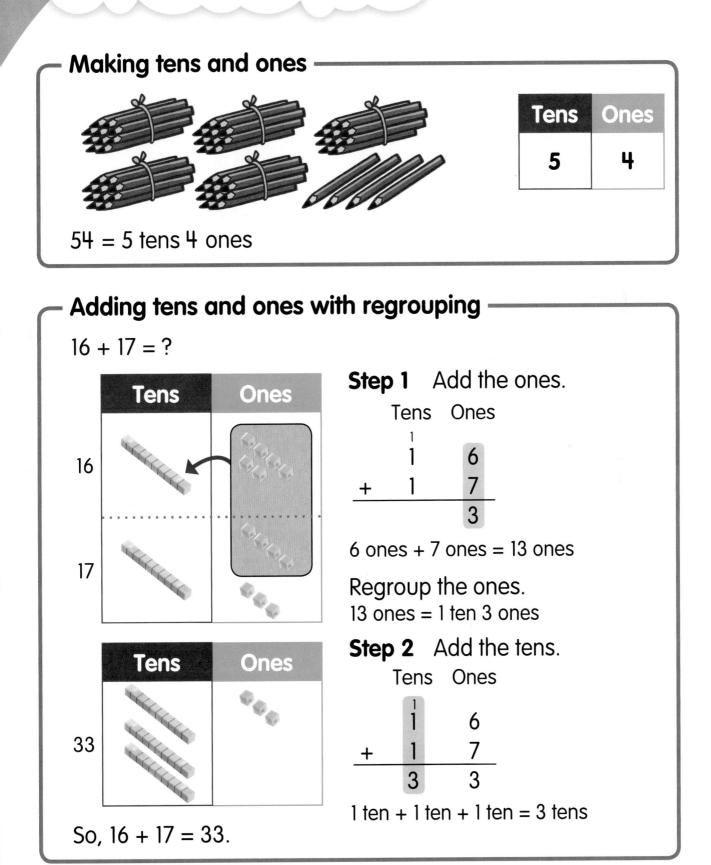

Tens	Ones
5	4

54 = 5 tens 4 ones

Adding tens and ones with regrouping

16 + 17 = ?

Tens	Ones
16	
17	

Step 1 Add the ones.

```
    Tens   Ones
     1
     1      6
  +  1      7
  _____
            3
```

6 ones + 7 ones = 13 ones

Regroup the ones.
13 ones = 1 ten 3 ones

Tens	Ones
33	

Step 2 Add the tens.

```
    Tens   Ones
     1
     1      6
  +  1      7
  _____
     3      3
```

1 ten + 1 ten + 1 ten = 3 tens

So, 16 + 17 = 33.

Subtracting tens and ones

$35 - 18 = ?$

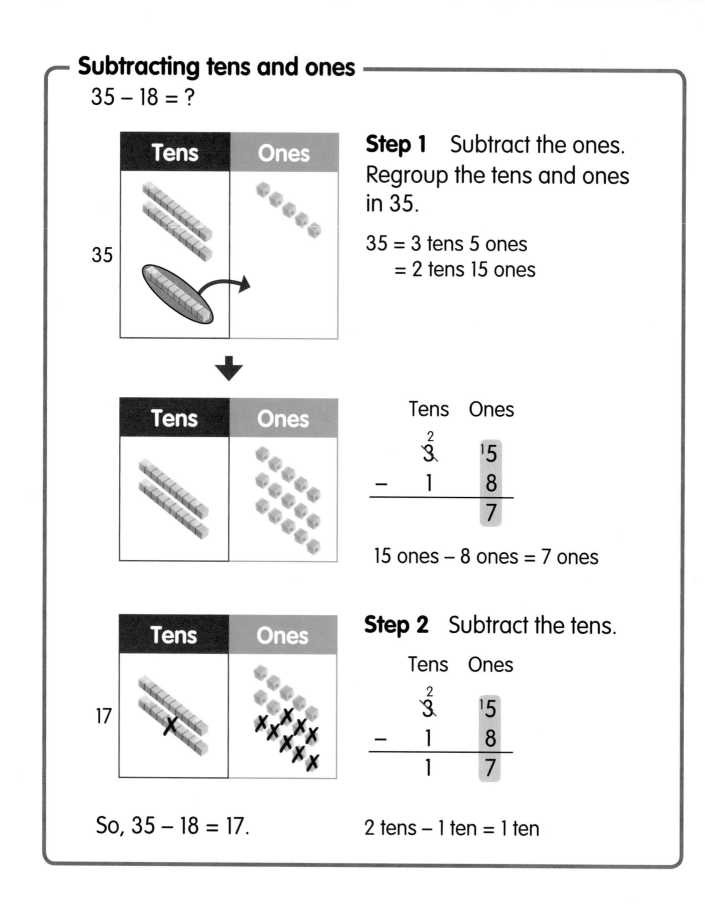

Step 1 Subtract the ones. Regroup the tens and ones in 35.

35 = 3 tens 5 ones
   = 2 tens 15 ones

15 ones – 8 ones = 7 ones

Step 2 Subtract the tens.

2 tens – 1 ten = 1 ten

So, 35 – 18 = 17.

Related addition and subtraction facts

$6 + 9 = 15$ ·················· $15 - 9 = 6$

$15 - 6 = 9$ ·················· $9 + 6 = 15$

Checking answers to addition and subtraction using related facts

If $39 - 14 = 25$, then $25 + 14$ should equal 39.
Check your answer by adding 25 and 14.
The answer is correct.

$$\begin{array}{r} 2\ 5 \\ +\ 1\ 4 \\ \hline 3\ 9 \end{array}$$

If $24 + 9 = 33$, then $33 - 9$ should equal 24.
Check your answer by subtracting 9 from 33.
The answer is correct.

$$\begin{array}{r} 3\ 3 \\ -\ \ \ 9 \\ \hline 2\ 4 \end{array}$$

✔ Quick Check

Find the missing numbers.

1

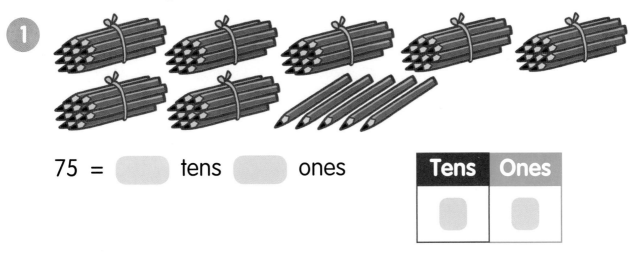

$75 =$ ⬭ tens ⬭ ones

Tens	Ones

Find the missing numbers.

2 $17 - \boxed{} = 9$

3 $\boxed{} + 5 = 16$

Show how to check that the answers are correct.

4
```
   2 4
 +   8
 -----
   3 2
```

5
```
   3 2
 - 1 3
 -----
   1 9
```

Add. Show how to check your answer.

6 $23 + 6 = \boxed{}$

7 $19 + 8 = \boxed{}$

8 $14 + 15 = \boxed{}$

9 $23 + 17 = \boxed{}$

Subtract. Show how to check your answer.

10 $37 - 5 = \boxed{}$

11 $30 - 8 = \boxed{}$

12 $25 - 14 = \boxed{}$

13 $32 - 16 = \boxed{}$

1 Addition Without Regrouping

Lesson Objectives

- Add a 2-digit number and a 1-digit number without regrouping.
- Add two 2-digit numbers without regrouping.

Learn **You can add ones to a number in different ways.**

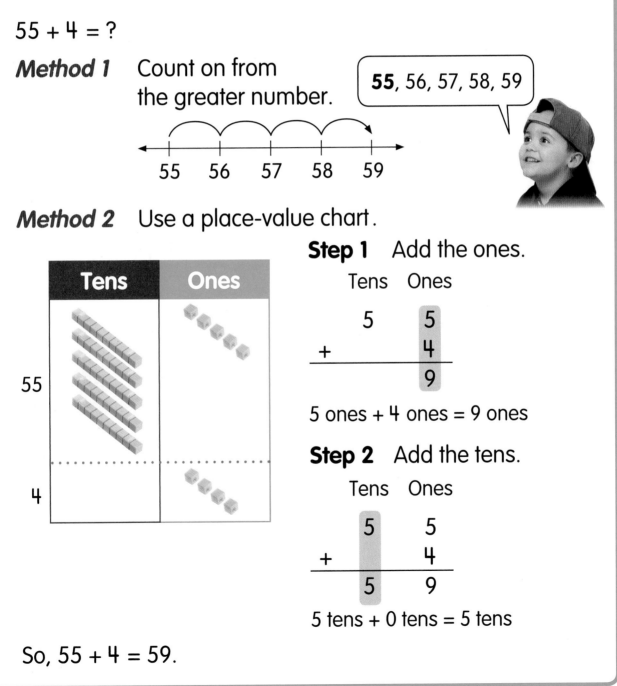

$55 + 4 = ?$

Method 1 Count on from the greater number.

55, 56, 57, 58, 59

55   56   57   58   59

Method 2 Use a place-value chart.

Tens	Ones
55	
4	

Step 1 Add the ones.

Tens   Ones

    5   5
+   4
         9

5 ones + 4 ones = 9 ones

Step 2 Add the tens.

Tens   Ones

    5   5
+   4
    5   9

5 tens + 0 tens = 5 tens

So, $55 + 4 = 59$.

Guided Learning

Complete.

1 82 + 7 = ?

Method 1   Count on from the greater number.

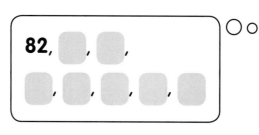

Method 2   Use a place-value chart.

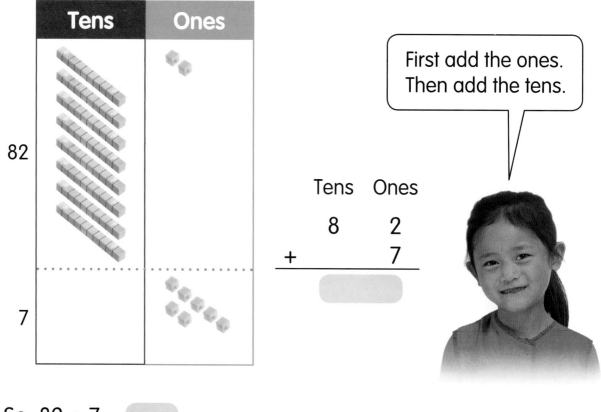

First add the ones.
Then add the tens.

Tens	Ones
8	2
+	7

So, 82 + 7 = ____.

You can use place-value charts to add tens.

$40 + 50 = ?$

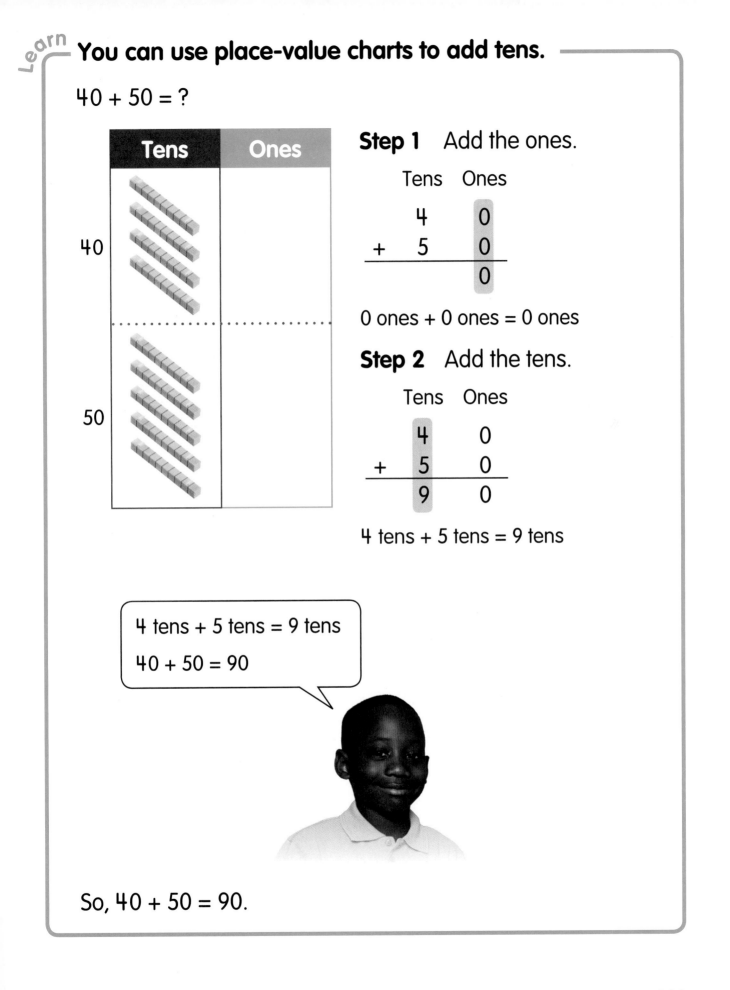

Tens	Ones
40	
50	

Step 1 Add the ones.

Tens   Ones

```
    4    0
+   5    0
_____
         0
```

0 ones + 0 ones = 0 ones

Step 2 Add the tens.

Tens   Ones

```
    4    0
+   5    0
_____
    9    0
```

4 tens + 5 tens = 9 tens

> 4 tens + 5 tens = 9 tens
> $40 + 50 = 90$

So, $40 + 50 = 90$.

Learn **You can use place-value charts to add tens to a number.**

46 + 30 = ?

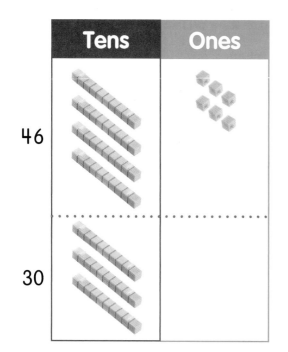

Tens	Ones
46	
30	

Step 1 Add the ones.

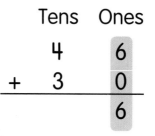

Tens Ones

```
     4    6
+    3    0
          6
```

6 ones + 0 ones = 6 ones

Step 2 Add the tens.

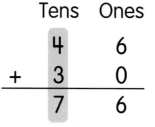

Tens Ones

```
     4    6
+    3    0
     7    6
```

4 tens + 3 tens = 7 tens

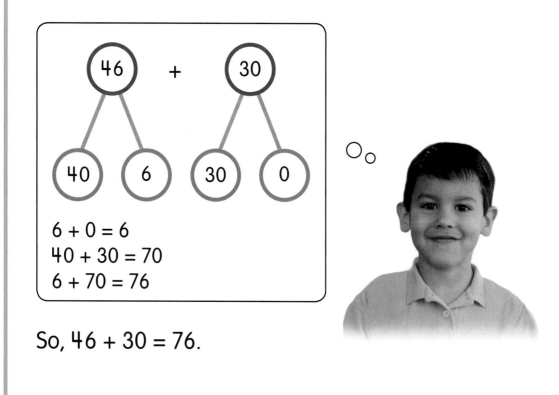

46 + 30

40   6   30   0

6 + 0 = 6
40 + 30 = 70
6 + 70 = 76

So, 46 + 30 = 76.

Guided Learning

Complete.

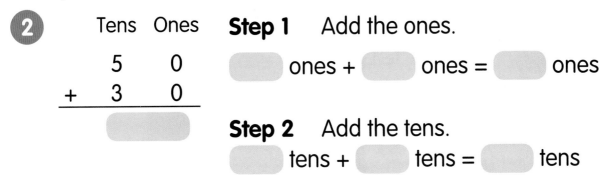

2

Tens	Ones
5	0
+ 3	0

Step 1 Add the ones.

⬜ ones + ⬜ ones = ⬜ ones

Step 2 Add the tens.

⬜ tens + ⬜ tens = ⬜ tens

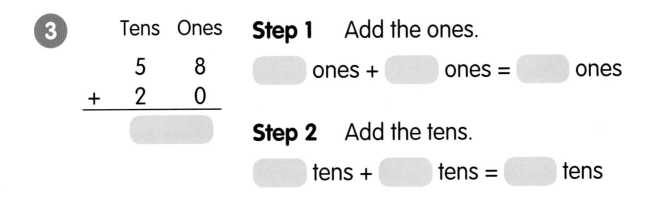

3

Tens	Ones
5	8
+ 2	0

Step 1 Add the ones.

⬜ ones + ⬜ ones = ⬜ ones

Step 2 Add the tens.

⬜ tens + ⬜ tens = ⬜ tens

Learn You can use place-value charts to add two numbers.

42 + 56 = ?

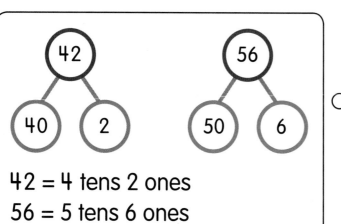

42 = 4 tens 2 ones
56 = 5 tens 6 ones

Tens	Ones
42 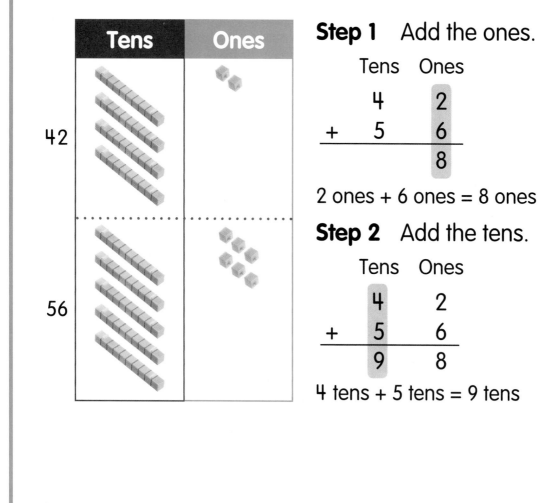	
56	

Step 1 Add the ones.

```
   Tens  Ones
     4    2
  +  5    6
  _____
          8
```

2 ones + 6 ones = 8 ones

Step 2 Add the tens.

```
   Tens  Ones
     4    2
  +  5    6
  _____
     9    8
```

4 tens + 5 tens = 9 tens

So, 42 + 56 = 98.

Guided Learning

Complete.

 4

Tens	Ones
5	3
+ 3	6

Step 1 Add the ones.

◯ ones + ◯ ones = ◯ ones

Step 2 Add the tens.

◯ tens + ◯ tens = ◯ tens

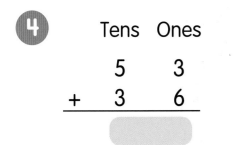

Let's Practice

Add by counting on.

1 62 + 6 = ◯

2 84 + 4 = ◯

Add.

3
Tens	Ones
4	6
+	3

4
Tens	Ones
2	0
+ 7	0

5
Tens	Ones
4	7
+ 5	0

6
Tens	Ones
3	2
+ 4	7

ON YOUR OWN

Go to Workbook B:
Practice 1, pages 161–164

2 Addition with Regrouping

Lesson Objectives

- Add a 2-digit number and a 1-digit number with regrouping.
- Add two 2-digit numbers with regrouping.

Learn **You can use place-value charts to add ones to a number with regrouping.**

66 + 7 = ?

66 = 6 tens 6 ones

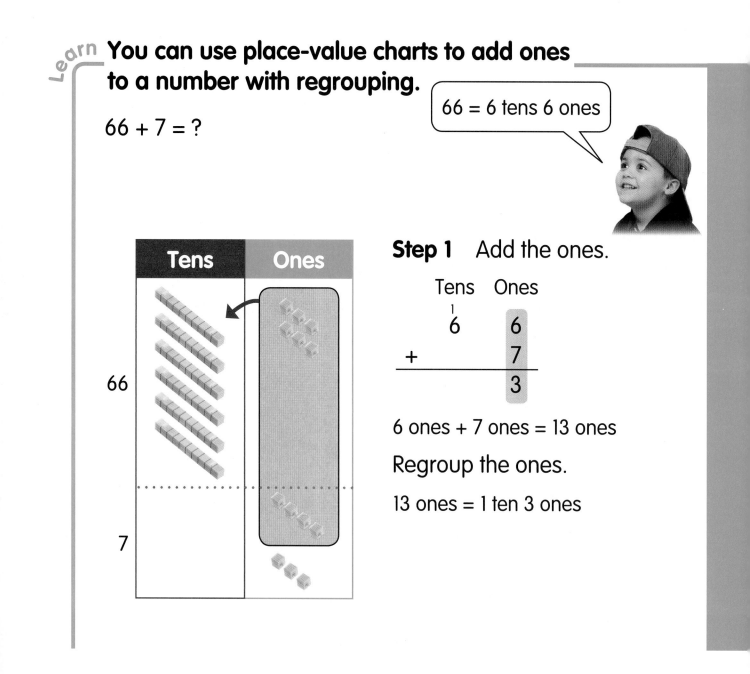

Tens	Ones
66	
7	

Step 1 Add the ones.

Tens   Ones

$\begin{array}{r} \overset{1}{6} \quad 6 \\ + \quad 7 \\ \hline \quad 3 \end{array}$

6 ones + 7 ones = 13 ones

Regroup the ones.

13 ones = 1 ten 3 ones

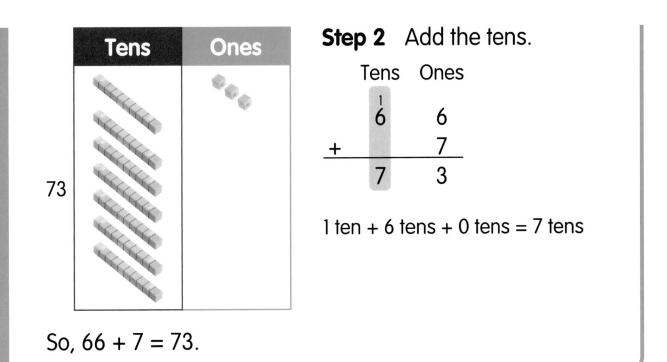

Tens	Ones

73

So, 66 + 7 = 73.

Step 2 Add the tens.

Tens   Ones

$$
\begin{array}{ccc}
 & \overset{1}{6} & 6 \\
+ & & 7 \\
\hline
 & 7 & 3 \\
\end{array}
$$

1 ten + 6 tens + 0 tens = 7 tens

Guided Learning

Add and regroup.

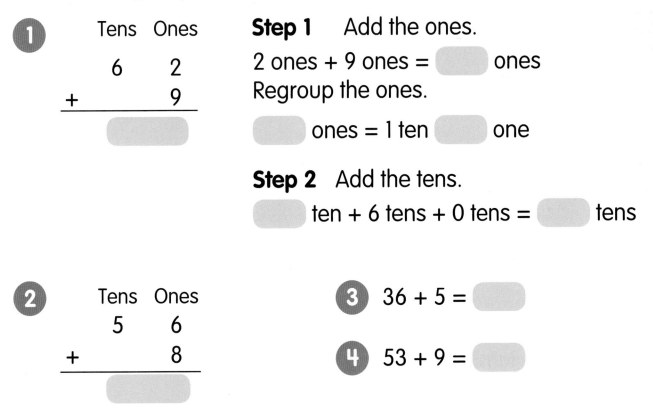

1

Tens   Ones

$$
\begin{array}{ccc}
 & 6 & 2 \\
+ & & 9 \\
\hline
\end{array}
$$

Step 1 Add the ones.

2 ones + 9 ones = ⬚ ones
Regroup the ones.

⬚ ones = 1 ten ⬚ one

Step 2 Add the tens.

⬚ ten + 6 tens + 0 tens = ⬚ tens

2

Tens   Ones

$$
\begin{array}{ccc}
 & 5 & 6 \\
+ & & 8 \\
\hline
\end{array}
$$

3 36 + 5 = ⬚

4 53 + 9 = ⬚

Hands-On Activity

Use a spinner.

spinner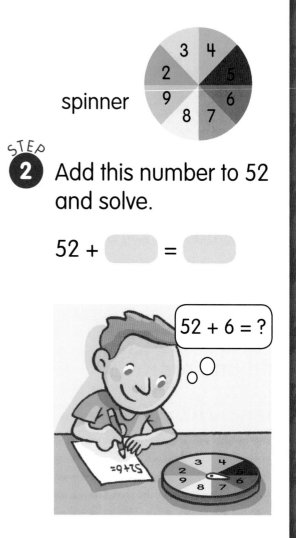

1 Spin to get a number.

2 Add this number to 52 and solve.

$$52 + \boxed{} = \boxed{}$$

6!

52 + 6 = ?

3 Spin to get another number.
Add this number to 64 and solve.

$$64 + \boxed{} = \boxed{}$$

4 Have someone in your group check your work.
Take turns to spin numbers and solve.

Learn You can use place-value charts to add numbers with regrouping.

33 + 18 = ?

33 = 3 tens 3 ones
18 = 1 ten 8 ones

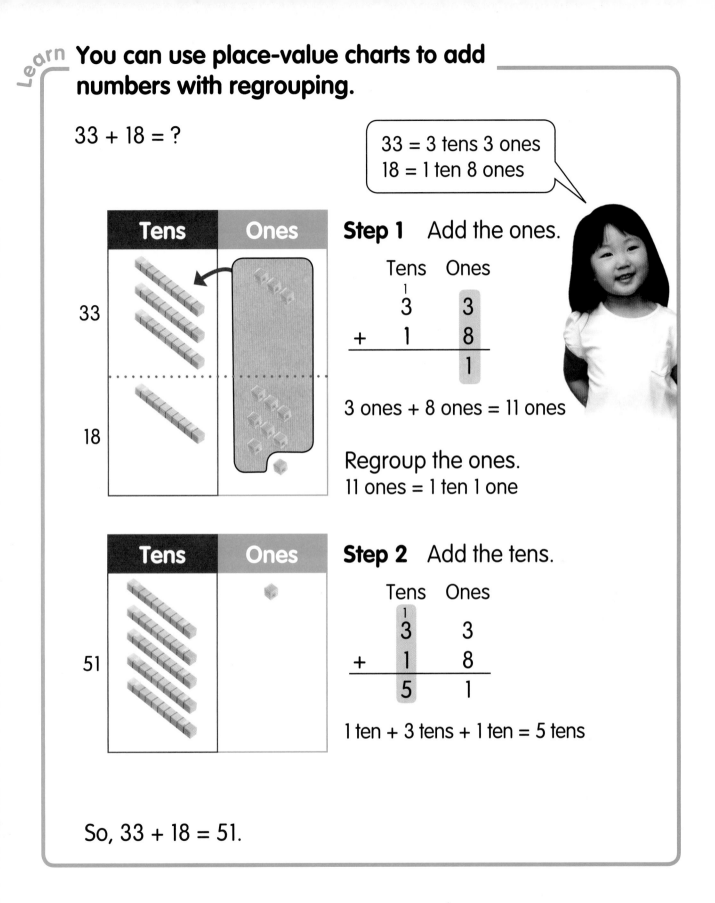

Tens	Ones
33	
18	

Step 1 Add the ones.

```
     Tens   Ones
      1
      3      3
  +   1      8
  _____
             1
```

3 ones + 8 ones = 11 ones

Regroup the ones.
11 ones = 1 ten 1 one

Tens	Ones
51	

Step 2 Add the tens.

```
     Tens   Ones
      1
      3      3
  +   1      8
  _____
      5      1
```

1 ten + 3 tens + 1 ten = 5 tens

So, 33 + 18 = 51.

Guided Learning

Add and regroup.

5

Tens	Ones
4	7
+ 3	8

Step 1 Add the ones.

[ ] ones + [ ] ones = [ ] ones

Regroup the ones.

[ ] ones = [ ] ten [ ] ones

Step 2 Add the tens.

[ ] ten + [ ] tens + [ ] tens

= [ ] tens

6

Tens	Ones
2	8
+ 1	4

7

Tens	Ones
5	4
+ 2	7

8

Tens	Ones
3	5
+ 3	6

9

Tens	Ones
4	9
+ 2	3

10

Tens	Ones
6	3
+ 2	8

11

Tens	Ones
7	7
+ 1	9

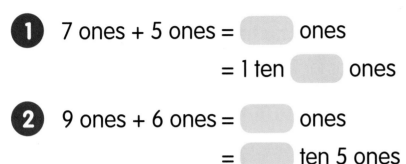

Let's Practice

Complete.

1 7 ones + 5 ones = [ ] ones

= 1 ten [ ] ones

2 9 ones + 6 ones = [ ] ones

= [ ] ten 5 ones

Add and regroup.

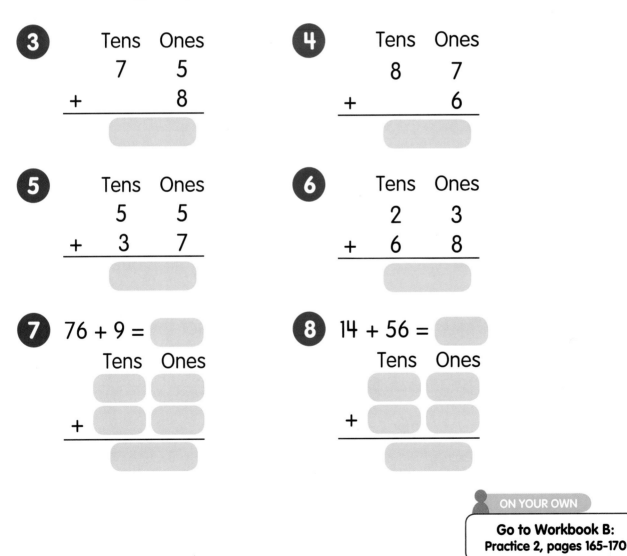

3
Tens	Ones
7	5
+	8

4
Tens	Ones
8	7
+	6

5
Tens	Ones
5	5
+ 3	7

6
Tens	Ones
2	3
+ 6	8

7 76 + 9 = [ ]

Tens	Ones
+	

8 14 + 56 = [ ]

Tens	Ones
+	

ON YOUR OWN

**Go to Workbook B:
Practice 2, pages 165-170**

LESSON 3 Subtraction Without Regrouping

Lesson Objectives

- Subtract a 1-digit number from a 2-digit number without regrouping.
- Subtract a 2-digit number from another 2-digit number without regrouping.

Learn You can subtract ones from a number in different ways.

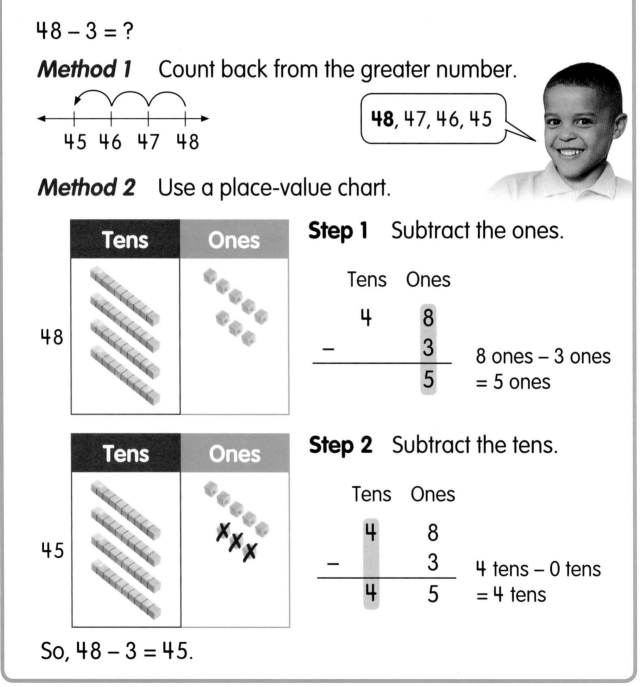

$48 - 3 = ?$

Method 1 Count back from the greater number.

45 46 47 48

48, 47, 46, 45

Method 2 Use a place-value chart.

Step 1 Subtract the ones.

Tens	Ones
4	8
–	3
	5

8 ones – 3 ones = 5 ones

48

Tens	Ones

Step 2 Subtract the tens.

Tens	Ones
4	8
–	3
4	5

4 tens – 0 tens = 4 tens

45

Tens	Ones

So, $48 - 3 = 45$.

Guided Learning

Subtract.

1 68 – 6 = ?

Method 1 Count back from the greater number.

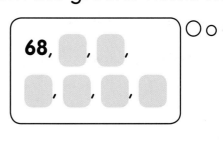

68, [ ] , [ ] ,
[ ] , [ ] , [ ] , [ ]

Method 2 Use a place-value chart.

First, subtract the ones.
Then, subtract the tens.

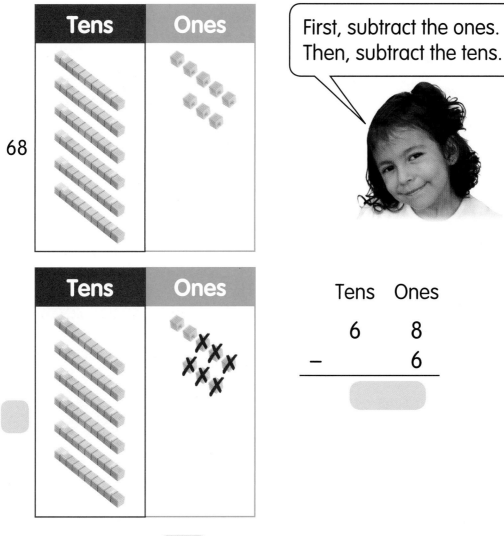

Tens	Ones

68

Tens	Ones

	Tens	Ones
	6	8
–		6

So, 68 – 6 = [   ] .

You can use place-value charts to subtract tens.

70 – 40 = ?

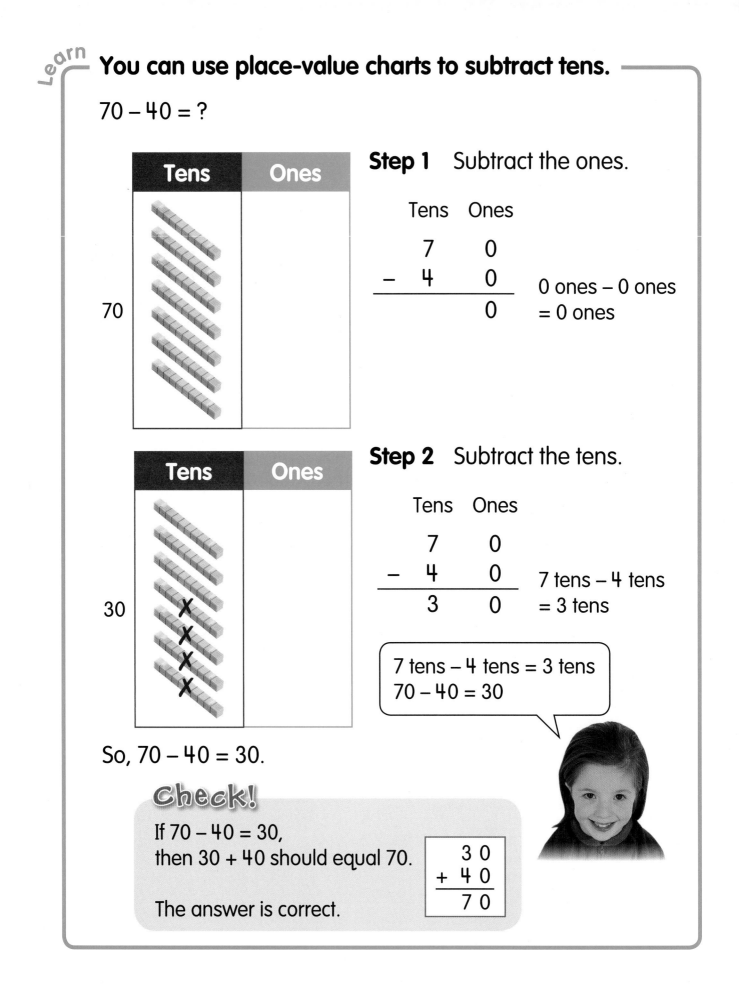

Step 1 Subtract the ones.

Tens Ones

7   0
–   4   0
_____
0

0 ones – 0 ones
= 0 ones

Step 2 Subtract the tens.

Tens Ones

7   0
–   4   0
_____
3   0

7 tens – 4 tens
= 3 tens

7 tens – 4 tens = 3 tens
70 – 40 = 30

So, 70 – 40 = 30.

Check!

If 70 – 40 = 30,
then 30 + 40 should equal 70.

3 0
+ 4 0
_____
7 0

The answer is correct.

Guided Learning

Subtract.

2 60 − 40 = ?

Tens	Ones
60	

First, subtract the ones. Then, subtract the tens.

Tens	Ones
20	

```
  Tens  Ones
    6    0
 −  4    0
  _____
```

6 tens − 4 tens = ⬜ tens

60 − 40 = ⬜

So, 60 − 40 = ⬜.

Check!

```
      ⬜
  +  4 0
  _____
    6 0
```

Learn **You can use place-value charts to subtract tens from a number.**

55 − 30 = ?

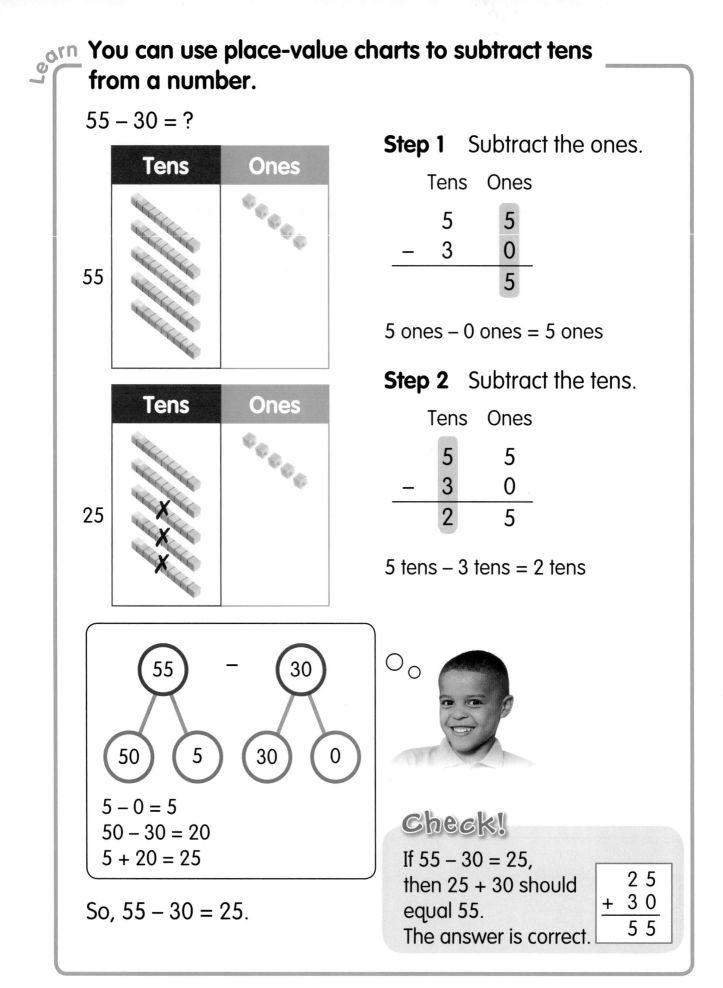

Tens	Ones
55	

Step 1 Subtract the ones.

	Tens	Ones
	5	5
−	3	0
		5

5 ones − 0 ones = 5 ones

Tens	Ones
25	

Step 2 Subtract the tens.

	Tens	Ones
	5	5
−	3	0
	2	5

5 tens − 3 tens = 2 tens

55 − 30

50   5   30   0

5 − 0 = 5
50 − 30 = 20
5 + 20 = 25

So, 55 − 30 = 25.

Check!

If 55 − 30 = 25,
then 25 + 30 should
equal 55.
The answer is correct.

	2	5
+	3	0
	5	5

238

Learn **You can use place-value charts to subtract one number from another.**

$58 - 24 = ?$

> $58 = 5$ tens 8 ones
> $24 = 2$ tens 4 ones

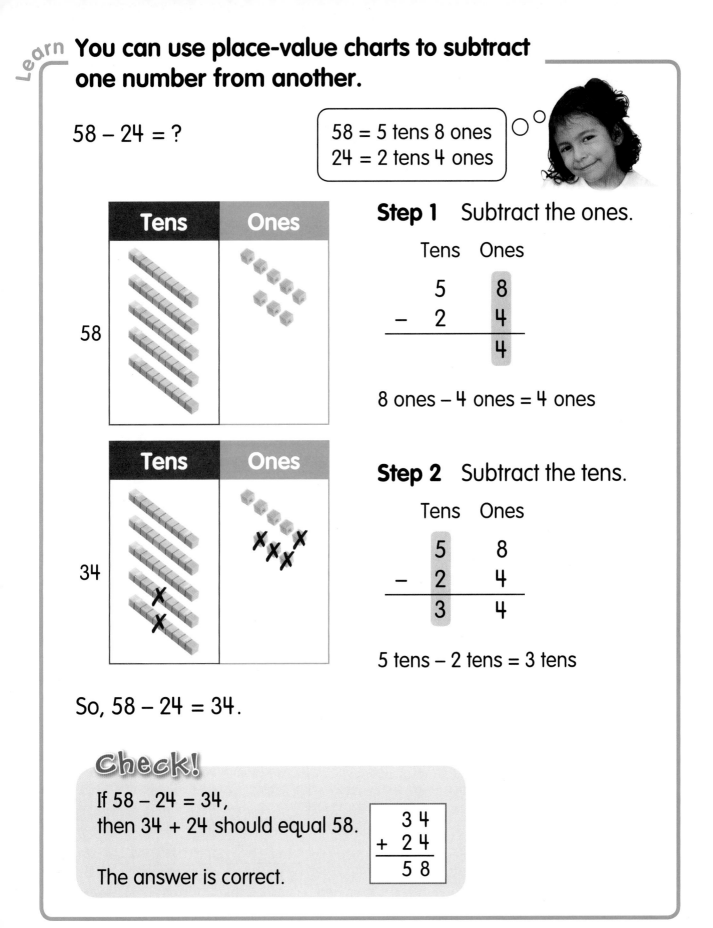

Tens	Ones
58	

Step 1 Subtract the ones.

	Tens	Ones
	5	8
−	2	4
		4

8 ones − 4 ones = 4 ones

Tens	Ones
34	

Step 2 Subtract the tens.

	Tens	Ones
	5	8
−	2	4
	3	4

5 tens − 2 tens = 3 tens

So, $58 - 24 = 34$.

Check!

If $58 - 24 = 34$,
then $34 + 24$ should equal 58.

```
   3 4
 + 2 4
 ─────
   5 8
```

The answer is correct.

Guided Learning

Complete.

2

Tens	Ones
7	2
− 4	0

Step 1 Subtract the ones.

( ) ones − ( ) ones = ( ) ones

Step 2 Subtract the tens.

( ) tens − ( ) tens = ( ) tens

Check!

```
   ( )
 + 4 0
 ─────
   7 2
```

○ ○

3

Tens	Ones
6	9
− 3	3

Step 1 Subtract the ones.

( ) ones − ( ) ones = ( ) ones

Step 2 Subtract the tens.

( ) tens − ( ) tens = ( ) tens

Check!

```
   ( )
 + 3 3
 ─────
   6 9
```

○ ○

Let's Practice

Subtract by counting back. Check your answer.

1 $87 - 4 =$ ⬚

2 $79 - 3 =$ ⬚

Subtract.

3

Tens	Ones
6	8
−	5

⬚

4

Tens	Ones
9	0
− 4	0

⬚

5

Tens	Ones
7	7
− 5	0

⬚

6

Tens	Ones
9	9
− 7	1

⬚

7 $53 - 2 =$ ⬚

Tens	Ones
⬚	⬚
− ⬚	⬚
⬚	

8 $89 - 23 =$ ⬚

Tens	Ones
⬚	⬚
− ⬚	⬚
⬚	

ON YOUR OWN

Go to Workbook B:
Practice 3, pages 171–174

Subtraction with Regrouping

Lesson Objectives

- Subtract a 1-digit number from a 2-digit number with regrouping.
- Subtract 2-digit numbers with regrouping.

Learn **You can use place-value charts to subtract ones with regrouping.**

$52 - 9 = ?$

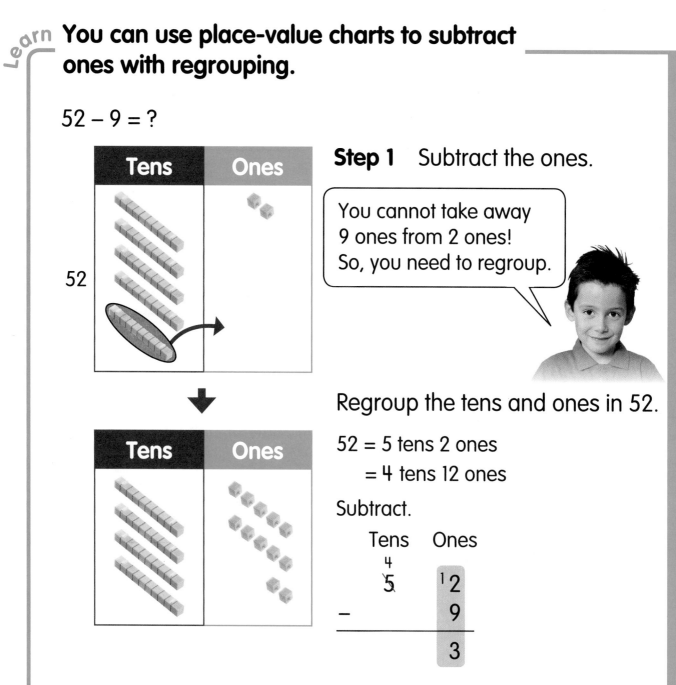

Step 1 Subtract the ones.

You cannot take away 9 ones from 2 ones! So, you need to regroup.

Regroup the tens and ones in 52.

$52 = 5$ tens 2 ones
$\quad = 4$ tens 12 ones

Subtract.

Tens Ones

$$
\begin{array}{cc}
 & \overset{4}{\cancel{5}} & \overset{1}{2} \\
- & & 9 \\
\hline
 & & 3 \\
\end{array}
$$

12 ones − 9 ones = 3 ones

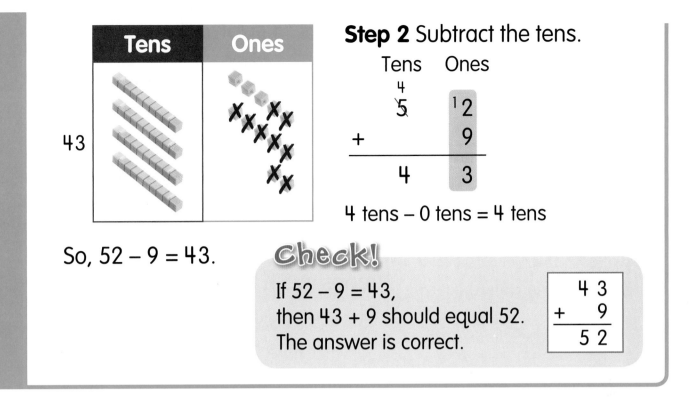

Tens	Ones

43

So, 52 − 9 = 43.

Step 2 Subtract the tens.

Tens   Ones

$\overset{4}{\cancel{5}}$ $^{1}2$

+   9

4   3

4 tens − 0 tens = 4 tens

Check!

If 52 − 9 = 43,
then 43 + 9 should equal 52.
The answer is correct.

```
  4 3
+   9
  5 2
```

Guided Learning

Regroup and subtract.

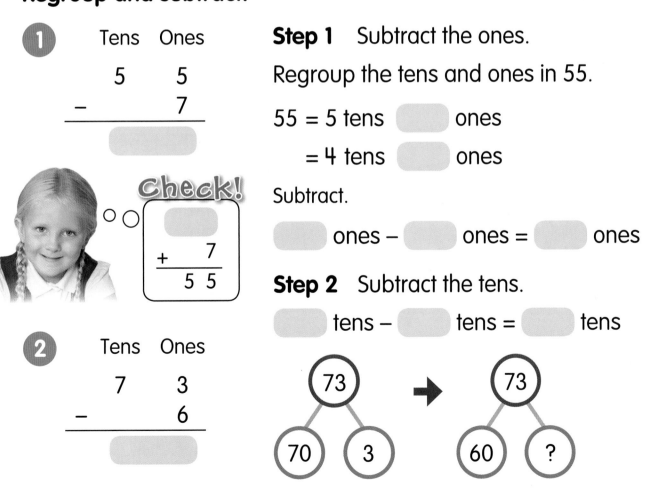

1

Tens   Ones

5   5

−   7

Check!

```
+    7
   5 5
```

2

Tens   Ones

7   3

−   6

Step 1 Subtract the ones.

Regroup the tens and ones in 55.

55 = 5 tens ⬭ ones

= 4 tens ⬭ ones

Subtract.

⬭ ones − ⬭ ones = ⬭ ones

Step 2 Subtract the tens.

⬭ tens − ⬭ tens = ⬭ tens

73 → 73

70 3   60 ?

Lesson 4 Subtraction with Regrouping   **243**

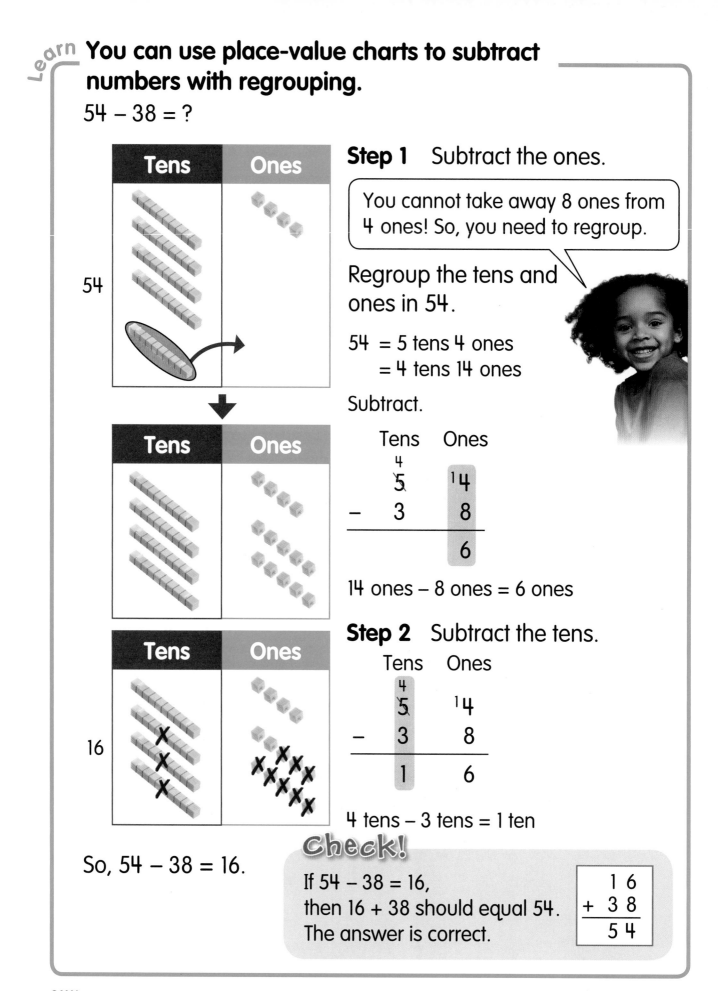

Learn **You can use place-value charts to subtract numbers with regrouping.**

54 − 38 = ?

Tens	Ones

54

Step 1 Subtract the ones.

You cannot take away 8 ones from 4 ones! So, you need to regroup.

Regroup the tens and ones in 54.

54 = 5 tens 4 ones
     = 4 tens 14 ones

Subtract.

```
   Tens   Ones
    4
    5      ¹4
 −  3       8
 ─────────────
            6
```

14 ones − 8 ones = 6 ones

Tens	Ones

Step 2 Subtract the tens.

```
   Tens   Ones
    4
    5      ¹4
 −  3       8
 ─────────────
    1       6
```

4 tens − 3 tens = 1 ten

Tens	Ones

16

So, 54 − 38 = 16.

Check!

If 54 − 38 = 16,
then 16 + 38 should equal 54.
The answer is correct.

```
   1 6
 + 3 8
 ─────
   5 4
```

Guided Learning

Regroup and subtract.

3

Tens	Ones
7	2
− 5	5

Step 1 Subtract the ones.

Regroup the tens and ones in 72.

72 = 7 tens ⬜ ones

= 6 tens ⬜ ones

Subtract.

⬜ ones − ⬜ ones = ⬜ ones

Step 2 Subtract the tens.

⬜ tens − ⬜ tens = ⬜ ten

4

Tens	Ones
6	2
− 5	8

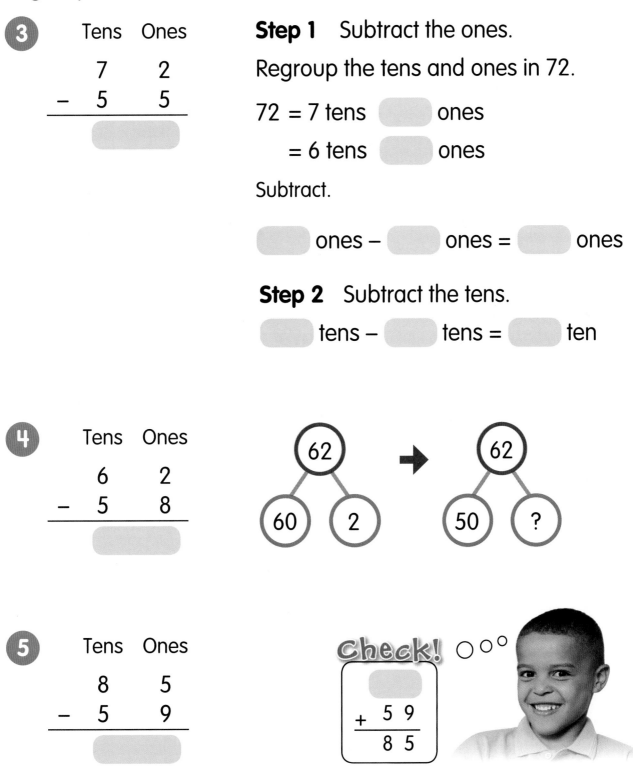

5

Tens	Ones
8	5
− 5	9

Check!

	⬜	
+	5	9
	8	5

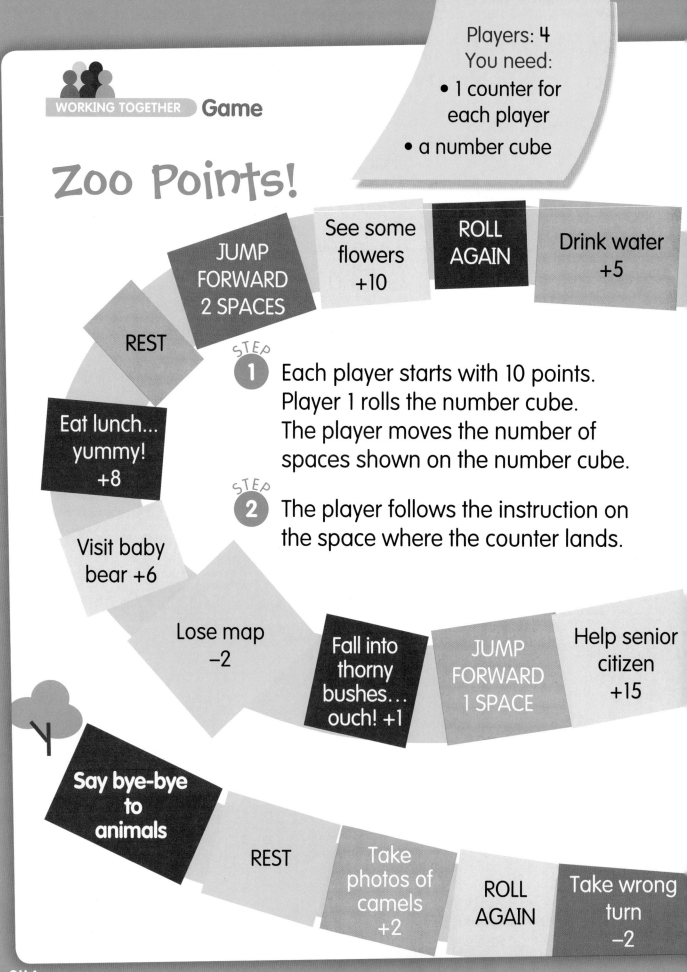

Players: 4
You need:
- 1 counter for each player
- a number cube

Zoo Points!

JUMP FORWARD 2 SPACES

See some flowers +10

ROLL AGAIN

Drink water +5

REST

STEP 1 Each player starts with 10 points. Player 1 rolls the number cube. The player moves the number of spaces shown on the number cube.

Eat lunch... yummy! +8

STEP 2 The player follows the instruction on the space where the counter lands.

Visit baby bear +6

Lose map −2

Fall into thorny bushes... ouch! +1

JUMP FORWARD 1 SPACE

Help senior citizen +15

Say bye-bye to animals

REST

Take photos of camels +2

ROLL AGAIN

Take wrong turn −2

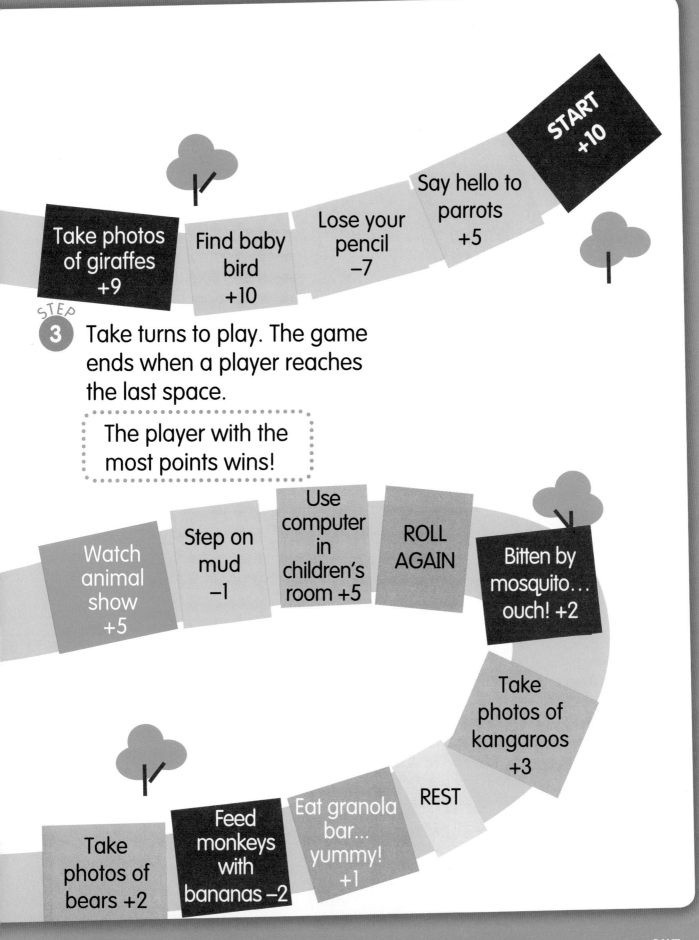

START
+10

Say hello to
parrots
+5

Lose your
pencil
−7

Find baby
bird
+10

Take photos
of giraffes
+9

STEP
3 Take turns to play. The game
ends when a player reaches
the last space.

The player with the
most points wins!

Watch
animal
show
+5

Step on
mud
−1

Use
computer
in
children's
room +5

ROLL
AGAIN

Bitten by
mosquito...
ouch! +2

Take
photos of
kangaroos
+3

REST

Take
photos of
bears +2

Feed
monkeys
with
bananas −2

Eat granola
bar...
yummy!
+1

Let's Practice

Regroup.

1 $82 = 8$ tens ▢ ones

$= 7$ tens ▢ ones

2 $75 = 7$ tens ▢ ones

$= 6$ tens ▢ ones

Regroup and subtract. Check your answer.

3

Tens	Ones
5	3
−	9

▢

4

Tens	Ones
9	2
−	6

▢

5

Tens	Ones
7	3
− 3	7

▢

6

Tens	Ones
9	0
− 5	4

▢

7 $64 - 6 = $ ▢

Tens	Ones
▢	▢
− ▢	▢

▢

8 $71 - 56 = $ ▢

Tens	Ones
▢	▢
− ▢	▢

▢

ON YOUR OWN

Go to Workbook B:
Practice 4, pages 175–180

PROBLEM SOLVING

Use each number once.

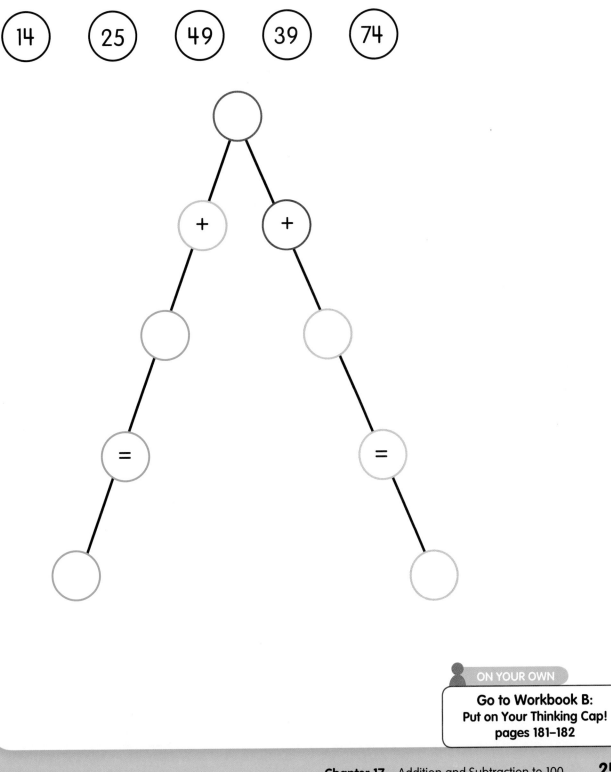

(14) (25) (49) (39) (74)

ON YOUR OWN

**Go to Workbook B:
Put on Your Thinking Cap!
pages 181–182**

Chapter Wrap Up
You have learned...

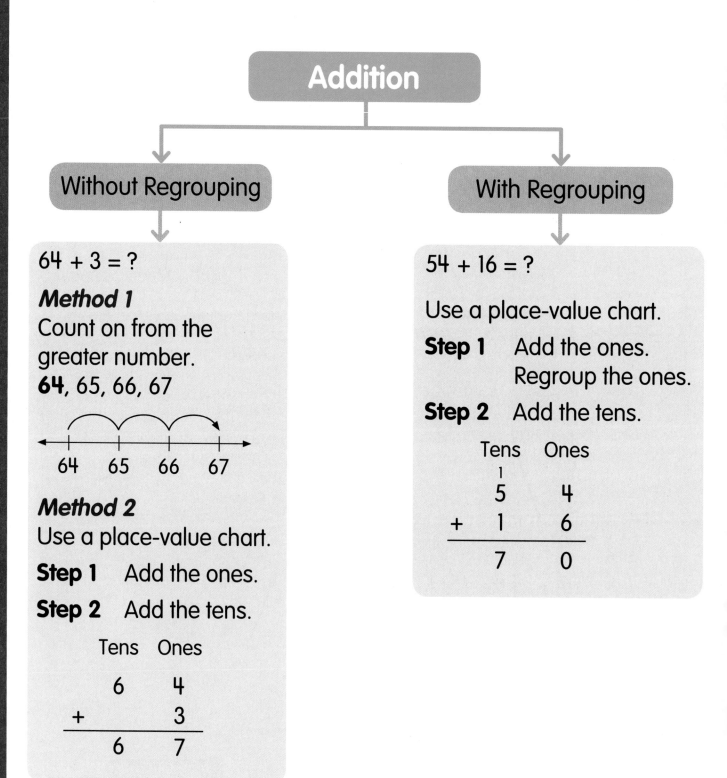

Addition

Without Regrouping

64 + 3 = ?

Method 1
Count on from the
greater number.
64, 65, 66, 67

64	65	66	67

Method 2
Use a place-value chart.

Step 1   Add the ones.

Step 2   Add the tens.

Tens	Ones
6	4
+	3
6	7

With Regrouping

54 + 16 = ?

Use a place-value chart.

Step 1   Add the ones.
Regroup the ones.

Step 2   Add the tens.

Tens	Ones
1	
5	4
+ 1	6
7	0

BIG IDEA

Numbers to 100 can be added and subtracted with and without regrouping.

Subtraction

Without Regrouping

75 − 2 = ?

Method 1
Count back from 75.
75, 74, 73

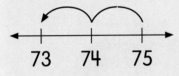

73   74   75

Method 2
Use a place-value chart.

Step 1 Subtract the ones.

Step 2 Subtract the tens.

Tens	Ones
7	5
−	2
7	3

With Regrouping

65 − 18 = ?

Use a place-value chart.

Step 1 Regroup the tens and ones in 65. Subtract the ones.

Step 2 Subtract the tens.

Tens	Ones
$\overset{5}{\cancel{6}}$	$^{1}5$
− 1	8
4	7

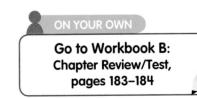

ON YOUR OWN

Go to Workbook B:
Chapter Review/Test,
pages 183–184

CHAPTER

18 Getting Ready for Multiplication and Division

We're catching ladybugs for a science lesson.

We've caught
3 + 3 + 3 + 3 = 12 ladybugs.

Let's put them into 2 boxes.

There are
6 ladybugs
in each box.

Lesson 1 Adding the Same Number

Lesson 2 Sharing Equally

Lesson 3 Finding the Number of Groups

BIG IDEAS

Multiplying is the same as adding equal groups. Dividing is the same as sharing things equally or putting things into equal groups.

Recall Prior Knowledge

Adding the same number

$2 + 2 = 4$

$2 + 2 + 2 = 6$

$3 + 3 = 6$

$3 + 3 + 3 = 9$

✔ Quick Check

Add.

1 $5 + 5 + 5 + 5 = $ [ ]

2 $4 + 4 = $ [ ]

3 $4 + 4 + $ [ ] $= 12$

4 $3 + 3 + 3 + $ [ ] $= 12$

LESSON 1

Adding the Same Number

Lesson Objectives

- Use objects or pictures to find the total number of items in groups of the same size.

- Relate repeated addition to the concept of multiplication.

Vocabulary
same
groups
each

Learn You can add the **same** number.

2 toys   2 toys   2 toys

> How many groups of toys are there?

> How many toys are in **each** group?

There are 3 **groups**.

Each group has 2 toys.

$2 + 2 + 2 = 6$

3 twos = 6

3 groups of 2 = 6

There are 6 toys in all.

> $2 + 2 + 2$ means 3 twos or 3 groups of 2.

Guided Learning

Complete.

1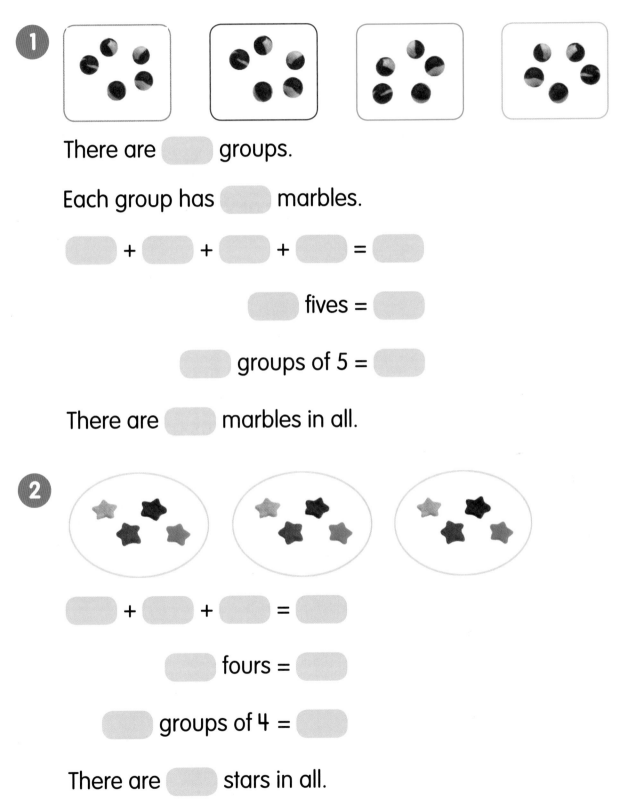

There are ⬜ groups.

Each group has ⬜ marbles.

⬜ + ⬜ + ⬜ + ⬜ = ⬜

⬜ fives = ⬜

⬜ groups of 5 = ⬜

There are ⬜ marbles in all.

2

⬜ + ⬜ + ⬜ = ⬜

⬜ fours = ⬜

⬜ groups of 4 = ⬜

There are ⬜ stars in all.

Hands-On Activity

1 Use 5 sheets of paper.
Put 2 counters on each sheet of paper.

◯ + ◯ + ◯ + ◯ + ◯ = ◯

◯ twos = ◯

◯ groups of 2 = ◯

2 Use 6 sheets of paper.
Put 3 counters on each sheet of paper.

◯ + ◯ + ◯ + ◯ + ◯ + ◯ = ◯

◯ threes = ◯

◯ groups of 3 = ◯

3 Use 3 sheets of paper.
Put an equal number of counters on each sheet of paper.

◯ + ◯ + ◯ = ◯

3 ◯ = ◯

3 groups of ◯ = ◯

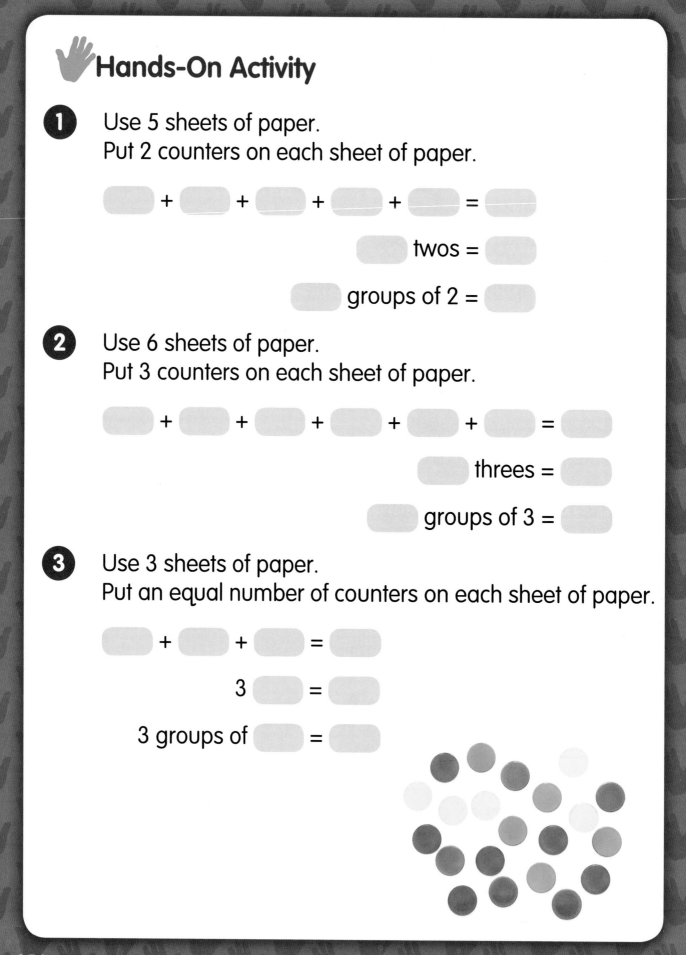

Let's Explore!

Use 12 counters.

Arrange them into rows in different ways.
Each row must have the same number of counters.
Then write three sentences for each arrangement.

Example

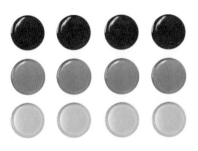

3 groups of 4 = 12
3 fours = 12
4 + 4 + 4 = 12

Use 18 counters.

Do the same as above.
How many sentences can you write?

READING AND WRITING MATH
Math Journal

Find the sentences that are false.
Then write true sentences.

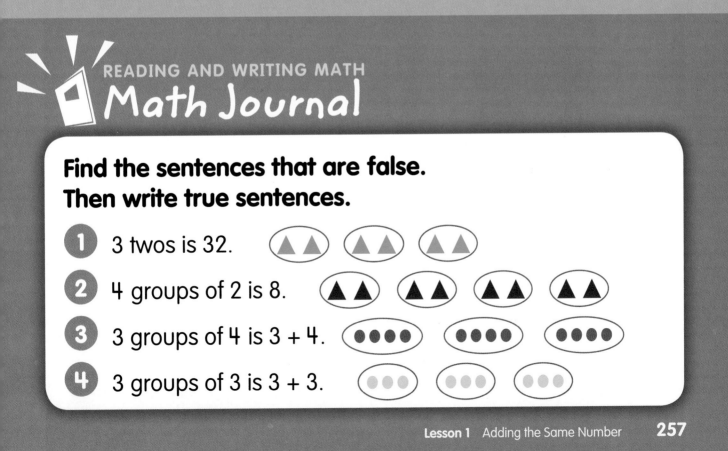

1. 3 twos is 32.
2. 4 groups of 2 is 8.
3. 3 groups of 4 is 3 + 4.
4. 3 groups of 3 is 3 + 3.

Let's Practice

Find the missing numbers.

1 $7 + 7 + 7 =$ [ ]

3 sevens = [ ]

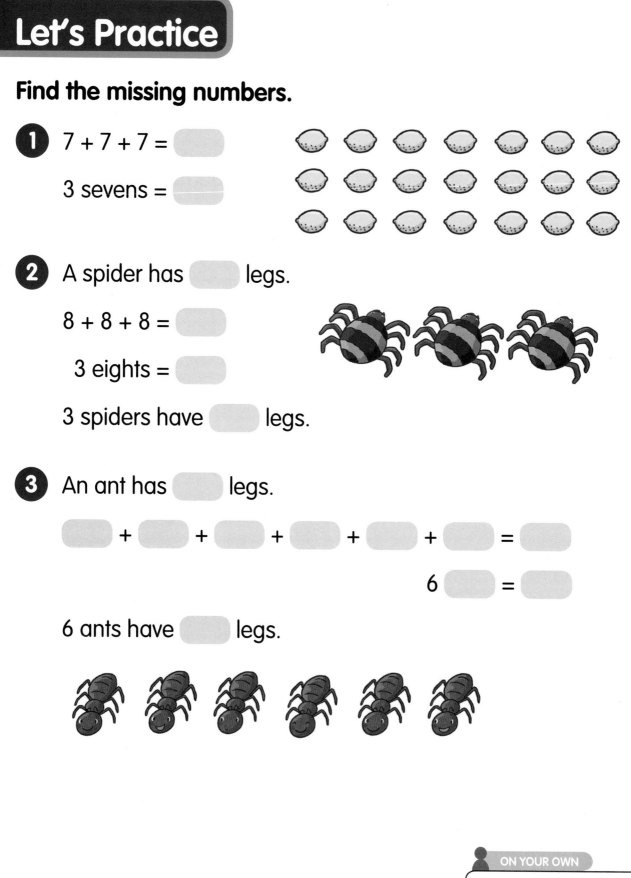

2 A spider has [ ] legs.

$8 + 8 + 8 =$ [ ]

3 eights = [ ]

3 spiders have [ ] legs.

3 An ant has [ ] legs.

[ ] + [ ] + [ ] + [ ] + [ ] + [ ] = [ ]

6 [ ] = [ ]

6 ants have [ ] legs.

ON YOUR OWN

Go to Workbook B:
Practice 1, pages 193–198

Sharing Equally

Lesson Objectives

- Use objects or pictures to find the number of items in each group when sharing equally.
- Relate sharing equally to the concept of division.

Learn **You can share equally.**

Mark has 6 muffins.
He has 3 friends.
He gives each friend the same number of muffins in a bag.

I tried putting 1 muffin into each bag.
I had 3 muffins left.

So, I put 1 more muffin in each bag. Now I have no muffins left.

Each friend gets 2 muffins.

Hands-On Activity

Use 20 counters and 4 sheets of paper.

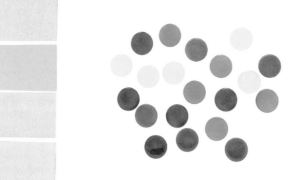

Put an equal number of counters on each sheet of paper.
Use all the counters.

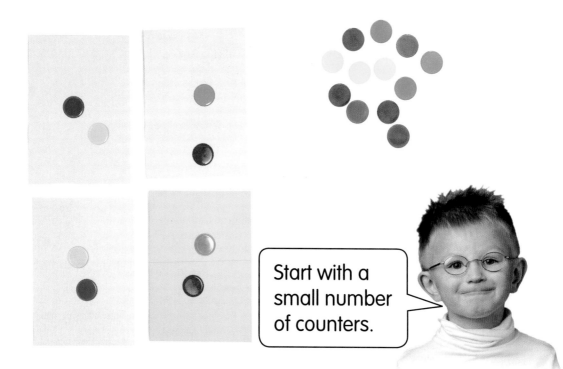

Start with a small number of counters.

How many counters are on each sheet of paper?

Guided Learning

Solve.

 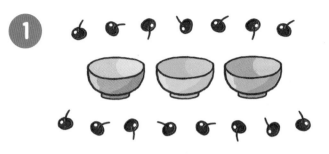

How many cherries are there in all ? ⬜

How many bowls are there? ⬜

Put the same number of cherries in each bowl.

Each bowl has ⬜ cherries.

Let's Practice

Complete.

1 Put 8 children into 2 equal groups.
How many children are in each group?

There are ⬜ children in each group.

2 There are 12 beads of different colors in a box.
Put the beads into 4 equal groups.
How many beads are in each group?

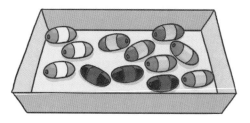

There are [____] beads in each group.

3 Mr. Armstrong has 18 crayons.
He gives the crayons equally to 6 children.
How many crayons does each child get?

Each child gets [____] crayons.

4 Mrs. Curley bakes 20 muffins.
She packs them into 5 boxes equally.
How many muffins are in each box?

There are [____] muffins in each box.

ON YOUR OWN

Go to Workbook B:
Practice 2, pages 199–206

Finding the Number of Groups

Lesson Objective

- Use objects or pictures to show the concept of division as finding the number of equal groups.

Learn

You can find the number of equal groups.

There are 12 eggs.

Put 4 eggs into each bowl.

How many bowls do you need?

First put 4 eggs into 1 bowl.

Do this until all the eggs are put into the bowls.

You need 3 bowls.

Guided Learning

Solve.

1 Kim has 15 toy cats.
She puts 3 toy cats on each sofa.
How many sofas does she need for all the toy cats?

She needs ⬭ sofas for all the toy cats.

🖐 Hands-On Activity

Use 20 counters and some cups.

1 Put 2 counters in each cup.
How many cups do you use?

2 Put 4 counters in each cup.
How many cups do you use?

3 Put 5 counters in each cup.
How many cups do you use?

4 Put 10 counters in each cup.
How many cups do you use?

Let's Explore!

WORK IN PAIRS

Use 24  .

Use all the  and put them into groups.

Each group must have the same number of  .

How many ways can you do it?

Math Journal

Draw the different ways you can group the  in the Let's Explore.

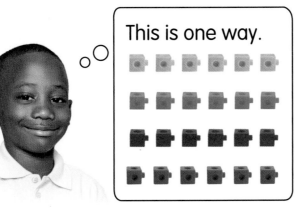

This is one way.

Solve.

1 Put 10 birds into groups.
Put 2 birds in each group.
How many groups of birds do you get?

2 A farmer has 15 sheep on his farm.
He keeps them in pens.
Each pen has 5 sheep.
How many pens are there?

3 Nate makes 24 puppets.
He puts 6 puppets in each box.
How many boxes does Nate use?

ON YOUR OWN

Go to Workbook B:
Practice 3, pages 207–212

Put On Your Thinking Cap!

PROBLEM SOLVING

Solve.

1 Alex has 3 rabbits.
   Which shows the number of legs Alex's rabbits have in all?

   $3 + 3 + 3 = 9$

   $3 + 3 + 3 + 3 = 12$

   $4 + 4 + 4 = 12$

2 Chris has 18 marbles.
   He puts them into groups.
   Each group has 5 marbles.

   a What is the greatest number of groups Chris can have?

   b How many marbles are not used?

   Draw pictures to help you or **act it out**.

ON YOUR OWN

Go to Workbook B:
Put on Your Thinking Cap!
pages 213–214

Chapter Wrap Up

You have learned...

BIG IDEAS

Multiplying is the same as adding equal groups. Dividing is the same as sharing things equally or putting things into equal groups.

to add repeated numbers.

5 + 5 + 5 means 3 fives.
5 + 5 + 5 = 15
3 fives = 15

to use a picture with equal groups of things and write an addition sentence.

3 + 3 + 3 + 3 = 12

to put or share things equally into groups.
Put 6 strawberries equally into 3 groups.
How many strawberries are there in each group?

The number of groups is given.

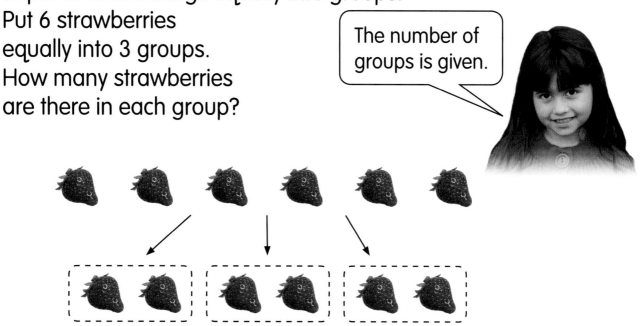

There are 2 strawberries in each group.

to group things equally and find the number of groups.

Put 9 strawberries equally into groups of 3. How many groups of strawberries are there?

The number of things in each group is given.

There are 3 groups of strawberries.

ON YOUR OWN

Go to Workbook B: Chapter Review/Test, pages 215–216

CHAPTER

19 Money

25¢ each

10¢ each

How many pennies do I need to buy 1 🐱 and 1 ✏️ ?

BIG IDEAS

Penny, nickel, dime, and quarter are coins that can be counted and exchanged. Money can be added and subtracted.

Recall Prior Knowledge

Knowing penny, nickel, dime, and quarter

penny

nickel

dime

quarter

These are the two faces of a penny.
A penny has a value of one cent or 1¢.

Using pennies to buy things

5¢

7¢

6¢

Name each coin.

Find the price.

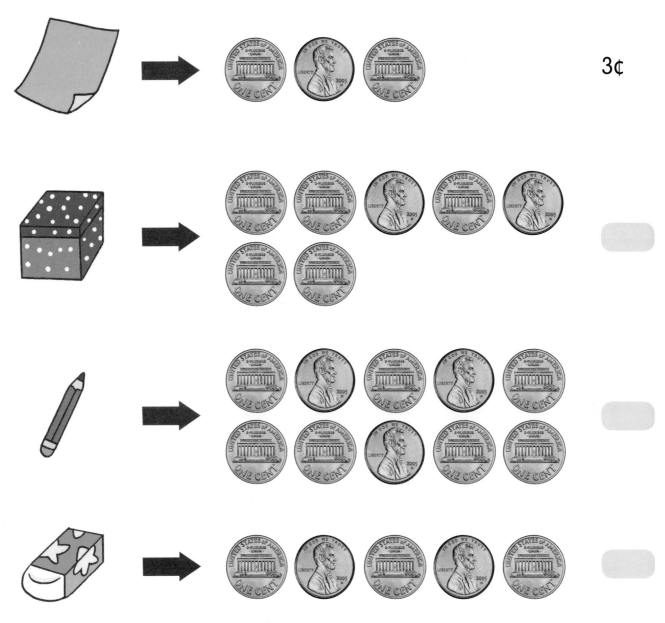

3¢

LESSON 1 · Penny, Nickel, and Dime

Lesson Objectives

- Recognize and name penny, nickel, and dime.
- Understand that '¢' stands for cents.
- Skip-count to find the value of a collection of coins.
- Exchange one coin for a set of coins of equal value.
- Use different combinations of coins less than 25¢ to buy things.

Vocabulary
cents
nickel
value
penny
dime
exchange

Learn · Know the penny, nickel, and dime.

These are the two faces of a **penny**.
A penny has a value of one **cent** or 1¢.

or

These are the two faces of a **nickel**.
A nickel has a value of five cents or 5¢.

These are the two faces of a **dime**.
A dime has a value of ten cents or 10¢.

¢ means cents!

Guided Learning

Complete.

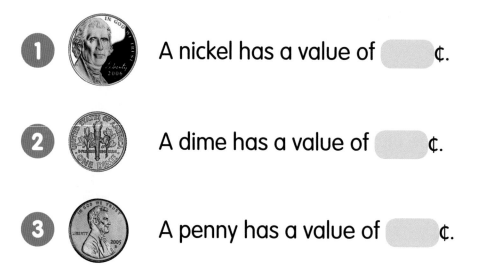

1 A nickel has a value of [　　] ¢.

2 A dime has a value of [　　] ¢.

3 A penny has a value of [　　] ¢.

4 How many pennies are there? [　　]

5 How many nickels are there? [　　]

6 How many dimes are there? [　　]

You can skip-count to find the value of a group of coins.

Skip-count to find the value of the coins.

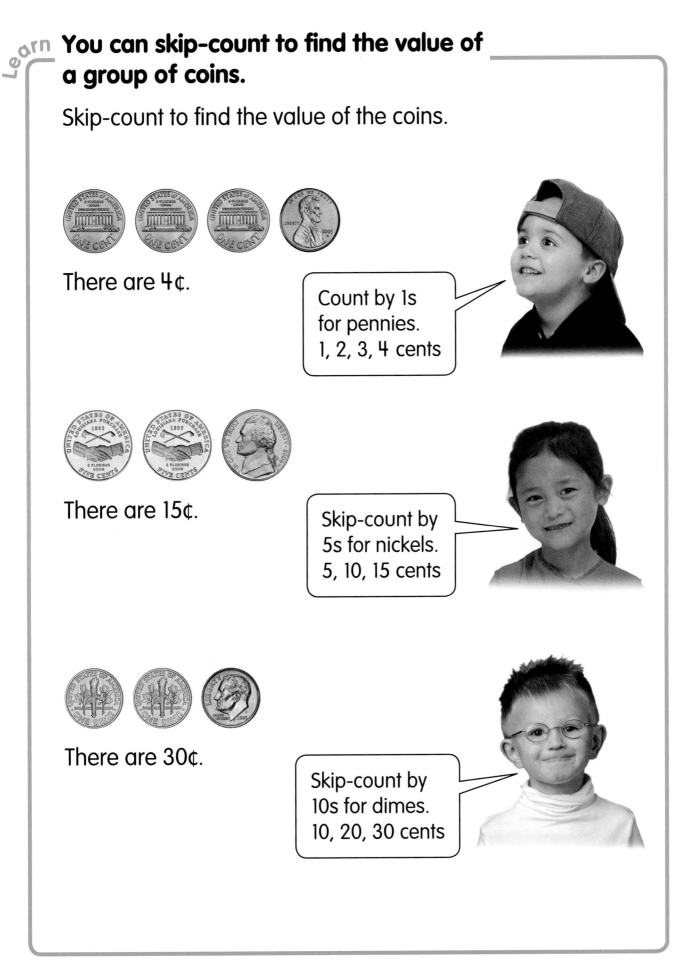

There are 4¢.

> Count by 1s
> for pennies.
> 1, 2, 3, 4 cents

There are 15¢.

> Skip-count by
> 5s for nickels.
> 5, 10, 15 cents

There are 30¢.

> Skip-count by
> 10s for dimes.
> 10, 20, 30 cents

Guided Learning

Complete.

7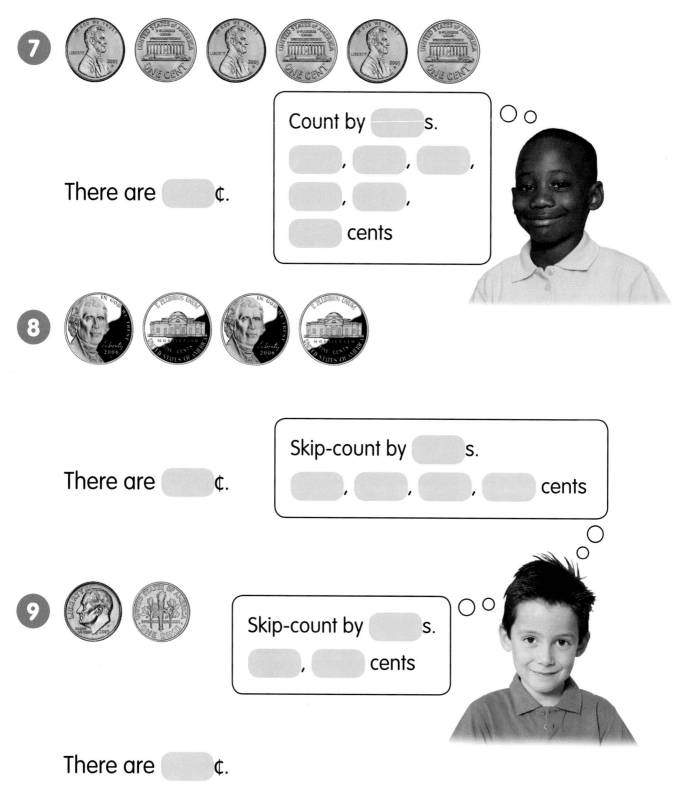

There are ⬚ ¢.

> Count by ⬚ s.
>
> ⬚ , ⬚ , ⬚ ,
>
> ⬚ , ⬚ ,
>
> ⬚ cents

8

There are ⬚ ¢.

> Skip-count by ⬚ s.
>
> ⬚ , ⬚ , ⬚ , ⬚ cents

9

> Skip-count by ⬚ s.
>
> ⬚ , ⬚ cents

There are ⬚ ¢.

You can find the value of a group of different coins.

Count on to find the value.
Begin with the coin of greater value.

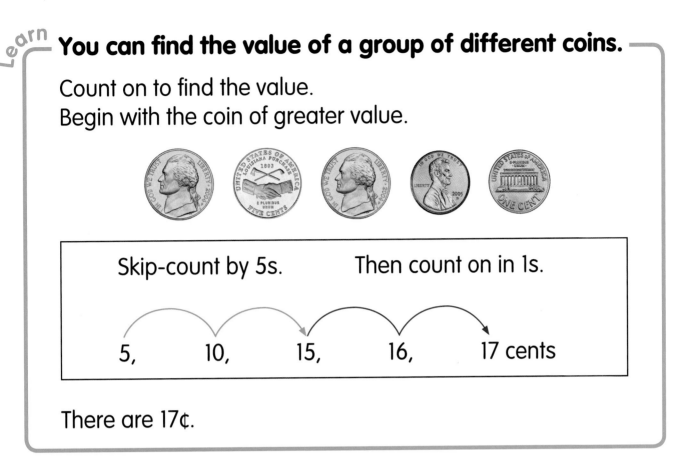

Skip-count by 5s.   Then count on in 1s.

5,   10,   15,   16,   17 cents

There are 17¢.

Guided Learning

**Find the value of the group of coins.
Begin with the coins of greater value.**

10

⬜, ⬜, ⬜, ⬜, ⬜, ⬜, ⬜ cents

There are ⬜ ¢.

11

⬜, ⬜, ⬜, ⬜, ⬜ cents

There are ⬜ ¢.

You can exchange one coin for a set of coins of equal value.

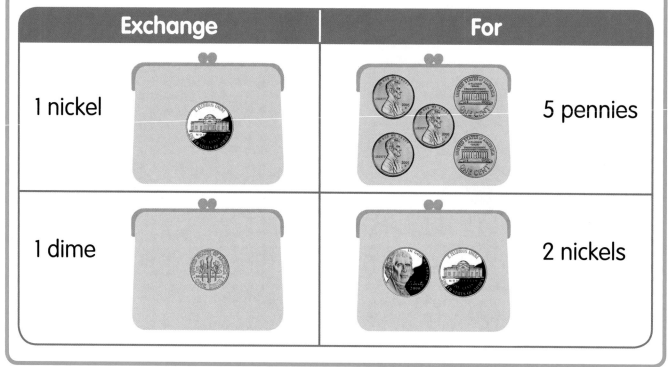

Exchange	For
1 nickel	5 pennies
1 dime	2 nickels

Guided Learning

Complete.

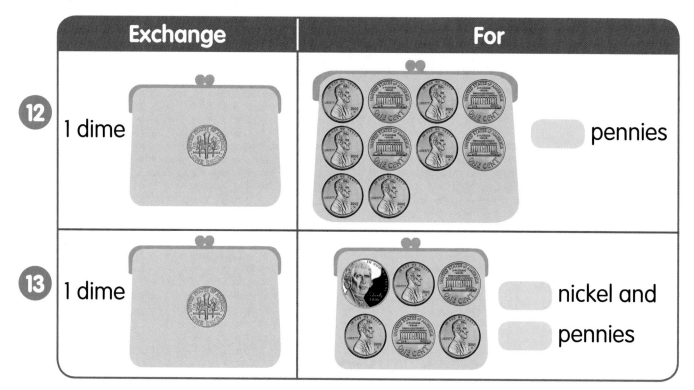

Exchange	For
12 1 dime	____ pennies
13 1 dime	____ nickel and ____ pennies

You can show the same amount of money using different groups of coins.

The children each want to buy a ball.

14¢   14¢   14¢

I'll pay with 14 pennies.

I'll pay with 2 nickels and 4 pennies.

I'll pay with 1 dime and 4 pennies.

Guided Learning

Complete.

14

The stamp is [ ] ¢.

15

The apple is [ ] ¢.

16

The pencil is [ ] ¢.

17

The ball of string is [ ] ¢.

Let's Practice

Answer the questions.

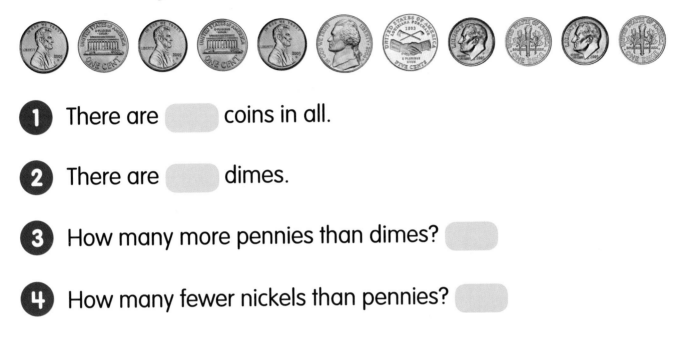

1 There are _____ coins in all.

2 There are _____ dimes.

3 How many more pennies than dimes? _____

4 How many fewer nickels than pennies? _____

Count on to find the value of each group of coins.

5

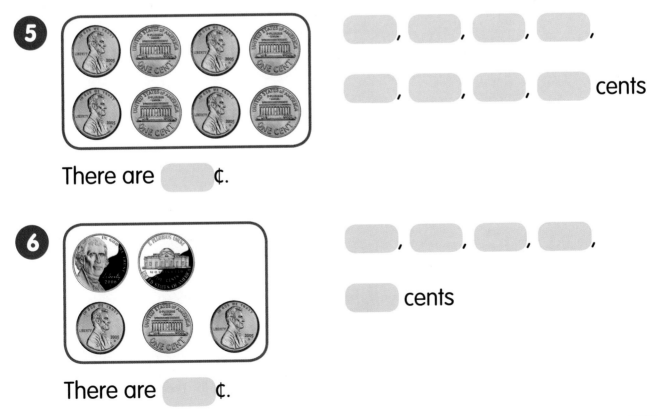

_____, _____, _____, _____,

_____, _____, _____, _____ cents

There are _____ ¢.

6

_____, _____, _____, _____,

_____ cents

There are _____ ¢.

Find the price.

7 🖍️ ➡️ 🪙🪙🪙 _____ ¢

8 🎈 ➡️ 🪙🪙🪙🪙 🪙🪙🪙 _____ ¢

Use pennies (1¢), nickels (5¢), and dimes (10¢) to match the price in 2 different ways.

Example

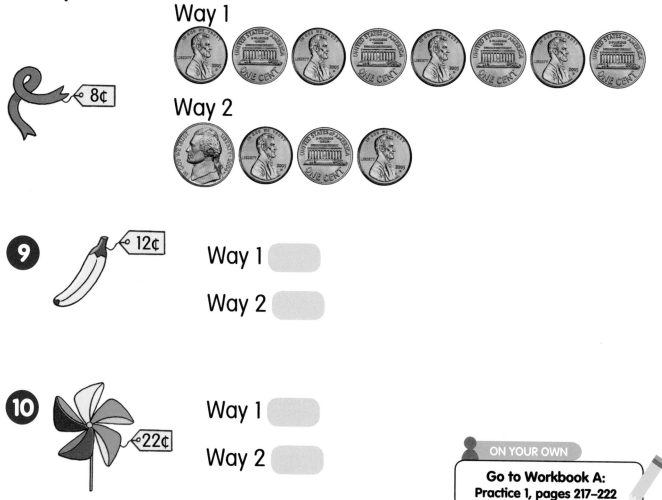

Way 1 🪙🪙🪙🪙🪙🪙🪙🪙

8¢

Way 2 🪙🪙🪙🪙

9 12¢   Way 1 _____

Way 2 _____

10 22¢   Way 1 _____

Way 2 _____

ON YOUR OWN

Go to Workbook A:
Practice 1, pages 217–222

Quarter

LESSON 2

Lesson Objectives

- Know and name a quarter.
- Exchange a quarter for a set of coins of equal value.

Vocabulary
quarter

Learn

Know another coin, the quarter.

 These are the two faces of a **quarter**.
The quarter has a value of twenty-five cents or 25¢.

You can exchange a quarter for other coins.

Exchange	For
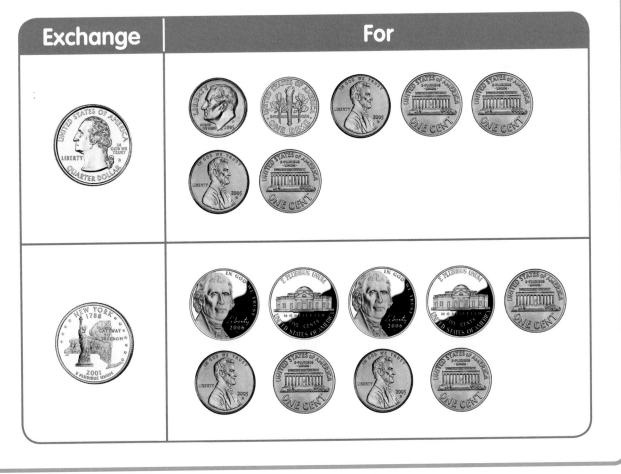	

Hands-On Activity

WORK IN PAIRS

Use pennies, nickels, and dimes to show 5 different ways to exchange a quarter for other coins.

Example

Exchange

Then draw (1¢), (5¢), (10¢) in a copy of the table to show your answers.

Exchange	For

Let's Practice

Complete.

1 One _____ has a value of 25¢.

2 How many quarters can you make with these coins? _____

Show 3 ways to pay for the keychain.

3 1 coin _____

4 5 coins _____

5 8 coins _____

25¢

ON YOUR OWN

Go to Workbook B:
Practice 2, pages 223–226

3 Counting Money

Lesson Objectives

- Count money in cents up to $1 using the 'count on' strategy.

- Choose the correct value of coins when buying items.

- Use different combinations of coins to show the same value.

Learn **You can count on to find the amount of money.**

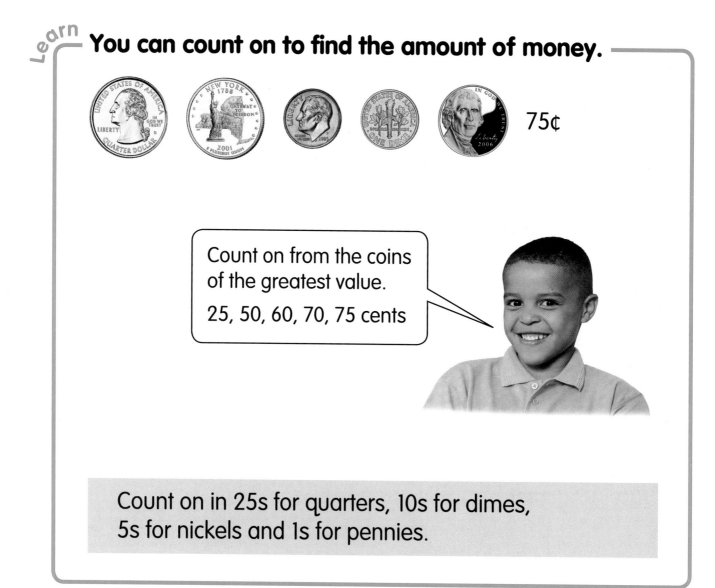

75¢

Count on from the coins of the greatest value.

25, 50, 60, 70, 75 cents

Count on in 25s for quarters, 10s for dimes, 5s for nickels and 1s for pennies.

Guided Learning

Complete.

Matt buys some things.
Count on to find the price of each keychain.

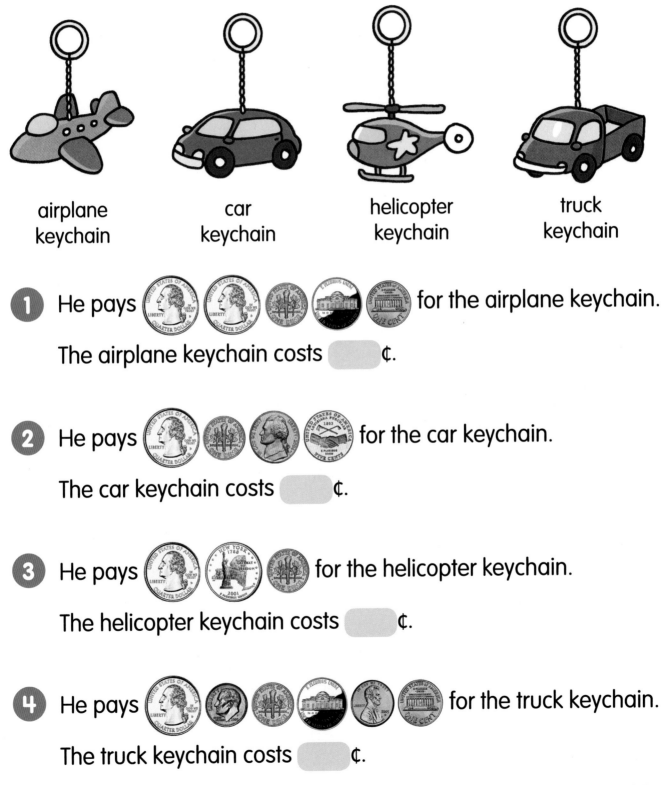

airplane	car	helicopter	truck
keychain	keychain	keychain	keychain

1 He pays 🪙🪙🪙🪙🪙 for the airplane keychain.

The airplane keychain costs ____ ¢.

2 He pays 🪙🪙🪙🪙 for the car keychain.

The car keychain costs ____ ¢.

3 He pays 🪙🪙🪙 for the helicopter keychain.

The helicopter keychain costs ____ ¢.

4 He pays 🪙🪙🪙🪙🪙🪙 for the truck keychain.

The truck keychain costs ____ ¢.

You can count a group of coins by arranging them in order first.

Ricky saved a dime last week.
This week, he added three nickels, one dime, and a quarter to his savings.
How much did he save in all?

He took out all the coins from his piggy bank.

He put the coins in order starting with the coin of the greatest value.

Then he counted on to find out how much he saved.

First count on by 10s.   Then count on by 5s.

25¢   35¢   45¢   50¢   55¢   60¢

He saved 60¢ in all.

Ricky used part of his savings to buy some marbles.
The marbles cost 50¢.
He took these coins from his piggy bank.

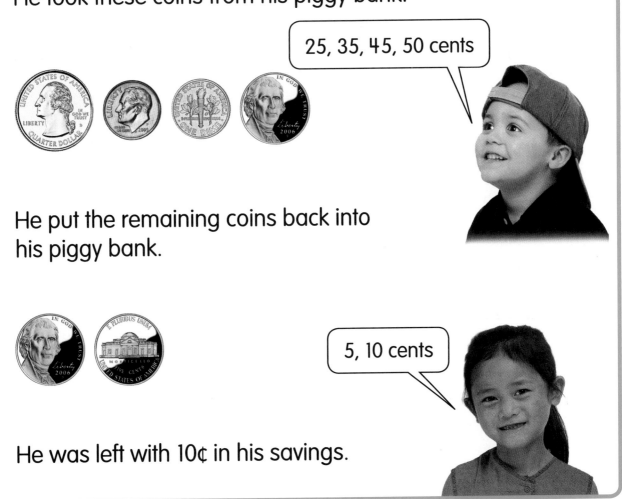

25, 35, 45, 50 cents

He put the remaining coins back into
his piggy bank.

5, 10 cents

He was left with 10¢ in his savings.

Guided Learning

Look at the coins.
Fill in the blanks.

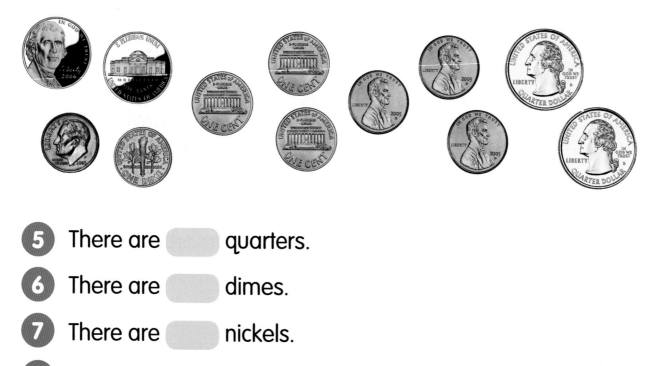

 5 There are [blank] quarters.

6 There are [blank] dimes.

7 There are [blank] nickels.

8 There are [blank] pennies.

Count on to find the total value.

9 There are [blank] ¢ in all.

Remember, count on from the coin of the greatest value.

Guided Learning

Complete.

10 Tell which of these coins make 62¢.

Use pennies, nickels, dimes, and quarters to show the given amount. Start with the coin of greatest value.

Example

50¢

11 72¢

12 96¢

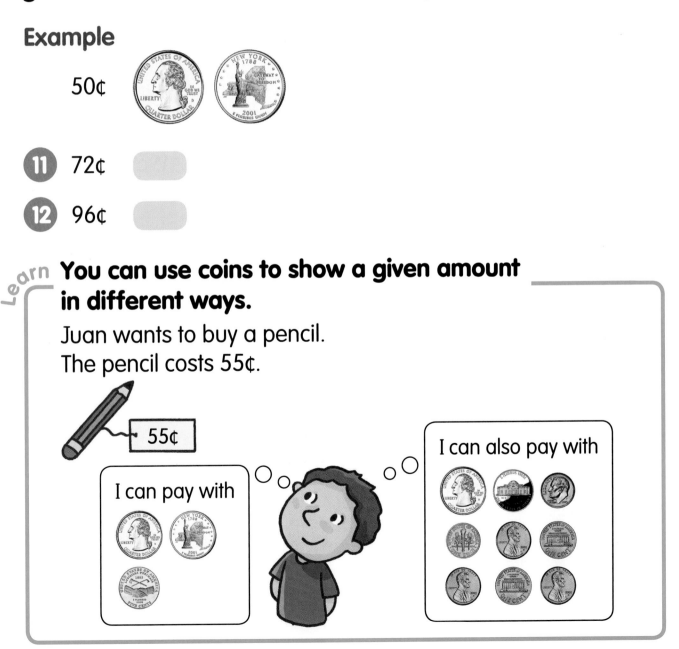

Learn **You can use coins to show a given amount in different ways.**

Juan wants to buy a pencil.
The pencil costs 55¢.

55¢

I can pay with

I can also pay with

Guided Learning

Use coins to show 2 ways of paying for each thing.

Example

Way 1

Way 2

85¢

13

95¢

Way 1 ⬜
Way 2 ⬜

14

86¢

Way 1 ⬜
Way 2 ⬜

15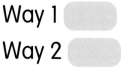

45¢

Way 1 ⬜
Way 2 ⬜

16

75¢

Way 1 ⬜
Way 2 ⬜

17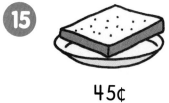

99¢

Way 1 ⬜
Way 2 ⬜

Say How Much!

Players: **4**
You need:
- A bag
- 2 quarters
- 2 dimes
- 2 nickels
- 2 pennies

How to play:

 STEP **1** Each player picks one coin without showing it to the other players.

STEP **2** On the count of three, all players place the coin they picked on the table.

 STEP **3** The first player to say the value of all four coins scores 1 point.

25¢! ? ? ?

The player who scores 10 points wins!

Let's Practice

Count on to find the value.

1

2

3

4

Arrange the coins in order from greatest to least value. Count on to find the value of all the coins.

5

6 The value of the coins is _____ ¢ in all.

Choose the correct purse to pay for each thing.

7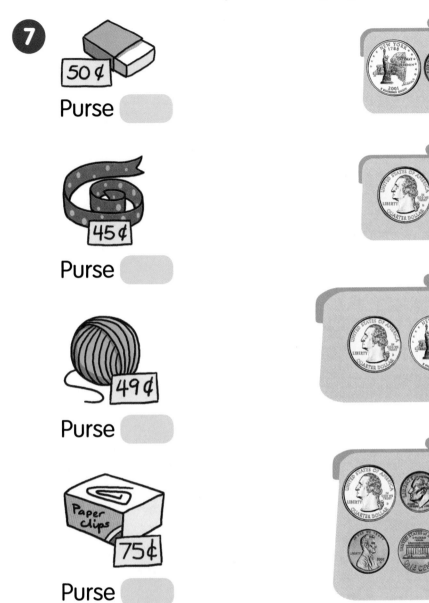

50 ¢

Purse

45 ¢

Purse

49 ¢

Purse

Paper Clips 75 ¢

Purse

A

B

C

D

Use coins. Tell 2 ways you can pay for the toy.

8

67¢	Way 1
	Way 2

ON YOUR OWN

Go to Workbook B:
Practice 3, pages 227–234

Adding and Subtracting Money

Lesson Objectives

- Add to find the cost of items.
- Subtract to find the change.
- Add and subtract money in cents (up to $1).
- Solve real-world problems involving addition and subtraction of money.

Vocabulary
change

Learn You can add and subtract money.

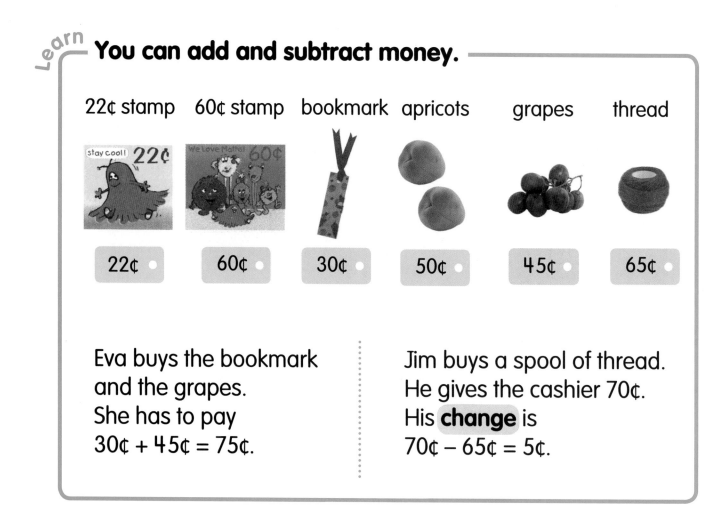

22¢ stamp	60¢ stamp	bookmark	apricots	grapes	thread
22¢	60¢	30¢	50¢	45¢	65¢

Eva buys the bookmark and the grapes. She has to pay
30¢ + 45¢ = 75¢.

Jim buys a spool of thread. He gives the cashier 70¢. His **change** is
70¢ − 65¢ = 5¢.

Guided Learning

Answer the questions.

You are at the store.

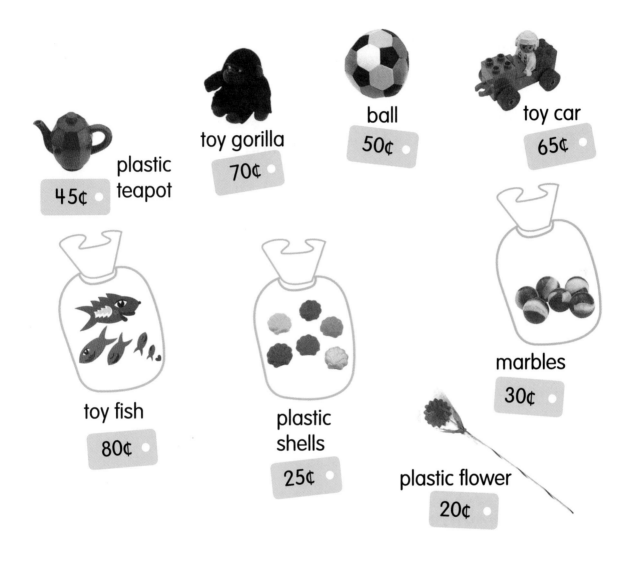

plastic teapot
45¢

toy gorilla
70¢

ball
50¢

toy car
65¢

toy fish
80¢

plastic shells
25¢

plastic flower
20¢

marbles
30¢

1 How much will a toy car and a bag of marbles cost?

2 What two things can you buy with only 45¢?

3 Four quarters are used to buy the toy fish.
How much change will you get?

You can solve real-world money problems.

Stickers

15¢

20¢

25¢

5¢

35¢

Mike buys the car, ship, and bicycle stickers.

15¢ + 20¢ + 5¢ = 40¢

He spends 40¢ in all.

Lily buys the car sticker.
She gives the cashier a quarter.

25¢ – 15¢ = 10¢

She gets 10¢ as change.

Salmah has 17¢.
She wants to buy the airplane sticker.

35¢ – 17¢ = 18¢

She needs 18¢ more.

Peter buys the bus sticker.
He has a nickel left.

25¢ + 5¢ = 30¢

He had 30¢ at first.

Guided Learning

Fill in the blanks.

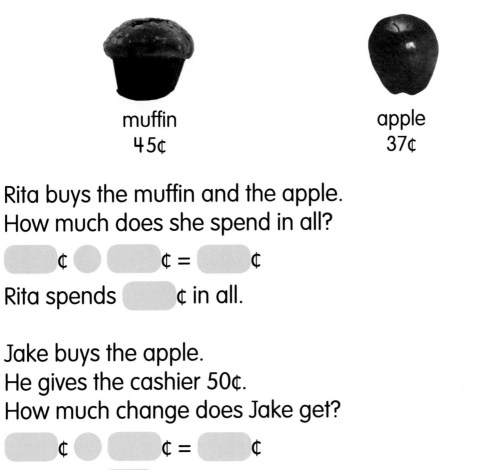

muffin
45¢

apple
37¢

4 Rita buys the muffin and the apple.
How much does she spend in all?

⬚ ¢ ⬚ ¢ = ⬚ ¢

Rita spends ⬚ ¢ in all.

5 Jake buys the apple.
He gives the cashier 50¢.
How much change does Jake get?

⬚ ¢ ⬚ ¢ = ⬚ ¢

Jake gets ⬚ ¢ change.

6 Gary buys the muffin.
Dawn buys the apple.
How much less does Dawn spend than Gary?

⬚ ¢ ⬚ ¢ = ⬚ ¢

Dawn spends ⬚ ¢ less than Gary.

7 After buying the apple, Louisa has 8¢ left.
How much did Louisa have at first?

⬚ ¢ ⬚ ¢ = ⬚ ¢

Louisa had ⬚ ¢ at first.

Let's Explore!

These are some things on sale.

bread
60¢

toy clock
65¢

pencil case
90¢

nuts
80¢

marbles
35¢

animal crackers
83¢

paper clips
20¢

ball
75¢

1. Paula wants to buy something to eat.
She has 80¢.
What can she buy?

2. Dwayne has 95¢.
After buying something to eat, he has 15¢ left.
What is the food that he buys?

3. Juanita has 4 quarters.
List any two things she can buy.
Then show how much she spends.

Let's Practice

Solve.

1 Gary buys an eraser and a pencil.
The eraser costs 40¢ and the pencil costs 35¢.
How much does Gary spend on these two items?

2 A marble costs 30¢.
Lisa buys the marble.
She has 15¢ left.
How much does Lisa have at first?

These are some things in a store.
Solve.

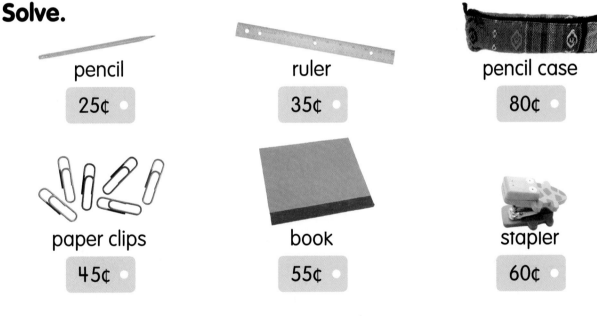

pencil
25¢

ruler
35¢

pencil case
80¢

paper clips
45¢

book
55¢

stapler
60¢

3 Tina has 80¢.
She buys two items.
List the items she could have bought.

4 Tim has 100¢.
He buys an item and has 20¢ left.
Which item has he bought?

ON YOUR OWN

Go to Workbook B:
Practice 4, pages 235–246

PROBLEM SOLVING
Answer the questions.

1 Look at the coins.
Which statements are correct?

a There are 3 dimes.

b There are only 3 nickels.

c You can exchange all of the coins for 9 dimes.

d You can exchange the 2 quarters for 50 pennies.

2 Ray has 2 coins under Cup A.
Amy has 4 coins under Cup B.
The coins in each cup add up to 50¢.

The coins can be  .

Which coins can be under Cup A?

Which coins can be under Cup B?

3

85¢

A pencil case costs 85¢.
James has some pennies, nickels, dimes, and quarters.
Show 3 ways that he can use his coins to buy the
pencil case.
What is the smallest number of coins he can use to buy
the pencil case?

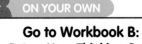

ON YOUR OWN

**Go to Workbook B:
Put on Your Thinking Cap!
pages 247–252**

Chapter Wrap Up

You have learned...

Money

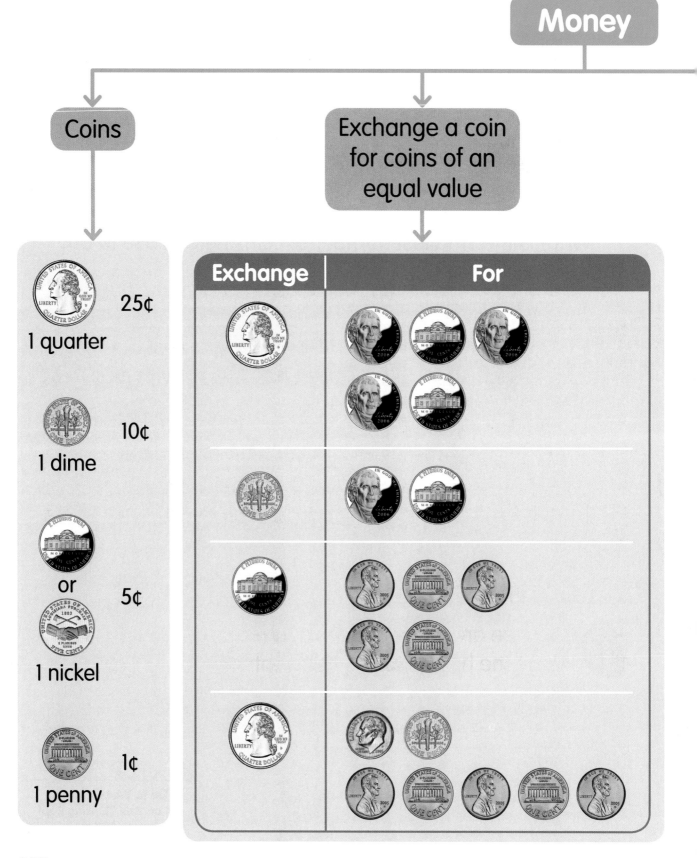

Coins

1 quarter	25¢
1 dime	10¢
1 nickel	5¢
1 penny	1¢

Exchange a coin for coins of an equal value

Exchange	For

BIG IDEAS

Penny, nickel, dime, and quarter are coins that can be counted and exchanged. Money can be added and subtracted.

Count a group of coins to find value

Add and subtract money

Solve real-world problems

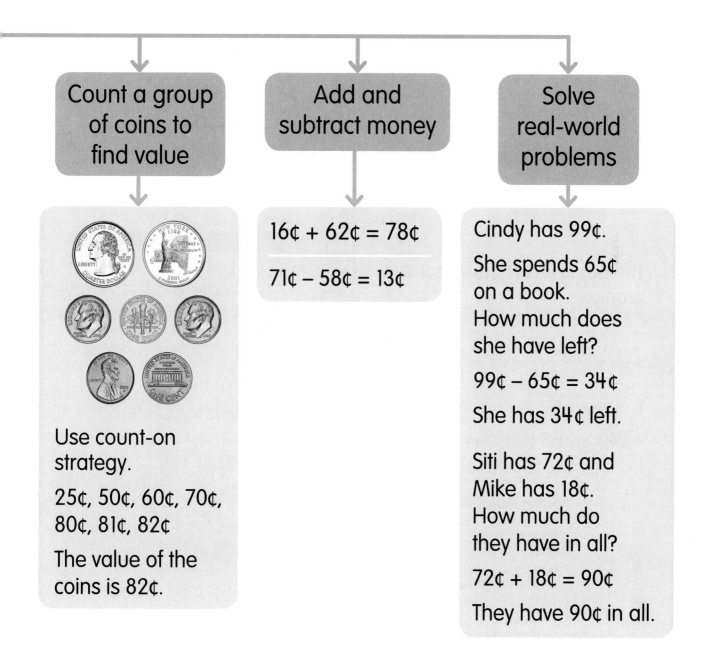

Use count-on strategy.

25¢, 50¢, 60¢, 70¢, 80¢, 81¢, 82¢

The value of the coins is 82¢.

16¢ + 62¢ = 78¢

71¢ − 58¢ = 13¢

Cindy has 99¢.

She spends 65¢ on a book. How much does she have left?

99¢ − 65¢ = 34¢

She has 34¢ left.

Siti has 72¢ and Mike has 18¢. How much do they have in all?

72¢ + 18¢ = 90¢

They have 90¢ in all.

ON YOUR OWN

Go to Workbook B:
Chapter Review/Test,
pages 253–254

Glossary

A

- **as heavy as**

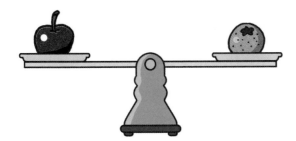

  The apple is as heavy as the orange.

B

- **bar graph**

  A bar graph uses the length of bars and a scale to show data.

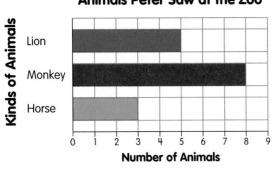

C

- **calendar**

  A calender shows the days, weeks, and months of a year.

- **cents**

  A unit of money.
  '¢' stands for cents.

- **colder**

  Some months are colder.

- **count back**

  $27 - 4 = ?$

  greater number

  Count back from the greater number to find the answer.

23	24	25	26	27

- **count on**

  $62 + 3 = ?$

  greater number

  Count on from the greater number to find the answer.

  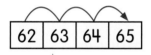

62	63	64	65

D

- **data**

  Data is information that has numbers.

Kinds of Sports	Tally	Number of Children
Soccer	⦀⦀ ⦀⦀	10
Basketball	⦀⦀ ⫿⫿⫿	8
Baseball	⫿⫿	2

- **date**

  The date for Fourth of July celebration in the year 2010 is **Sunday, July 4, 2010**.

- **days**

  There are seven days in one week.

JULY						
Sunday	Monday	Tuesday	Wednesday	Thursday	Friday	Saturday

  days

- **digital clock**

  Clock that shows time in digital form.

- **dime**

  A dime has a value of ten cents or 10¢.

- **doubles fact**

  6 + 6 = 12

  8 + 8 = 16

  The numbers that are added together are the same.

E ———————

- **each**

  There are four muffins on each plate.

- **eighty**

Count	Write	Say
	80	eighty

- **equally**

  Having the same amount or number.

  You can put 12 ladybugs equally into 2 boxes.

- **estimate**

  You can estimate the number of things.

  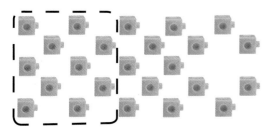

  There are about 20 ▣.

  The actual number of ▣ is 24.

- **exchange**

  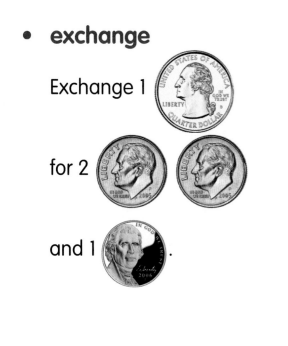

  Exchange 1 [quarter]

  for 2 [dimes]

  and 1 [nickel].

- **fewer, fewest**

  Eggs Laid This Week

  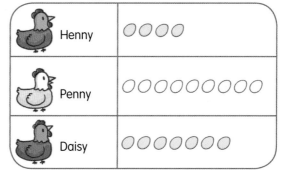

  Daisy laid fewer eggs than Penny.
  Henny laid the fewest eggs.

- **fifty**

Count	Write	Say
[blocks]	50	fifty

- **forty**

Count	Write	Say
[blocks]	40	forty

G

- **greater than**

Tens	Ones
2	7

Tens	Ones
2	3

27 > 23

- **groups**

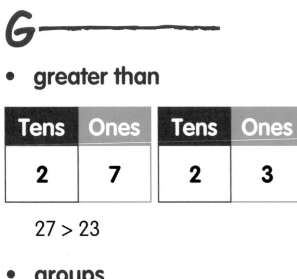

There are 3 groups.
Each group has 7 apples.

H

- **half hour**

See **half past**.

- **half past**

When the minute hand is at 6, we say it is half past the hour.

It is half past 5.

- **heavy, heavier, heaviest**

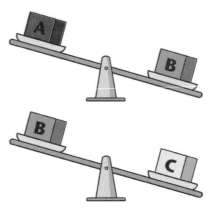

Box A is heavy.
Box B is heavier than Box A.
Box C is the heaviest.

- **hour hand**

The hour hand is the short hand on the clock.

Hour hand

L

- ## light, lighter, lightest

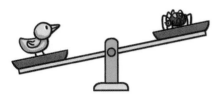

is light.

is lighter than the .

is the lightest.

M

- ## mentally

  You can add and subtract numbers mentally.

- ## minute hand

  The minute hand is the long hand on the clock.

- ## months

  There are twelve months in one year.

January, February, June, July, November and December are examples of months.

- ## more, most

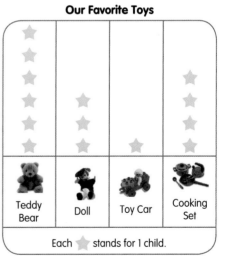

3 more children like cooking sets than toy cars.
The most popular toy is the teddy bear.

N

- **nickel**

or

A nickel has a value of five cents or 5¢.

- **ninety**

Count	Write	Say
	90	ninety

- **number line**

  The numbers are arranged in order to form a regular pattern. A number line can be used to count on and count back.

  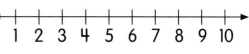

O

- **o'clock**

  When the minute hand is at 12, tell the time as o'clock.

  It is 2 o'clock.

- **one hundred**

  10 tens = 1 hundred

  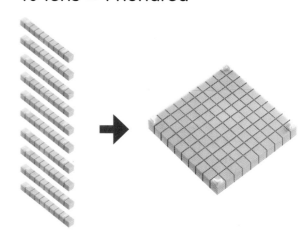

P ————

penny

A penny has a value of one cent or 1¢.

picture graph

A picture graph uses pictures or symbols to show data.

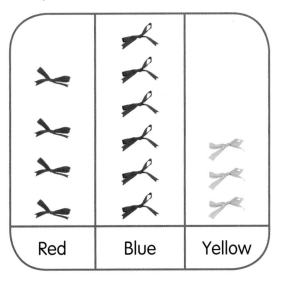

| Red | Blue | Yellow |

place-value chart

A place-value chart shows how many tens and ones there are in a number.

Tens	Ones

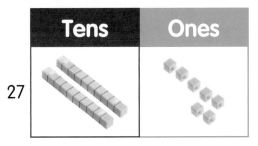

27

In the number 27, there are 2 tens and 7 ones.

Q ————

quarter

A quarter has a value of twenty-five cents or 25¢.

R

- **regroup**

  You regroup when you change 10 ones to 1 ten or 1 ten to 10 ones.

  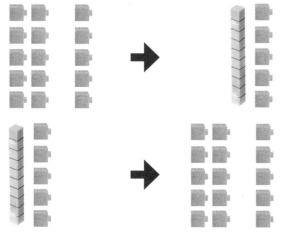

S

- **same**

  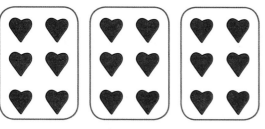

  6 + 6 + 6 = 36

  There are the same number of hearts in each group.

- **seasons**

  There are 4 seasons in one year.

  Spring   Summer

  Fall   Winter

- **seventy**

Count	Write	Say
	70	seventy

- **sixty**

Count	Write	Say
	60	sixty

- **share**

3 children share 6 balloons equally.
Each child gets 2 balloons.

T

- **tally chart**

Kinds of Sports	Tally
Soccer	⸝⸝⸝⸝⸝ ⸝⸝⸝⸝⸝
Basketball	⸝⸝⸝⸝⸝ ///
Baseball	//

- **tally mark**

A tally mark / is used to record each piece of data. 5 tally marks is shown like this ⸝⸝⸝⸝⸝.

⸝⸝⸝⸝⸝ // stands for 7.

- **thirty**

Count	Write	Say
	30	thirty

- **twenty-one**

Count	Write	Say
	21	twenty-one

- **twenty-nine**

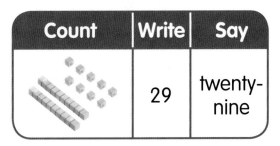

Count	Write	Say
	29	twenty-nine

U

- **unit**

  A unit is used to measure how heavy a thing is. 1 🔲 stands for 1 unit.

  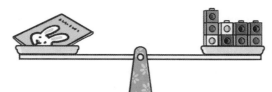

  The book weighs about 9 units.

V

- **value**

  The value of a coin is how much money it is worth.

W

- **warmer**

  Some months are warmer.

- **weeks**

  See **days**.

- **weight**

  A weight of an object is the measure of how heavy it is.

Y

year

  See **months**.

Index

A

Pages listed in regular type refer to Student Book A.
Pages listed in blue type refer to Student Book B.
Pages in *italic type* refer to Workbook (WB) A.
Pages listed in *blue italic type* refer to Workbook (WB) B.
Pages in **boldface** type show where a term is introduced.

Pages listed in regular type refer to Student Book A.
Pages listed in blue type refer to Student Book B.
Pages in *italic type* refer to Workbook (WB) A.
Pages listed in *blue italic type* refer to Workbook (WB) B.
Pages in **boldface** type show where a term is introduced.

Pages listed in regular type refer to Student Book A.
Pages listed in blue type refer to Student Book B.
Pages in *italic type* refer to Workbook (WB) A.
Pages listed in *blue italic type* refer to Workbook (WB) B.
Pages in **boldface** type show where a term is introduced.

Ⓜ

R

Pages listed in regular type refer to Student Book A.
Pages listed in blue type refer to Student Book B.
Pages in *italic type* refer to Workbook (WB) A.
Pages listed in *blue italic type* refer to Workbook (WB) B.
Pages in **boldface** type show where a term is introduced.

Photo Credits

cover: ©Houghton Mifflin Harcourt, *2tl:* ©Marshall Cavendish Education, *2tr:* ©Digital Stock (Animals in Action) Photo CD, *2ml:* ©Digital Stock (Four Seasons) Photo CD, *2mr:* ©iStockphoto.com/pixhook, *4ml:* ©Marshall Cavendish Education, *4m:* ©Marshall Cavendish Education, *4mr:* ©Comstock Klips Photo CD, *4tl:* ©Corel Everyday Objects Photo CD, *4tm:* ©Marshall Cavendish Education, *4tr:* ©Wikipedia Commons/Rudolf Stricker, *7ml:* ©Marshall Cavendish Education, *7mr:* ©Marshall Cavendish Education, *7br:* ©iStockphoto.com/Marilyn Nieves, *8:* ©Marshall Cavendish Education, *8tr:* ©Corel Everyday Objects Photo CD, *9:* ©Marshall Cavendish Education, *10:* ©Marshall Cavendish Education, *13ml:* ©Marshall Cavendish Education, *13mr:* ©iStockphoto.com/Kyu Oh, *13bl:* ©Marshall Cavendish Education, *15t:* ©Marshall Cavendish Education, *15m:* ©Houghton Mifflin Harcourt, *16:* ©Marshall Cavendish Education, *17:* ©iStockphoto.com/Tracy Whiteside, *18:* ©Marshall Cavendish Education, *19tl:* ©Corel Everyday Objects Photo CD, *19tm:* ©Marshall Cavendish Education, *19tr:* ©Marshall Cavendish Education, *20t:* ©Marshall Cavendish Education, *20b:* ©Houghton Mifflin Harcourt, *25:* ©Marshall Cavendish Education, *30:* ©Marshall Cavendish Education, *31t:* ©Marshall Cavendish Education, *31br:* ©iStockphoto.com/Thomas Perkins, *34t:* ©Comstock Klips Photo CD, *34m:* ©Marshall Cavendish Education, *34b:* ©Comstock Klips Photo CD, *36tr:* ©Image Source Photo CD, *36mr:* ©Image Source Photo CD, *36br:* ©Stockbyte Photo CD, *37:* ©Image Source Photo CD, *38:* ©Marshall Cavendish Education, *45m:* ©iStockphoto.com/Stuart Monk, *45br:* ©Stockbyte Photo CD, *50tr:* ©iStockphoto.com/Tracy Whiteside, *50br:* ©iStockphoto.com/Marilyn Nieves, *51:* ©iStockphoto.com/Marilyn Nieves, *57m:* ©Stockbyte Photo CD, *57br:* ©iStockphoto.com/Marilyn Nieves, *58:* ©iStockphoto.com/Thomas Perkins, *59:* ©Stockbyte Photo CD, *60tr:* ©iStockphoto.com/Tracy Whiteside, *60ml:* ©iStockphoto.com/Jarek Szymanski, *60mr:* ©Image Source Photo CD, *60bl:* ©Jupiter Images Photo CD, *61:* ©Comstock Klips Photo CD, *62:* ©Jupiter Images Photo CD, *66bl:* ©iStockphoto.com/Jeff Strauss, *66br:* ©Image Source Photo CD, *67:* ©Jupiter Images Photo CD, *68tr:* ©iStockphoto.com/Nathan Maxfield, *68mr:* ©Stockbyte Photo CD, *68b:* ©Jupiter Images Photo CD, *69tr:* ©Image Source Photo CD, *69br:* ©iStockphoto.com/Stuart Monk, *70:* ©iStockphoto.com/Thomas Perkins, *71:* ©Stockbyte

Photo CD, *74mr:* ©Stockbyte Photo CD, *74br:* ©iStockphoto.com/Marilyn Nieves, *77:* ©Stockbyte Photo CD, *84:* ©iStockphoto.com/Nathan Maxfield, *85m:* ©Jupiter Images Photo CD, *85br:* ©Image Source Photo CD, *86mr:* ©iStockphoto.com/Marilyn Nieves, *86br:* ©Image Source Photo CD, *87tr:* ©iStockphoto.com/Miroslav Ferkuniak, *87bl:* ©iStockphoto.com/Jeff Strauss, *88tr:* ©Image Source Photo CD, *88mr:* ©Stockbyte Photo CD, *88bl:* ©iStockphoto.com/Thomas Perkins, *89:* ©iStockphoto.com/Kyu Oh, *90mr:* ©iStockphoto.com/ Marilyn Nieves, *90b:* ©iStockphoto.com/Jarek Szymanski, *91:* ©Jupiter Images Photo CD, *92m:* ©iStockphoto.com/Tracy Whiteside, *92b:* ©Stockbyte Photo CD, *96:* ©Stockbyte Photo CD, *98:* ©Image Source Photo CD, *101:* ©Jupiter Images Photo CD, *102t:* ©Jupiter Images Photo CD, *102br:* ©Image Source Photo CD, *103tr:* ©Image Source Photo CD, *103mr:* ©iStockphoto.com/Thomas Perkins, *103br:* ©iStockphoto.com/Stuart Monk, *104tr:* ©Jupiter Images Photo CD, *104b:* ©Stockbyte Photo CD, *105t:* ©iStockphoto.com/Kyu Oh, *105m:* ©Jupiter Images Photo CD, *105bl:* ©Image Source Photo CD, *106:* ©Image Source Photo CD, *107tr:* ©Image Source Photo CD, *107mr:* ©Jupiter Images Photo CD, *107br:* ©iStockphoto.com/Marilyn Nieves, *108:* ©iStockphoto.com/Jeff Strauss, *109tr:* ©iStockphoto.com/Kyu Oh, *109mr:* ©Jupiter Images Photo CD, *109br:* ©Image Source Photo CD, *113:* ©iStockphoto.com/Miroslav Ferkuniak, *114:* ©Stockbyte Photo CD, *115:* ©Image Source Photo CD, *116:* ©Image Source Photo CD, *124:* ©Image Source Photo CD, *125:* ©Stockbyte Photo CD, *128:* ©iStockphoto.com/Tracy Whiteside, *129:* ©iStockphoto.com/Jeff Strauss, *134:* ©iStockphoto.com/Nathan Maxfield, *138mr:* ©iStockphoto.com/Jarek Szymanski, *138br:* ©iStockphoto.com/Marilyn Nieves, *143mr:* ©iStockphoto.com/Thomas Perkins, *143br:* ©Image Source Photo CD, *148:* ©Jupiter Images Photo CD, *150:* ©Image Source Photo CD, *156:* ©Jupiter Images Photo CD, *158:* ©iStockphoto.com/Marilyn Nieves, *160:* ©Image Source Photo CD, *161:* ©Corel Stock Photo Library CD, *162:* ©Image Source Photo CD, *166:* ©iStockphoto.com/Jeff Strauss, *167:* ©Marshall Cavendish Education, *170:* ©Stockbyte Photo CD, *173:* ©Stockbyte Photo CD, *176:* ©iStockphoto.com/Thomas Perkins, *182:* ©iStockphoto.com/Nathan Maxfield, *184mr:* ©iStockphoto.com/Tracy Whiteside, *184bl:* ©Jupiter Images Photo CD, *185tr:* ©Stockbyte Photo CD,

Acknowledgements

The publisher wishes to thank the following organizations for sponsoring the various objects used in this book:

Accent Living
Metal ball p. 7
Green bowl p. 263
Cats on sofa p. 264

Growing Fun Pte Ltd
Base-ten cubes and blocks – appear throughout the book

Hasbro Singapore Pte Ltd
For supplying Play-Doh™
to make the following:
        Clay stars p. 255

Lyves & Company Pte Ltd
Puppet doll p. 38

Noble International Pte Ltd
Unit cubes – appear throughout the book

The publisher also wishes to thank the individuals who have contributed in one way or another, namely:
Model Isabella Gilbert
And all those who have kindly loaned the publisher items for the photographs featured.